STUDIES IN IMPERIALISM

general editor John M. MacKenzie

When the 'Studies in Imperialism' series was founded more than twenty years ago, emphasis was laid upon the conviction that 'imperialism as a cultural phenomenon had as significant an effect on the dominant as on the subordinate societies'. With more than fifty books published, this remains the prime concern of the series. Cross-disciplinary work has indeed appeared covering the full spectrum of cultural phenomena, as well as examining aspects of gender and sex, frontiers and law, science and the environment, language and literature, migration and patriotic societies, and much else. Moreover, the series has always wished to present comparative work on European and American imperialism, and particularly welcomes the submission of books in these areas. The fascination with imperialism, in all its aspects, shows no sign of abating, and this series will continue to lead the way in encouraging the widest possible range of studies in the field. 'Studies in Imperialism' is fully organic in its development, always seeking to be at the cutting edge, responding to the latest interests of scholars and the needs of this ever-expanding area of scholarship.

Silk and empire

Manchester University Press

AVAILABLE IN THE SERIES

Silk and empire

Brenda M. King

MANCHESTER UNIVERSITY PRESS
Manchester and New York

distributed exclusively in the USA by Palgrave

Published by **MANCHESTER UNIVERSITY PRESS**
OXFORD ROAD, MANCHESTER M13 9NR, UK
and ROOM 400, 175 FIFTH AVENUE, NEW YORK, NY 10010, USA
www.manchesteruniversitypress.co.uk

Distributed exclusively in the USA by
PALGRAVE, 175 FIFTH AVENUE, NEW YORK, NY 10010, USA

Distributed exclusively in Canada by
UBC PRESS, UNIVERSITY OF BRITISH COLUMBIA,
2029 WEST MALL, VANCOUVER, BC, CANADA V6T 1Z2

British Library Cataloguing-in-Publication Data
A catalogue record for this book is available from the British Library

Library of Congress Cataloging-in-Publication Data applied for

ISBN   0 7190 6700 6   hardback
EAN   978 0 7190 6700 6

First published 2005

14 13 12 11 10 09 08 07 06 05   10 9 8 7 6 5 4 3 2 1

Typeset in Trump Mediaeval
by Graphicraft Limited, Hong Kong
Printed in Great Britain
by CPI, Bath

For my family

CONTENTS

LIST OF FIGURES

LIST OF PLATES

The plates can be found between pp. 12 and 13

GENERAL EDITOR'S INTRODUCTION

Among the exhibits at the Great Exhibition of 1851 was a piece of silk from Messrs Redmayne and Son of London showing a 'graceful running pattern' of the rose, the shamrock and the thistle.* Here in a luxurious fabric, the visitors to the Crystal Palace could behold a symbol of the apparently successful British Union which had come to dominate a global empire, not least in India. The bourgeois among those visitors may well have noted it as something they would like to possess, for one of the characteristics of the expanding nineteenth-century bourgeoisie in Britain, as elsewhere in Europe, was a desire to acquire those luxury items that had previously been restricted to the rich upper-class elite of past ages. Silk was indeed just such a product and it came to symbolise wealth and taste. It embraced the intriguing natural aspects of sericulture, transformed through refined techniques and the artist's hand into a fabric which combined technical facility with aesthetic worth.

As Brenda King points out, historians, both of empire and of design, have paid comparatively little attention to silk. Economic historians have been much more interested in volume products, like cotton or jute, while consumables or medicines, like tea, coffee, sugar or quinine, have always featured more prominently among the 'fruits of empire'. Yet silk stuffs seemed to symbolise everything that Europeans imagined about the Orient: richness, craftsmanship, refined taste, and exceptional beauty of design. In the nineteenth century, a more complex relationship emerged than a mere effort to relocate silk production in Europe. That was certainly part of it, and the damp North-West of England seemed an ideal place (for many years my office at Lancaster University virtually looked out on a former silk factory in the village of Ellel). But the connections were also a matter of exchange and learning, in respect of techniques, patterns, designs, and creative values.

In all of these, the exhibition, the museum, the college of design, the craft workshop, the larger-scale factory, and the shop displaying wares founded on eastern trades, each of them such striking characteristics of nineteenth-century Britain, were key. And among individuals enthralled by silk, Sir Thomas Wardle, a classic entrepreneur of the North-West of England, was a central figure. He visited India in order to observe and learn. He brought together all the interests and institutions through which silks could be created and appreciated. He had connections with so many of the significant designers of the nineteenth century, not least William Morris of the Arts and Crafts movement. And his combination of aesthetic appreciation with hard-headed business acumen ensured a premier position for his products.

Brenda King's book is the first sustained study of these developments. The fascination with silks which she recounts is now best understood through the remarkable collections in museums in Manchester, London and elsewhere. She brings a considerable knowledge and a wealth of detailed understanding to the phenomenon of silk as a luxury East–West trade in production, technique and design. In doing so, she creates a significant revision of the crudely binary ideas of Edward Said and his followers. Here was a milieu in which there was a genuine respect for an Eastern product and the craftsmanship associated with it, while a striking debt was created in terms of techniques and design values. The additional complexities of the relationship emerge in the fact that the main threat ultimately came not from the industrial and imperial power of the West but from the emergence of new techniques, and also synthetic products, promoted by other Asiatic powers, Japan and China. Silk thus very well illustrates the multilateral channels through which influences, ideas, and production of a fabric like silk can flow. Brenda King's book reveals much of interest and value to historians of empire, of Orientalism, of English industry and its rivalries with France, as well as of art and design.

John M. MacKenzie

* Illustrated in *The Great Exhibition: A Facsimile of the Illustrated Catalogue of London's 1851 Crystal Palace Exposition*, New York, Gramercy Books, 1994, p. 202.

GLOSSARY OF TEXTILE TERMS

Batik   An Indonesian word commonly used in Europe and English-speaking countries to describe resist dyeing where a resist medium (usually molten wax) is applied to woven cloth by means of special tools, brushes or stamps.

Block-printing   Printing dyes, mordants or a resist medium (such as gum) onto a textile by means of relief-carved wooden block (a different block for each colour). In India, the blocks are usually 23 or 30 centimetres (9 or 12 inches) square in size.

Brocade   Figured textiles with the patterning woven in supplementary, usually discontinuous, weft threads.

Brocaded   A pattern made by wefts which only go to the width of the motif and are then turned back.

Calico   A plain weave, opaque cotton fabric.

Cocoon   The hardened pupa case of moths and butterflies, here referring to that created by silkworms. It consists of hundreds of metres of continuous filament (silk) which can be reeled from the cocoon after boiling.

Complementary threads/elements   Threads usually of contrasting colours woven into a textile to create a pattern. Unlike supplementary threads, they are structurally integral parts of the weave, and their removal damages and weakens the fabric.

Continuous threads   Those threads that extend the full length or width of the textile.

Cords   Refers to the threads of the figure harness on the drawloom which control the pattern in the width of the fabric. The greater the number, the finer and more elaborate could be the design.

Count, thread   The number of warp and weft threads found in a specified linear measurement, such as a centimetre or inch. A high thread count usually denotes fine, thin threads (or else medium-sized threads in a very dense weave). Thus a 200-count cotton has 100 warp and 100 wefts per inch (39 warp/39 weft per centimetre).

Cutwork   Warp or weft floats (at the back of the textile) cut away by hand, so that the pattern may appear as if woven in discontinuous supplementary-weft technique (a more time-consuming process).

Damask   A weave and, by extension, a fabric which was usually (but not essentially) self-coloured. The pattern is created by the contrast in the reflection of light from the warp to the weft – the vertical and horizontal elements. The meaning is unchanged since the eighteenth century.

Discontinuous weft   A weft thread that does not extend the full width of the textile. Usually of a contrasting colour to the ground threads (if supplementary) or to surrounding weft threads (if tapestry-woven).

Drawloom   Believed to be of Sassanian Persian origin (c. AD 200). The fully developed drawloom uses a double harness set, one providing the weave,

[xii]

the other the figured patterning. Drawlooms developed differently in the Far East, Middle East and Europe, until the early nineteenth century invention of the Jacquard loom, most drawlooms required 'drawboys' who activated the pattern harness by lifting sets of threads. Today, Indian figured textiles woven commercially are usually created on Jacquard looms.

Figured fabric A textile in which patterning is woven into the cloth rather than painted, printed, dyed or embroidered. Figured textiles are popular, but erroneously, called 'brocades'. They include those fabrics with continuous or discontinuous supplementary warp and weft patterning; sammitas and lampas, velvets, etc. Historically figured fabrics were woven using traditional drawlooms (*naksha, jala*); today Jacquard attachments are generally used.

Filament A continuous fibre created by natural (e.g. silk) or man-made processes. In silk cocoons, one or two filaments are created by the caterpillar to form the cocoon; in synthetic fibres the filament is created by being extruded through a 'spinneret'.

Gauze In true gauze weaves the warps are crossed and uncrossed between the wefts at intervals to create a transparent openwork fabric. The name is also given to plain-woven fabrics where the warps do not cross, but are often 'paired', creating uneven spacing in the weave between the series of warp threads. (This makes the textile look more transparent than it otherwise would be).

Jacquard A punch-card pattern-selecting device for handlooms or powerlooms, which was originally invented to replace the drawboy. It was refined and patented by J.M. Jacquard in 1804. Its speed and ease of use has made the older drawlooms obsolete throughout most of India.

Lampas A figured textile that has patterning created through at least two different warps and wefts in the weaving. Warp-faced and weft-faced integrated weave structures form the motifs, typically polychrome, using plain weaves and satins.

Lustring A lightweight crisp silk popular in the seventeenth and eighteenth century with a lustre given by preliminary treatment of the warp.

Mordant A colourless chemical (metallic oxide) that is necessary to bind dye to a cellulose fibre such as cotton or linen. The two most common mordants in India are (1) aluminium sulphate (alum), which binds, for instance, alizarin dyes to cotton and produces bright colours; and (2) iron-based compounds which in alizarin create the darker hues.

Muslin Fine, sheer, often transparent cotton fabric. Usually has high thread counts, ranging from about 150 to 300.

Organzine Undegummed, twisted silk warp threads used to create organza. The silk filling yarn (wefts) used with organzine, called tram, is not so highly twisted.

Plain weave An over-one, under-one weave structure. Also called tabby weave.

Powerloom A loom powered by steam or electricity, making it much faster to use than a handloom.

Raw silk Undegummed silk; where the sericin has not been removed from the filaments.

Reel   Process by which silk filaments, in groups of six or more, are unwound from their cocoons and wound onto a circular contraption, which is also called a reel.

Resist dyeing   Any form of dyeing where the dyestuff is prevented from adhering to selected areas of the thread or woven textile.

Satin   A weave, and by extension, a fabric with a smooth surface in which the warp threads cover the wefts completely.

Selvage   The outer edge of a textile parallel to the warp. It is made by the weft threads wrapping round the outermost warp threads. Often the group of warps threads at the selvage are more densely set than the rest of the fabric, making the selvage stronger than the inner cloth.

Shafts   'Foot-figured' silks were made without the drawloom mechanism. The warp was entered on the heddles of a series of wooden battens which were operated by treadles to give simple geometric designs.

Shuttles   The weaver creates the textile by lifting alternate warp threads and passing the shuttle containing the weft from side to side of the loom. Tiny shuttles were used for brocading (see above). The designer had to let the weaver know how many shuttles would be needed in each line of the design – to work out the cost.

Silk   Natural fibre produced by silkworms. Originally cultivated by the Chinese about 2500 BC. Many filaments are used to create a single fine thread, which, when woven, creates a thin, lustrous fabric.

Silkworm   The caterpillars of moths of *Bombidiceae* and *Saturnidae* families, from which silks are derived.

Spin/spun   Fibres of limited length (e.g. cotton, wool, linen) can be carded (aligned so the fibres lie parallel to each other) and then drawn out and twisted to form thread. The process is called spinning.

Supplementary warp or weft   Supplementary threads are those added to a textile that already has one set of warp and weft threads. If supplementary threads are removed from a woven textile, the remaining fabric will still be complete.

Tie-dye   Called *bandhani* (G) in western India. Resist patterning created on an already-woven textile by tying selected sections of cloth with thread, so preventing the dye from entering the tied areas.

Tissue   The generic name in England for a silk with two warp and two weft systems. There were many varieties. A single tissue had one pattern weft from selvage to selvage and thus had one colour in the pattern, a double tissue had two colours, etc. Tissues could, however, be brocaded – and still be tissues. The French term for this, lampas, has not changed in meaning.

Twill   A weave and, by extension, a fabric, in which the warp and weft interlace at one or more removes as the textile progresses. It was a supple material used for linings and softly draped fabrics.

Warp   Set of parallel threads mounted on a loom frame, kept in supply on a warp beam. In India, handweavers make warps long enough to make three to six saris at a time. (The length of the warp determines the overall length of the woven cloth coming off the loom.)

[xiv]

Warp-faced weave A cloth wherein the warp threads predominate on the face of the fabric. In terms of fabric count, this can also result from there being either considerably more warp threads than weft, or else much thicker warp threads than weft.

Weft A set of threads that runs at right angles to the warp, interworking with them to create various structures of weaves, such as plain or twill weave.

Weft-faced weave A cloth wherein the weft threads predominate on the face of the fabric. In terms of fabric count, this is produced by there being either more weft threads than warp, or else thicker weft threads than warp.

Whitework Embroidery using white threads upon a white fabric, which is usually fine and translucent so the embroidery will stand out.

Wild silk Silk from the products of silkworms that are not varieties of *Bombyx mori*. Because their filaments are flat and spiral instead of circular or triangular, and their sericin is difficult to remove, they usually cannot be mechanically reeled or woven on powerlooms. Sometimes the spun threads from the broken ends and 'floss' from *B. mori* cocoons are also – erroneously – called wild silk instead of raw silk. Indian wild silks include *tasar, muga* and *eria (endi)*.

Yarn-dyeing The yarn used to weave a textile is dyed before it is woven (as warp or weft).

GLOSSARY OF INDIAN TEXTILE TERMS

(A) Assamese; (B) Bengali; (G) Gujarati; (H) Hindi; (Ja) Jaintia; (Ka) Kannada; (Ko) Khondi; (M) Malay; (Pk) Prakrit; (Sk) Sanskrit; (Ta) Tamil; (Te) Telugu

Aar   A hooked needle (awl) used for chain-stitch embroidery.
Abrawan   (H) Flowing water. Very fine transparent fabrics of cotton or silk.
Atlacho, alacha   Striped silk cloth used for making trousers (Sindhi).
Ajanta   A series of elaborately carved and painted caves in western Maharashtra which were used as Buddhist temples c.100 BC to AD 500.
Al   Root of plants of the *Morinda* family containing red dye.
Alizarin   Red dye obtained from the madder plant, *Rubia tinctorum*.
Amru   (H) Figured silk that only has coloured silks, not zari, in its construction.
Arakku   (Ta) Lac. Used to describe red saris dyed with lac.
Badla, kamdaani   Flattened gold or silver wire used for embroidery.
Bagh   A shawl of which the surface is entirely covered with floss-silk embroidery in surface darn-stitch (Punjab).
Baluchar   (B) Amru sari traditionally from Baluchar, West Bengal.
Bandhani   (H, G) Tie-dye technique in which patterns are formed by resist-dyeing dots. Bandana (H).
Batik   (Ja) From *tic* 'dot'. Cotton cloth decorated by a complex process of repeated wax-resisting and dyeing. The wax may be put on with a spouted applicator (*canting*), which produces *tulis* ('hand-drawn' batik), or with a copper stamp (*cap*), a method chiefly associated with Java.
Bhat   (G) Pattern. Used in describing *patolu* patterns, probably derived from *bharat*.
Buta   (H) Large, usually floral or foliate motif created in corners and endpieces of saris. From Persian *buteh*.
Buti   (H) Small, usually floral motif usually created as a repeat against a plain ground. See *Buta*.
Butidar   (B) Amru sari from west Bengal with many *buti* in field.
Chadar   (H) Common north Indian name for shawl or upper wrap, literally a sheet or cloth.
Chikankiri   (H) Whitework embroidery from Lucknow.
Choli   (H) Tight-fitting tailored blouse worn with most modern saris.
Dariyai   (H) Type of *tasar* silk sari worn by Brahmins in eastern Madhya Pradesh. Name *daryai* mentioned in Mughal accounts of silk cloth, so may be an old name signifying good-quality silk cloth.
Dhoti   (H) Male lower garment wherein untailored cloth is draped and drawn between the legs.
Dukula   (Ka) Fine silk cloth.
Dupatta   (H) Two cloths (referring to cloth being folded in two when worn). Veil worn with *salwar kameez*.

Endi, eria (H, B, A) Heavy wild silk produced in eastern and north-east India, usually makes *chadars* and other heavy textiles. From cocoons of *Philosamia ricini* which produces silk ranging from white to brick red.

Gorad (B) Undyed silk sari with simple border, often used as a *puja* sari.

Ikat (M) Literally 'to bind'. Cloth in which the pattern is pre-dyed by resist-binding bundles of yarns in the warp or weft threads. When done in both, as in *patola* the process is known as double ikat.

Indigo From Sanskrit *nila* and Arabic *al-nil*, via the Portuguese *anil*; widely referred to in trade records as *nil*. A dye extracted from the leaf of *Indigofera tinctoria*, producing a great variety of hues of blue.

Jaal, jaala, jaali (H) Net, mesh. Any net-like design, large or small.

Jamdani (H, B) Fine transparent cotton muslin with discontinuous supplementary-weft motifs woven in heavier cotton threads.

Kalabattun (G, H) Old-fashioned term for gold-wrapped thread once commonly used in the western region. Alternative name for *kamdani* embroidery.

Kalamkari (H) Painted cloth. A special pen (*kalam*) is used to draw freehand designs in ink or resist medium (e.g. wax, resin).

Kalga (H) Curvilinear *buta* with hook-like end, also called mango (*aam*), *konia*, paisley design. Name derived from Urdu *galb* (hook). *Kalka.*

Kamdani (H, G) Embroidery using fine *zari*, often created on fine sheer fabrics.

Kameez (H) Cut and sewn top traditionally worn by western Indian Muslim women.

Kantha (B) Embroidered quilt made from used clothing.

Kincab, Kimkhab (H) Figured silk with more *zari* than silk showing in the fabric surface.

Konia, kona (H, M, G) Corner. Name given to *kalga* design when placed in corner of sari between endpiece and border. *Konya* (H).

Kosa (Sk) Silk-moth cocoon. Name for *tasar* in parts of eastern Deccan.

Lac (H) Red dye derived from secretions of insect *Lacifer lacca*, common in eastern Deccan.

Lahariya, laheriya (H, G) Waves. Striped tie-dye pattern.

Lungi (H) 2.7 metre (9 foot) wrap covering legs from waist down, commonly worn by men as well as some women in various ethnic groups. Name derived from *lunga* (Sk) cloth, as in *lungda* (sari).

Marorhi Embroidery using couched gold-wrapped thread.

Masuria (H) 'Muslim cloth'. Fine muslin from Kota (Rajasthan) with alternating silk and cotton threads, name related to *mashru*, a heavy silk/cotton cloth worn by Muslims.

Minakari (H) Inlay or enamelling. Supplementary coloured silks woven onto a golden ground.

Muga (A) Light brown. Golden-coloured wild silk grown almost exclusively in Assam (*Antheraea assama*).

Mukta (H) Freedom. *Tasar* silk fabric made from spun threads from cocoons where the moth had escaped; consequently the name 'freedom'.

Naksha (H) Traditional drawloom of northern India which uses warp-lifting devices based upon threads tied to each warp thread. Called *adai* (Ta/Te) in the northern Tamil weaving belt, and *jala* (O) in eastern Deccan.

Odhani (G, M) Large 2.7 metre (9 foot) half-sari worn as veil in western India; name also means sheet. *Orhna, orhni* (H), *odhvu, odhnu, odhaavvu, odho* (G), *orna* (B), *orani, orona* (A).

Pat Silk thread.

Patolu (G) Combined (warp and weft) ikat silk saris once made for export to South-East Asia, now only made for home market. Pl. *Patola*.

Patta (Sk) Silk, upper garment, veil, cloth. *Paata* (Ko) cloth.

Phulkari 'Flower work'. Floss silk embroidery on cotton done in the Punjab for women's shawls and garments.

Piece goods Cloths intended for attire, supplied to order in measured lengths.

Rangrez Western Indian caste of dyers. From *rang* (H) colour.

Sari (H) An untailored length of cloth, typically 5–6 metres, worn by women as a wrapped garment, sometimes extended over the head.

Soosi Striped material made of cotton or cotton and silk, used mainly for women's trousers (*shalwar*).

Tarbana (H) Woven water. Tissue sari with warp of silk and weft of fine *zari*.

Tasar (H, M) Most widely produced type of wild silk, form cocoons of various *Antheraea* spp., such as *A. mylitta, A. pernyi.*

Valli (Ta) Foliate floral creeping vine design, from *veelli* (Pk).

Zardozi (H) Embroidery using *zari*, both *muka* and *kamdani*. Zardoshi (H).

Zari (H) Gold-wrapped thread, usually a core silk or cotton thread (*asara*) around which wound a fine, flattened gilded silver wire. *Jari*.

PREFACE AND ACKNOWLEDGEMENTS

This book owes its origin to some collections of magnificent Indian silks that exist in England. One collection has been especially inspiring; it is a group of costly and complex silks collected in India in 1885–86 by the silk dyer Thomas Wardle and now in the Whitworth Art Gallery, Manchester. The collection was first displayed at the Colonial and Indian Exhibition, London (1886) followed by Manchester's Royal Jubilee Exhibition (1887). The collection represents Indian silk production at the end of the nineteenth century and is testimony to the fine skills of weavers, dyers and embroiderers. Most items are saturated with rich colour and many have gold and silver ornamentation. Predominantly they are items of traditional Indian dress; saris, wide shawls and turbans with just a few tailored items included.

This primary evidence in the form of silk cloth provides a wealth of information that helps us to address a whole series of questions concerning the interplay between aesthetics, trade and the British Empire. Undoubtedly these magnificent textiles offered a huge amount of aesthetic pleasure, as they were the best possible examples of their type. When the cloth is linked to other sources, however, including a wide range of contemporary documentation, much of which has never been evaluated, we gain a wider context and can learn a great deal about the societies that produced and valued it. We can also enhance our understanding of collections, exhibitions and display. Business records, backed up with publications by leaders in the field of design, newspapers, trade journals, correspondence and transcripts of public lectures, reveal the complex negotiations that characterised the trade in silk between England and India. In particular they exemplify concerns surrounding the meeting of tradition with modernity during the period of the Raj.

The long history of Indian silk production is a rich field with considerable scope for further investigation. Silk was a labour intensive, luxury commodity that still provided livelihoods for hundreds of thousands of workers in Indian and England during the late nineteenth and early twentieth century. It played an important role in the economy of both countries, whole regions were devoted to the production of silk yarn and cloth, which dominated the lives of the people who lived there and demanded great skills from the work-force. Silk was more than a source of income, however. It was important in other ways; it provided beautiful, practical textiles, often with a significant cultural value.

During research for my doctoral thesis[1] I became aware that many collections of Indian silks in English museums, particularly the provincial collections, were unexplored and their importance unrecognised. These collections had a particular significance when they were formed; they are significant now, however, for different reasons. They are a powerful reminder of the era of the British Empire and symbolise the strong bond that existed between India and England, a trading relationship long overlooked.

PREFACE AND ACKNOWLEDGEMENTS

I could not have explored the silk collections without the cooperation of a number of individuals and institutions. The curators and conservators of textiles at the Whitworth Art Gallery Manchester have been unfailingly helpful; Frances Pritchard in particular has given unstinting help, expertise and encouragement over many years. Staff at Macclesfield Silk Museums have also cooperated fully. I would like to thank Professor Anne Morrell, a friend and renowned expert on Indian textiles, who has been characteristically generous with her knowledge, time and donations, and John Newell, Chairman of Leek Historical Trust for his enthusiasm and faith in me. I would also like to extend my thanks to the Pasold Research Fund, whose generous financial support has allowed the inclusion of colour plates in this publication.

Note

1   *Collections of Indian Silk Textiles and Their Connection With the English Silk Industry 1830–1930*, London, The Royal College of Art, 2000.

INTRODUCTION

In order to fully understand the huge impact of India's role in the global silk trade and the intense design debates of nineteenth-century Europe it is necessary to be aware of the technical, aesthetic and cultural values embedded in Indian silks. The influence of India's designs in Europe went far beyond that of fashionable exotica; there is overwhelming evidence for the positive and unbroken appreciation of India's silk textiles over centuries by industrialists, educators, designers, theorists, museum curators and consumers.

Through collections of Indian silks made in the nineteenth century we can explore the high regard in which India's textiles were held. The North-West of England is particularly rich in under-explored textile archives and their associated documents.[1] Manchester, for example, currently houses magnificent and representative collections of Indian silks from the mid-nineteenth to early twentieth century. These silks were collected for specific purposes. They reflect the size and diversity of India's handmade silk industry and are testimony to a wide range of traditional and complex weaving, printing, dyeing and embroidery skills. What then was their relevance to the Manchester region, widely known for the mass production of cheaply printed cottons that dominated the English economy?

These collections of textiles were formed at a time when design for industry was a subject of intense discussion in England. A better understanding of universal design principles was considered necessary for competitive advantage against foreign imports. This was, furthermore, a time when textile manufacturers were calling for the provision of regional textile museums to assist their understanding of successful design. India's role in the intense design debates in England of the nineteenth century is fully explored in this context.

India's designs and raw materials had a significant effect on commercial designs in the manufacturing world. Due to the survival of the finest craft skills, India was recognised for its centres of excellence in silk production, which created every form of silk yarn and complex silk cloth. Many distinguished artists and theorists upheld Indian design as exemplary in every respect. Walter Crane, Henry Cole, Lewis F. Day, Owen Jones and William Morris were just a few of the prominent promoters of India's designs. Principles of timeless, universal design principles were seen to be evident, the command of complex textile technology, the unparalleled use of colour and the

[1]

continuation of traditional design motifs were acknowledged as universally important and promoted widely. This book emphasises the impact that Indian textiles had on the English silk industry, design education, museum collections and the Arts and Crafts Movement.

The role that small manufacturers played in international trade demonstrates that the era of empire has to be understood in the context of the small business and regional interests, as well as the global economy. The 1870s and 1880s were crucial decades marking major difficulties for both the English and Indian silk industries. Both nations struggled to survive in the face of fierce competition from foreign imports; a mutually dependent relationship developed in a way that confirmed the beneficial aspects of commerce being conducted within the framework of the empire. Product innovation, the understanding of new technologies, the role of institutions, and a widespread understanding of appropriate design, were strategic in the fight for commercial survival in England and India. The crucial positions that a number of manufactures held in international trade are exemplified through the story of Thomas Wardle (1831–1909), owner of a modest silk dyeing company. Wardle (see Figure 1), from Leek, Staffordshire, taught William Morris (1834–96), a major figure in the Arts and Crafts Movement, to dye yarn and print cloth. Morris visited Wardle at his Staffordshire dye works a number of times between 1875 and 1878. The English Arts and Crafts Movement was mainly concerned with the revival of handicrafts relating to architecture and the applied arts; it was most active during the second half of the nineteenth century.

Although he shared the same moral values there is a great deal more to Wardle and his involvement with the Arts and Crafts Movement. He was also an expert on Indian sericulture and spent decades researching the properties of India's silks and dyestuffs. He became an advocate of these silks because he wanted people to take advantage of what lay in front of them. He was consistent in his desire to use India's silks for the benefit of its people in the first instance; he wanted to preserve what was working well and used recent European innovation as the best means of survival and ultimately growth for India's silk production. His were reasonable and achievable goals, yet success was by no means guaranteed; he was well aware that human agency was the key to future success. He was sent to India on a rescue mission where he put his scientific knowledge to great use. He made an exhaustive trawl through the major European silk centres, acquiring the latest technology from France and Italy in order that India could compete, both in its home industry and in the global silk trade. Wardle's work to reinstate the Kashmir silk industry was at great personal cost and effort, it was a great achievement mainly

1 Portrait of Sir Thomas Wardle, 1904.

driven by humanitarian imperatives. He was widely acknowledged as the person who gave most help to India's declining silk industry and gave it a more prominent place in international trade. His is a remarkable success story that demonstrates that there are many colonial experiences that reflect the different values of societies, including their patterns of trade.

Poor understanding of sericulture, backward technology and little exploitation of its vast resources of wild silks had led to India becoming a net importer of foreign silk yarn, mainly from China and Bokhara, as its own thread production fell. Wardle wanted to create a system of manufacture that would leave India more independent of foreign imports and therefore less vulnerable to external market forces. He was very aware that the need for change was urgent; the Indian silk industry would die if it did not adapt to new technologies. Unemployment in both India and England was, therefore, a driving force for change, as was the production of beautiful and well-made things. Competitive advantage was essential for Indian silk producers and the encounter between western science and eastern products, which Thomas Wardle organised, helped to ensure the continuation of India's craft skills in the face of fierce competition. Although greater stability could be achieved by better control over silk yarn production, Wardle recognised that a new system would only work on India's terms, and that these might rest on different assumptions. Through the agency of Thomas Wardle, Indian silk producers acknowledged and accepted the immediate benefit of improved technology from France, Italy, Germany and England.

There was simultaneously great tension in the European silk trade created in part by the influx of silk from China and Japan. Growing globalisation had to some degree increased the mutually dependent nature of the silk trade in Europe. One of Wardle's aims was to remove barriers that may have prevented the free flow of information between those involved in silk production and encouraged rival countries to pool their resources.

Textile archives clearly demonstrate that several modest, but important, English textile manufacturers valued the preservation of more time-consuming and, therefore, more costly craft skills in their workforce. The evidence confirms that many small manufacturers aimed to create textiles in which artistic value was recognised and they strove for perfection in their pursuit of goods that were well designed and well made. Wardle was a manufacturer who aimed for ethical business practice and produced well-made beautiful objects. Other manufacturers shared his views, following Ruskinian principles in many aspects of their production. In an age characterised by widespread technological progress, silk manufacturers maintained craft skills concurrently with technological advancement, well into the twentieth century. Was William Morris really such a rebel, 'against the age', far removed from the values of other textile producers? The evidence suggests that a number of arts and crafts designers and textile manufacturers co-existed in a mutually collaborative climate, which aimed to satisfy the demands of a particular consumer group.

English silk manufacturers were suffering in the face of fierce competition from imported French silks. Desperate to break the monopoly of French silks, they looked to India where the continuation of craft skills, an understanding of design principles and use of colour was considered to be exemplary. India's textiles had provided the West with exemplars in design, construction and utility since at least the seventeenth century; they are still a rich source of stimuli to designers worldwide. This sustained success has been due to a large extent to the flexibility of Indian designs which could readily adapt to international market forces. By the end of the nineteenth century, India's designs were well integrated into Western design practice. The result of this interchange was a wonderful choice of practical and luxurious English textiles. Many of the textile designs produced in England have, however, been seen as merely unthinking Western interpretations of 'Oriental' designs, or as evidence of fleeting fashions, reflecting Western whims for the exotic. It has, moreover, been assumed that India's textiles have been collected and exhibited in the West solely for the purpose of indiscriminate commercial gain.[2] This is an important misunderstanding, as it has been widely accepted that English manufacturers used Indian designs primarily to better penetrate the Indian market, and that this had led to the destruction of India's own textile industries. There has been the belief that, as a consequence, India's ancient textile traditions were ruined by European industrial expansion and colonialism during this period. Debates continue over the extent of the decline.

However, there were complex conditions that contributed to the changes in textile production in India and variations existed from region to region. There are Indian economic historians who claim that 'at least as far as handloom weaving was concerned, the initial decline quite clearly slowed down or reversed by the end of the nineteenth century'.[3] Judgements on this matter depend heavily on the data utilised. Roy emphasises that textile history in India has yet to address the points of continuity between the pre-and post-1800 histories in detail. The long-term impact of European trade has not yet had an important role in research.[4] There are so many variables affecting the collection and presentation of data on India's import and export trade, and on production and consumption, that accuracy is difficult. There is, however, a sizeable amount of evidence from English archives, which provides great insight into the importance that Indian silk textiles had for the West, forcing us to question the received ideas referred to above. This evidence clearly indicates that great efforts were made to retain and support the Indian silk industries.

The history of Indian silk has been overshadowed by the greater economic importance of cotton in imperial history. There is a huge amount of literature devoted to cotton and the empire; a prevailing theme throughout many of the publications is of the British efforts to open up India as the biggest export market for Lancashire's mass-produced cotton goods.[5] In the case of silk the received wisdom about imperial exploitation of the colonial dependency is questioned. India traded textiles with other cultures for centuries before it traded with Europe. This trade lasted throughout the era of empire and continues

[5]

today. Simplistic assumptions about the exploitation of Indian textiles workers by Western businessmen are undermined by the history of silk production. Silk tied India and Britain together in a complex and symbiotic trading relationship. The story here will weaken negative assumptions about Britain's trading relationship with India, as Wardle, acting on behalf of Indian and English authorities, engaged with Indian silks to the greater benefit of both.

Although the textile industry was a major employer throughout the Victorian era, little is known about the training of textile designers. Good design was, however, a major weapon in the fight against massive imports of French silks during this period. Drawing on little-known archive material it is possible to demonstrate how designers were educated for the silk trade in major centres of production. Educationalists, artists, designers and manufacturers worked together towards a common goal and India's design heritage played an exemplary role for them all.

The nineteenth century was a time of influential international exhibitions and the founding of many major museums. India was given huge prominence in major international exhibitions; its goods were fêted, they gained prestigious awards and made a huge impact on the general public. India's luxurious silks, which were displayed in numerous exhibitions, were collected afterwards and many have survived in British archives. The importance of much of this archive material has remained unrecognised.

The lack of a comprehensive history of the English silk industry is surprising as is the positioning of Indian silk history in the era of empire. This history specifically addresses the production and consumption of silk in an integrated manner. In particular it deals with silk's aesthetic values in the context of modern technological advances, social forces, tensions between business practice and ethical production and global trade; in doing so it reflects a growing interest in the regionalisation of imperial history. Previous histories of the English silk industry are fragmentary and it is a largely neglected area of cultural history.[6] Even though design was a significant factor in the marketplace, there are economic histories that do not address aesthetics; and there are a small number which deal with the aesthetic aspects, but which do not include the vital economic base upon which production was predicated. Throughout this period English consumers imported French silks in vast quantities. This exacerbated the strains on the English silk industry, which, unlike cotton with its economies of scale, was more subject to fashionable trends and subsequent periodic booms and busts. English silk design eventually developed its own characteristics, reflecting the values of designers, manufacturers and a distinctive consumer group. Good design was a key factor, yet only a few theorists could provide clear definitions of what they felt this to be. Besides William Morris, a key spokesperson on design values was the less-well known, but influential silk manufacturer, Thomas Wardle. His work and writings make him a key figure in this publication.

By pulling together a number of disparate histories this book contributes to a better understanding of English and Indian silk industries. The broad sweep is deliberate as such wide-ranging evidence sustains the notion that there area number of neglected contexts for evaluating India's silk textiles. By advancing our understanding across a variety of fronts it is possible to demonstrate the pervasiveness of the idea that Indian silks displayed universal principles to a number of key people.

The book is divided into two parts covering broad themes, as follows. Part I summarises the Anglo-Indian silk trade and the global context for silk production. Chapter One focuses on the state of sericulture in England from the early nineteenth century to the early twentieth century. Chapter Two is concerned with design issues in the English silk industry and the threat from mainland Europe, especially France. It includes the importance of international museums and exhibitions for the textile industries. It also summarises English design education, which was identified as contributing to the weakness of design skills. Case studies of Manchester Municipal School of Art, Bradford Technical College and Macclesfield School of Art examine significant information in the form of cloth samples, student notebooks and educational publications, which reveal how design education for the textiles industry operated in major centres of silk production and how Indian silks were used as exemplars. Chapter Three provides a short overview of silk textile production in India where cloth is central to the culture. Although many splendid publications cover a vast range of India's textiles, this survey provides a brief introduction and context for those who may be unfamiliar with the high quality fabrics, exemplary designs and excellent manual skills in weaving, embroidery, printing and dyeing. Chapter Four explains the state of sericulture in India from the early nineteenth century to the early twentieth century.

Part II focuses on Thomas Wardle and brings him in from the margins. Chapter Five covers his background influences and highlights the role of the small business in international trade. It details his aesthetic sense, in particular his appreciation of traditional Indian textile designs and techniques. Chapter Six centres on Wardle's travels in India and his role in the modernisation of its silk industry. A major interest is the collecting of silks in India, the displaying of those silks in England and the politics of display that were involved.

Three major international exhibitions are highlighted: the Paris International Exposition of 1878, the Colonial and Indian Exhibition of 1886 and the Manchester Royal Jubilee Exhibition of 1887. The roles of major exhibitions are discussed in the context of the silk trade during the era of the British Empire. The magnificent Indian silk collection in the Whitworth Art Gallery, Manchester, is given prominent coverage; case studies of other Indian silk collections are included. Chapter Seven considers the Arts and Crafts Movement in the context of English silk production. It focuses on William Morris, the Leek Embroidery Society and Liberty and Co. The Conclusion discusses the wealth of evidence in the form of objects and texts, which are the legacies of the silk trade between England and India. The most important evidence used for this publication is in the form of the many nineteenth-century Indian silk textiles that survive in the provinces and in London.

The provincial collections have never previously been fully re-searched, although they are clearly an important resource for histor-ians and designers. They are, for the most part, collections acquired by leading English institutions directly from major exhibitions during this period. International exhibitions have been identified as forma-tive events in design development, yet some, such as Manchester's Royal Jubilee exhibition (1887), have not hitherto been researched. Many of the specialised textile collections formed by national and provincial museums were collected to serve practical commercial con-cerns, one of which was the promotion and support of a local, regional or national industry. Although there is a growing body of literature, which explores the politics of museum collections and exhibitions,[7] the textile archives used for this research have not been previously assessed in this manner.

Seen from an English perspective the accumulated evidence of both objects and documents confirms that a wide range of institutions and individuals valued the same technical expertise and pattern-making elements in Indian silks. Individually, the collections discussed here demonstrate why Indian silk textiles were valuable to a specific insti-tution. Collectively they show patterns and regularities in collecting policies. By linking formerly disparate collections it is possible to confirm the centrality of India's textile designs and to underscore the widespread and consistent nature of their influence. Although other cultures and eras provided important sources of inspiration to England's textile industries, India offered the widest range of textile techniques as well as providing a long-standing record of excellence in dyeing.

The main themes of this book are competitiveness and commercial survival through collaboration, making things well, understanding appropriate design principles, the importance of design education to commercial success and the role of the textile museum. The most important theme, however, is that there are many experiences that make up the British Empire and that the role of individuals can be as important as the role of major institutions.

NB It is important to note that when discussing Indian silks that there are two distinct types: the 'domesticated' or mulberry-feeding silkworms (*Bombycidae*) and the 'wild' or non-mulberry feeding silkworms (*Saturnidae*). Mulberry feeding and non-mulberry feeding are more accurate terms than domesticated or wild, as certain 'wild' varieties have undergone a degree of husbandry over the centuries. Very early references to Indian silk usually indicate the non-mulberry feeders, as the cultivated silkworms of commerce did not arrive from China until possibly the second century BC. 'Wild' and 'cultivated' are the more commonly used terms in publications, however, and are less clumsy for repetitive use, therefore, they will be used within. Furthermore, this is an English history; Scotland had its own connections with India's textile industry.

Notes

1 I refer to archives in The Whitworth Art Gallery, Manchester; the Gallery of Costume, Platt Hall, Manchester; Manchester Metropolitan University; Macclesfield Silk Heritage Museum, Cheshire; Salford Museum; Bradford and Ilkley Technical College; the Local History Collection, Leek Library, Staffordshire.
2 Banham, Macdonald and Porter, 1991, p. 48.
3 Roy, 1996, p. 13.
4 Ibid.
5 Twomey, 1983, p. 37.
6 I refer to Warner, 1921; Mathias, 1969; Coleman, 1969; Berg, 1994; Federico, 1997.
7 Barringer and Flynn (eds), 1998; Elsner and Cardinal (eds); Hooper-Greenhill, 1992; Karp and Lavine (eds), 1990; Pearce, 1992.

PART I

The Anglo-Indian silk trade

COLOUR PLATES 1 AND 2

Macclesfield School of Art, student's design on paper for woven silk, 1910

Macclesfield School of Art, student's design woven in silk, 1920s

Brocaded *tasar* silk samples, woven in Macclesfield, 1885

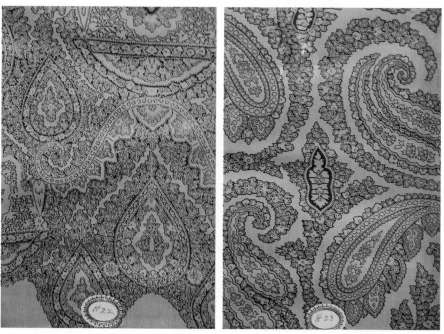

Silk printed in Macclesfield with 'Indian' designs, 1930s–40s

Silk printed in Macclesfield with 'Indian tie-dye' and 'Kashmir' inspired designs, 1930s–40s

A *patolu* sari, India, 1885

Kinkab, detail, red silk and gold thread, India, 1885

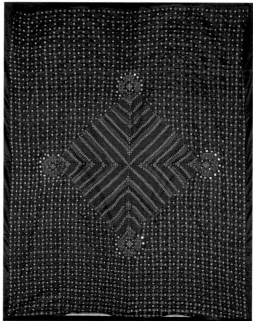

Embroidered shawl, Kutch, India, 1885

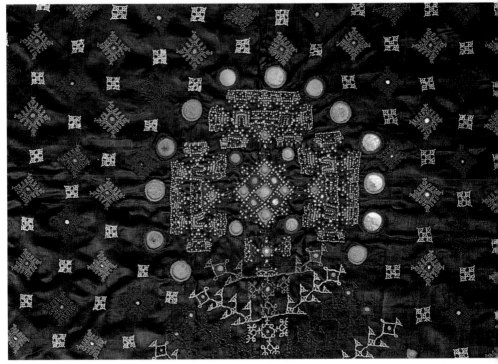

Detail of Embroidered shawl, Kutch, India, 1885

Macclesfield School of Art, student's design woven in silk, 1920s

William Morris designs printed by
Thomas Wardle on Indian silk cloth, c.1878

Greek embroidery on silk brocade (detail), c.1880

Leek embroidery, 'Indian Poppy' on Indian *tasar* silk (detail), c.1880

Leek embroidery (detail) on Indian *tasar* silk, border inspired by Indian designs, c.1880

CHAPTER ONE

The state of silk manufacturing in England from 1830 to 1930

Throughout the nineteenth century the textile industries in Europe were central to economic developments worldwide. The English silk industry of this period is, however, an under-researched field and few previous works have addressed this subject in an integrated manner.[1] Surprisingly, even though design was a significant factor for consumers, scholars of economic history have paid little attention to the aesthetic aspects of silk production, in particular the role of colour, which was such a vital element in the marketplace.

During the eighteenth and nineteenth centuries, English silk manufacturing saw its highest achievements and its most serious problems; by the last quarter of the nineteenth century it was an industry in decline. Throughout the nineteenth century the English silk industry remained structurally diverse and geographically scattered. Silk production in one form or another existed mainly in small pockets in Cheshire, Coventry, Derbyshire, Essex, Greater Manchester, Hampshire, Leicester, Nottingham, Norfolk, Yorkshire, Staffordshire, Scotland and Ireland. Although the expansion, which had begun in the eighteenth century, continued, the 1860 Chevalier-Cobden Treaty with France was to prove a watershed. This commercial treaty with France was disastrous for the English silk industry. It removed protection from English silk cloth and exposed a then fragile industry to the full onslaught of foreign competition. Richard Cobden's vision placed great confidence in free trade as a defender of peace and prosperity.[2] His theory was that non-interventionist trade would connect corresponding economies, extending the trade between them in such a way that war would be improbable. However, several petitions from struggling silk manufacturers to Parliament opposed it. The terms of the treaty regarding the silk trades allowed French silk goods into England free of charge while English silk goods were to be subject to a duty in France not exceeding 30 per cent *ad valorem*.[3] The consequence was a major contraction of English silk production as more than 250 silk manufacturers were badly affected by the more open competition from France.

The English silk industry was the subject of much debate in the nineteenth century as English consumers imported vast quantities of French silks. Even though they were more expensive, they were considered to be superior on a number of counts, and their designs in particular were preferred to English ones. This exacerbated the strain on the English silk industry, which, unlike cotton with its economies of scale derived from mass production, was a luxury product subject to changes in fashion, which brought about periodic booms and busts.

Large supplies of cheap labour, often children, meant that manually operated winding and throwing mills continued long after water and steam power appeared in the cotton industry. Moreover, the yarn produced by these mills was still bought by handloom weavers, working at home or in small workshops. Records show that Manchester and its environs alone still had approximately 8,700 handloom weavers working at the end of the nineteenth century. As Warner argues, the lack of cohesion and unity of effort, in political, economical, technical and educational matters, was undoubtedly a source of weakness.[4] This was the case whether judged relative to the prosperity of silk workers in other countries, or to those engaged in the other branches of the textile industries in Great Britain and Ireland.

Provincial as well as foreign competition reduced the Spitalfields silk weavers to sweated labour by the early nineteenth century. After the rapid entry of cheaper labour from redundant cotton handloom weavers in the 1820s, the status of silk weavers in Macclesfield and Manchester took a similar course. By far the biggest growth in weavers was in greater Manchester; Jacquard looms were operating there from 1823, thereafter there was regular production of figured silks.[5] Having survived free trade initiatives in 1820s and 1845, the expansion, which had begun under eighteenth century protection, continued. However, the Cobden Treaty was a heavy blow. The industry at that point was diverse in character; it was composed of companies scattered across twenty-two counties, some of which carried out numerous processes while others were more specialised. 'Hard' silk (a yarn that still retained the silk-gum on the thread), was used by some manufacturers for cheaper goods such as plain umbrellas and dress silks. 'Soft' silk (a yarn that had the gum removed), was utilised for more general weaving. The more recent and swiftly expanding business of spun silk used silk waste for the manufacture of velvets, plushes and upholstery trimmings. Many English textile manufacturers considered that the powerloom could never be successfully adapted to elaborate silk weaving. Although large numbers of handloom weavers were still employed as outworkers, increasing numbers of weavers were operating powerlooms in large factories to produce cheaper plain silks.

In England silk was classed as 'small manufactures' compared to the thriving cotton and woollen industries. The silk industry was, therefore, given little consideration by those outside the trade, especially politicians, compared to the huge interest accorded to the more prosperous sector concerned with mass-produced textiles such as cotton. The consequence was that the Spitalfields silk industry virtually disappeared. Many middlemen and retailers prospered, however. They filled their warehouses and shops with cheaper goods from France made specifically for the purpose, at less difficulty and threat to themselves than hitherto; and they were sold alongside cheap stock from Spitalfields firms that had closed. This influx of cheaper French silks hastened the extinction of those English manufacturers who made similar goods, which for some time had been the mainstay of Spitalfields weavers.

After the 1860s, protective tariffs remained in place in a number of European countries. Many European manufacturers, moreover, operated with newer and better machinery and/or lower labour costs. During the final decades of the nineteenth century the silk industries of France, Germany, Switzerland, Japan and America grew rapidly, supplying their home markets and competing with English goods in export markets. French and Swiss silk textiles were exported to Britain in increasing quantities. The worldwide expansion of silk manufacturing did prevent raw silk prices from falling, although ominously the centre of the European raw silk market moved from London to Lyons. The inadequacies of English technical education and weak designs became more obvious than ever. Consequently, all parts of the English silk industry faced a series of grim challenges from 1860 onwards. Different reactions to these challenges moulded the future of the industry. Spun and hard silks were less affected, but falling prices, foreign competition and increasing tariff barriers exacerbated the general slump. The number of artisans engaged in English silk production fell to about a quarter of the number employed in 1850, mostly due to the contraction of handloom weaving. At the same time, the imports of silk textiles reached five times the volume of domestic production. The overall result was that silk manufacturers were drastically reduced in number. Towards the end of the nineteenth century, however, those who had captured a specialised segment of the market had survived (see Chapter Six). Macclesfield remained the strongest of the provincial centres, although marginal products were weeded out of production.

Thomas Wardle was a key figure in the development of the English silk industry at a crucial time. He was elected as the first President of the Silk Association of Great Britain and Ireland when it was formed in 1887, an office which he kept until his death in 1909. The association was formed in order to promote and develop the silk industry in all its branches at a time when it was causing deep concern. Membership included silk manufacturers, merchants, dyers and finishers and others who were interested in the well-being of the industry. Silk manufacturers were acutely aware that their industry was not maintaining equilibrium and might become fixed in a position where it would be beyond rescue. The best they could try to do was to prevent disaster; some were more concerned with preventing further decline than with huge profit margins. Technical instruction was given a high profile and largely due to the efforts of the association the important Municipal School of Technology was founded in Manchester.[6]

The desire to preserve the English silk industry was very clear, and many manufacturers refused to consider that Britain would be forced by French imports to abandon silk production. They recognised that it was not simply a matter of reducing wages to make English silk goods cheaper to produce and subsequently be more competitive on price. There was a clear and constantly stated need to substitute imported French silk goods with well-designed English silks that would satisfy the discerning English consumer. The production of a better product would lead to greater employment in the silk industry and prevent the poverty that followed unemployment. It was crucial to raise the image of English silks to encourage fashionable English consumers to purchase them. The formation of the Ladies' National Silk Association in 1890 set out to promote British silks to British women. The first President was HRH Princess Mary Adelaide, Duchess of Teck; she was succeeded by her daughter the Princess of Wales.

Exhibitions of British silk were organised by this association at prestigious addresses in London, aiming to draw the public's attention to the fact that British manufacturers could produce excellent silks for furnishings and dress. Although the stratagems were a down-to-earth response to fundamental global changes and the unprecedented level of international competition, one question dominated: just how much must the domestic economy be forced to adjust to the dictates of the international economy? In 1905 the Silk Association successfully appealed against proposed increased tariffs by the French Senate on silks entering France. The tariffs, if adopted, would have seriously damaged the British silk industry, particularly the producers of black silk crape who had a large export trade with France.

In addition to these pragmatic services, which helped to reinvigorate the silk industry, the Silk Association also provided an important means of inter-communication between its widely scattered members, which had not previously existed, and operated for the benefit of them all. They shared the same concerns and often the same values, and it was increasingly obvious that they needed to tackle huge practical problems together, if they were to stimulate design education to improve English silk designs as well as produce beautiful fabrics. In 1886 the *Report of the Royal Commission on Depression in Trade*[7] revealed that many Macclesfield manufacturers were well aware of the minutiae of international trade and foreign markets and had a working knowledge of business practices, as well as art and technical education in France, Germany, Italy and Switzerland. The importance of good technical education was clearly understood, as was the role of trade museums in generating a sense of good design. They shared similar concerns, had analysed the reasons for silk industries decline and offered well-thought-out solutions.

Many silk manufacturers and design theorists who were consistent in their thinking and who wanted to make beautiful things in an ethical manner followed the ethics of the Arts and Crafts Movement. They shared the same moral values as Morris and Ruskin, only differing in the best way to maintain skills. Some leading English designers adopted an aesthetic that derived from the Arts and Crafts Movement (see Chapter Six). England became a less successful market for French exports when a preference for different styles heralded a period of change towards the end of the century. This was a time when French silk patterns, particularly those for furnishings, did not change dramatically and many designs inspired by the eighteenth century continued to be produced in France until well into the twentieth century. Features of the distinctly new style Art Nouveau, which took many of its features from Arts and Crafts design and oriental influences, were evident in English designs from the 1880s and were also in demand in France. English consumers demanded softer silks for dress and furnishings, with an increasing range of fashionable colours. Surviving evidence in the form of manufacturers' pattern books reveals that a huge range of designs were manufactured throughout the first quarter of the twentieth century, indicating that a variety of tastes were catered for. Handloom weaving was still practised, albeit for a highly specialised market, as late as the 1930s in Sherborne in Dorset and as late as the 1980s in Macclesfield, when one handloom weaver was still working.

Notes

1 A notable exception is *English and American Textiles* by Schoeser and Ruffey, 1989.
2 Richard Cobden (1804–65), English economist and politician, known as the 'Apostle of Free Trade', was financially involved with the cotton industry.
3 Chadwick, *The Silk Manufacturers*, p. 14.
4 Warner, 1921, p. 151.
5 The Jacquard loom was invented by Charles Marie Jacquard (1752–1834) in France in 1801–8. It was a major technological development which greatly reduced the time needed for weaving complex patterns.
6 This became known as UMIST.
7 *The Royal Commission on Depression in Trade. Report of Evidence of a Deputation from Macclesfield on the Decline of the English Silk Trade*, 1886.

CHAPTER TWO

Design issues in the English
silk industry

The period that began with William Ewart's work towards the Parliamentary Commission on Art and Design Education between 1834 and 1936[1] and ended with the Gorrell report on Art and Industry in 1932,[2] was a time when trade between India and England underwent changes and the English textile industries were identifying new markets for their products. It was a time of intense interest in art and technical education and increased interaction between art schools and industry, when India's textile designs provided models for best practice and had a unitary significance in different regions and institutions. Industrialists and educators aimed to balance production with consumption and improvements in art and technical education were seen as crucial elements in the battle to retain a hold over world markets. Concern over design education was related to the series of international exhibitions and coincided with the growth of museums. All of these developments were directed towards producing a better-trained workforce for industry, rather than an individual worker's self-improvement.

A wide range of primary evidence ranging from textbooks and students' notebooks to cloth samples woven by students attending art schools and technical schools,[3] has given new insights into the teaching of textile design in the nineteenth century.

Extensive reports in trade journals such as the *Textile Recorder* and journals for theorists such as the *Journal of Design* and the *Journal of Decorative Art*, along with minutes and other documents relating to the individual institutions are important sources of information relating to textile designs and trade matters. Publications by designer-educators, aimed at artisans training for the textile industries, provide a clear picture of late nineteenth-century industrial and theoretical attitudes. Statements about Victorian design values, however, carry little meaning unless we can comprehend how the objects under discussion relate to the theories. The publications were, therefore, examined alongside contemporary textiles in order to arrive at an understanding of what the theorists meant by true and false principles of design and how they related to design education. Collections of Indian textiles in teaching institutions provide invaluable primary sources, as do samples of English silk textiles produced during the period. When texts and objects are examined together they have the potential to give us a clearer understanding of what was meant by 'good' design principles than either would when studied alone.

Due to rapidly increasing changes in the methods of production during the nineteenth century, artisans designing for the textile industry needed to respond to new technologies and more complex markets. As a result, art and technical education became formalised and more detailed. As we have seen, French silk goods posed the greatest threat to the English silk industry. In 1847 Manchester manufacturers alone were spending about £20–30,000 per annum on imported French designs in order to provide consumers with the patterns they demanded.[4] In addition, competition from Germany, Switzerland and the USA increased towards the end of the century. In the face of such fierce competition, powerful English textile manufacturers attempted to galvanise the government into action in order to improve design and technical education. The Parliamentary Commission on Art and Design Education (1835–36) resulted in a national system of art and technical education, which was centrally organised by the Board of Trade. In 1836 the Central School of Art and Design[5] was founded, swiftly followed by a branch in Spitalfields, then the centre of English silk production. There followed a period when schools of design were opened in manufacturing areas throughout the country. However, the result was often an erratic distribution of institutions, which in some cases duplicated the Mechanics' Institutes, already in place.[6] Overall standards in the schools were inconsistent and became a matter for public concern.

The problem of what to teach and to whom was one that had been recognised earlier when Mechanics' Institutes were established. This continued, amid a great deal of confusion surrounding the curriculum of the schools of design in their early years. However, there was 'an important discussion of principle, a debate concerning the nature of art schools, which turned on the question of whether they should be workshops or academies'.[7]

There was an established precedent of manufacturers' involvement in education, in industrial regions. The Manchester Mechanics' Institute had involved local industrialists and had been influential in producing an informed workforce for the local industries. However, each local textile industry was differently structured and attitudes towards the education of artisans depended on the type of product being manu-factured. The more enlightened manufacturers took many factors into account when they became involved with local education; furthermore, they often needed to battle with their more indifferent colleagues. Generally, as Rifkin observes, 'The Utopian dream of a wise and cultiv-ated workforce enters profoundly into the cultural make-up of the industrial managers and entrepreneurial classes'.[8] And, if industrialists and design educators did not always agree about how to achieve this Utopian dream in Manchester, they remained equally convinced of the important role which Indian textiles had to play in design educa-tion. As we shall see, Indian textiles remained a constant factor in the debate over the teaching of design.

Despite the fact that the schools of design were the result of both state provision and the support of manufacturers, after a decade or so there were still no obvious discernible benefits for the luxury indus-tries such as silk. This was all too evident when English textile manu-factures were displayed at the Great Exhibition, and theorists such as Henry Cole (1808–82) and Richard Redgrave (1804–88) among others, pronounced the schools of design failures in the *Journal of Design*, which Cole founded. Cole and his supporters introduced reforms and proposed a new ethos that revolved around theories of appropriate design. Publications followed in which true and false principles of design were discussed. Alongside discourses on aesthetics were others concerned with foreign competition, the realities of production, profit and loss and the relationship between production and consumption. Overall, foreign competition was the strongest motivating force for change.

At the mid-point of the nineteenth century, the supremacy of the British textile industry lay in its highly industrialised sectors. The manufacture of dyed and printed cotton cloth was mechanised and intensive factory production, with its economies of scale, meant that it was more cost-effective and price was a deciding factor for the consumer of cotton. English silk production, on the other hand, still depended on a great deal of hand technology and a division of labour that created a lower profit margin. The production of costly luxury silk goods had more to fear from foreign goods, as superior designs were their main attraction, and more to gain, therefore, from improved design education. Consequently, although they occupied a smaller sector of the market, silk manufacturers were a driving force for educational reform. They knew only too well that French designers' superior skills were the result of training that allowed for greater in-dividual creativity. Most French designers were capable of practising all aspects of the silk weaving process, as well as producing designs on paper; whereas the English system rested on a greater division of labour skills. Furthermore, in Lyons, the heart of the French silk region, there was a fine design school and famous school of flower painting, geared entirely to the local industry.

Throughout this period of intense debate, Indian textiles carried considerable weight as exemplars of good design and utility. The technical and design characteristics found in Indian textiles provided a unifying element in that design theorists, textile producers and consumers all admired them. This was the case for many major European textile-manufacturing countries and most types of textile manufacture. Indian textiles widely influenced woven, printed and embroidered textile production in France, Germany, Austria, Switzerland and America. Indian designs maintained a relevance to aesthetic and technical education throughout the period under discussion, although one can detect shifts in their importance that corresponds to different moments of international competition. At different times it was their patterns, their handling of colour, the usefulness of different types of silks, the fact that they signified the continuation of time-honoured craft skills and a traditional way of life, which took precedence in debates.

Manchester School of Art, Macclesfield School of Art and Bradford Technical College provide interesting case studies relating to the debates surrounding design theories. All three schools were concerned with silk production, all three had dynamic tutors who published seminal works on design for artisans, and all three acknowledged the influences of collections of Indian textiles. Although they are typical of all art and technical schools in some ways, each institution had its own distinct and local concerns. Using primary sources it is possible to account for the differences between these institutions, with special reference to the importance of Indian design as a stable and continuous factor during a period of educational and industrial change.

Case study: the Manchester School of Art

The Manchester School of Art opened in 1838. Its early history was stormy and the cause of much consternation in the city. Prior to this Manchester had a history of enlightened art patronage and workers' education.[9] During the period under review the institution changed its location, name, size, financial status and the types of education it offered. The Manchester School of Design, as it was first known, soon became an art school with an inclination towards life drawing. By 1840 many of the classes reflected a desire to break down the barriers between the training of a designer and the training of a fine artist.[10] During its formative years local businessmen seemed unwilling to support the school and at one point sent only 6 out of a possible 400 workers. It seemed that the school had very little to offer the local cotton industries where cheapness rather than design was the main selling factor. Unlike silk producers, cotton manufacturers were unwilling to pay for educated designers and the workers were not eager to learn. Furthermore, this was a nationwide problem. It became obvious that there were difficulties in accepting either of two possible approaches: courses devised for the specific needs of local manufacturers, or one general course responding to many needs.

In 1847 John Grogan, Headmaster of the Manchester School of Art, suggested that pupils should be given a general curriculum rather than a specialist one. Grogan considered that cultivation of the mind was the root of successful designing and that this could be applied to whatever branch of manufacturing a student chose to enter. In 1849 the Manchester School was reported in the *Journal of Design and Manufactures* to be the 'unfortunate Manchester School', and in a state of complete subordination to the Science and Art Department in London. It was 'the most signal failure, whilst it ought to be the most important school we have'; ineffective 'for those classes for whose benefit the school was established'.[11] In the same edition of the *Journal* a number of mass-produced English textile designs came under scrutiny and several of them described as brilliant, although not novel, were identified as inspired by Indian design. The thousand years of continuity behind Indian design was considered 'a tolerable proof of its goodness'.

The year after Manchester's Royal Jubilee Exhibition (1887), the Manchester School was reported, 'pre-eminently as the one that has made the most rapid strides, and achieved the greatest success'.[12] It followed the South Kensington system, earning its grants by working to the rules set by the central authority. It had previously been governed by a graduate of that system and became more successful in achieving consistently good examination results. Manchester's success was due to the newest head of school, R.H.A. Willis, who brought about radical changes, raising the school's status.[13] The school's standing became one of the highest under the jurisdiction of the Science and Art Department. The history of ornament was a strong element in the design classes, and students were directed to study the best examples of work in their chosen field. It was the principals of design evident in antique objects that were studied, and not simply their appearance, which could be copied. The tutors considered that this would create a wide and liberal basis for designers' ideas to grow.

The Arts and Crafts Movement was an influential force in Manchester, with powerful and articulate spokespersons, who advocated a hands-on approach to designing. This was a counterpoint to the non-specific teaching in most art schools; too many students ended up with no experience of making an object or understanding either the principles of design or the production processes. Although the Arts and Crafts Movement was highly influential it was still surprising to some that the Manchester School of Art took on so many elements of its thinking, considering the huge emphasis placed on mass-production in the north-west region. A number of influential local industrialists were, however, firm supporters of Arts and Crafts principles and philanthropic supporters of the arts.

As the Manchester School gained increasing independence from the curriculum imposed by the Department of Science and Art, it recruited prominent artists to its staff, and they developed the teaching along lines approved by local businessmen. Leading members of the Arts and Crafts Movement best fitted the teaching role as far as silk manufacturers was concerned. During the 1890s the prominent Head Master, Richard Glazier, was also eager to propel the school towards the crafts.[14] Glazier published a number of volumes, several of which (including *A Manual of Historic Ornament* and *Historic Textile Fabrics* (1899)), became respected textbooks. Indian designs figured prominently in these publications.

In 1892 Walter Crane, known today primarily for his book illustrations, but also for designs for textiles and ceramics,[15] was offered the post of Director of Design at Manchester. Crane was also a writer and painter and had been the first President of the Art Workers' Guild (1884), and first President of the Arts and Crafts Exhibition Society (1889–90). No artist of his status would have enmeshed themselves in the difficulties of running a major art school unless they had a profound interest in art education. Crane was, by then, known as a crusader for art education reform and challenged the power that South Kensington exercised over the curriculum.[16] Crane's appointment was symptomatic of the provincial schools forming their own opinions on education. He was clearly expected to establish a teaching system that would encourage students to work imaginatively. During his period as Director of Design (1893–97), Crane developed many of his theories relating to design education and presented these to the governing body and students.

Crane felt it was important to include a section in the Manchester curriculum devoted to colour; this was entitled 'Study in Colour: Harmonies Derived from Nature'. It was innovative as few schools officially recognised the importance of colour in design. He defined this area of study as that which included the arrangement of patterns and schemes of decoration with selected tints and harmonies. Under

Crane students quickly gained a wider choice and greater freedom of expression. They were encouraged to aim for good style and artistic expression above mere surface finish and neat execution. Hopes were raised for the school's future success.

Insight into Crane's teaching at Manchester can be gained by examining three of his publications which became set books of design theory: *Recommendations and Suggestions* (1893), *The Bases of Design* (1898) and *Line and Form* (1900). These volumes aimed to develop an understanding of universal design principles. Both *Line and Form* and the *Bases of Design* promoted Indian textile designs as exceptional. In Crane's view their importance lay in the ways in which the flora of India was transformed into another existence in cloth. In particular it was the 'small rich detail and variety'; the 'inventive spirit' in the treatment of colour, and the 'delicate subsidiary pattern of Indian designs' of which Crane approved.[17] He argued that the lack of shading was vital to a successful pattern and promoted the Indian exemplars as displaying principles that students of design should aim to understand completely. He urged student designers to make themselves familiar with them in order to acquire a comprehension of the 'intricacy in colour and pattern', not in order to copy mindlessly.

The lines and forms in Indian textiles demonstrated many possibilities in pattern. In the 'palmette'[18] motif alone Crane found a capacity that could be utilised to the utmost potential. The longevity of the 'palmette' motif was, to some extent, dependent on its symbolic importance, although Crane considered it was most likely to be due to the beauty of its contour. Its significance in a textile pattern consisted of 'its graceful swirling mass . . . its bold and sweeping curves, for its value as an inclosing form for small floral fittings'.[19] It was, however, to be used as a model that should be adapted in fresh ways to produce new varieties of ornament.

The appointment of so prominent an artist and free thinker to run an influential school focused the art establishment's attention on Manchester. The increased success of Manchester students in national competitions indicates that central authorities approved of the new curriculum. By the end of Crane's Manchester tenure, however, changes had taken place and South Kensington had become increasingly sympathetic to the growing interest in handicrafts. His appointment at Manchester was, therefore, probably not as radical as it first appeared, but was in line with changes already taking place in London and Birmingham. When Crane was appointed as Director of the new Royal College of Art in 1898, he was by then accepted as a campaigner for changes in the schools of art.

Lewis Forman Day was an enormously influential and successful practising designer, who lectured at the Manchester School of Art. Day was well known as a designer of textiles, embroidery, wallpaper, stained glass and book covers. He was also a journalist, art critic and design historian. From 1881 he was Artistic Director of Turnbull and Stockdale, a prominent textile company, and produced freelance designs, including some for Thomas Wardle. In 1884 he was Master of the Art Workers' Guild and was a founder member of the Arts and Crafts Exhibition Society (1888). Day was a collector of embroidered textiles and made generous gifts of some of his collections to the Manchester Art School Museum, notably collections of Japanese prints and Indian embroideries.[20]

Day wrote extensively, aiming much of his published work at students of art and design. Like Crane and others before him, he was at pains to demonstrate appropriate principles inspired by nature, in order that students might produce designs of their own. He covered aspects of pattern and ornament in great detail, including: *Some Principles of Every-Day Art* (1882), *The Anatomy of Pattern* (1887), *The Planning of Ornament* (1887), *The Application of Ornament* (1888), *Line and Form* (1900), *Art in Needlework* (1900), *Pattern Design* (1903) and *Nature and Ornament* (1908). *Nature and Ornament* (1908) contained many references to the value of Indian design and its underlying principles of pattern making. It was considered to be his best publication and became a standard work of reference for design students for some time afterwards. Day wrote *Pattern Design* from the perspective of a practitioner with an obvious feeling for the evolution of a design, from the starting point to the finished result. This too became a popular textbook, which was reprinted many times.

The Manchester Municipal School of Art gallery

The 1880s was a particularly interesting period for the school, when an art gallery with a study collection was planned. Throughout this period of change the curriculum shows a strong emphasis on antique designs, and historic ornament. The Textile Court was the largest space in the new gallery; a permanent display of textiles was envisaged:

> [A] selection of the Decorative Textile Works from Persia and India ought to be acquired at once to hang in frames on the walls of the New School. . . . these designs may not always suit the taste of the present, but as time goes on, and when the population becomes more cultivated in art matters, they will certainly become duly recognised and appreciated, and would form the basis of education for the future designers of this country.[21]

On the east and north walls of the Textile Court a collection of woven textiles was displayed; some items were from the Bock Collection, an extensive range of woven silks, with some wool, linen and cotton. The collection, which included a number of interesting Indian textiles, had been purchased in 1883 by the Manchester Corporation. It had been chosen to 'represent the perfect mastery of the material, whilst the beauty and diversity of the ornamentation indicated the skill and resource of the craftsman'.[22] Alongside the above were examples of the finest Indian textiles loaned from South Kensington Museum's circulation department arranged on the walls, and in four glass cases. The loan collections changed annually.

Given Manchester's position as the chief centre of the cotton industry it is hardly surprising that a large section of the gallery was dedicated to textiles. However, it was perhaps surprising that so many leading Arts and Crafts designers were represented in the exhibits, given that the bulk of Manchester's textile production was mass-produced. Walter Crane had always been convinced of the value of museums for design education. His 'Suggestions for the School', stated:

> [A] museum of carefully selected examples of the best kinds of design in various materials . . . would be a most important and necessary thing in connection with the School of Art. It would indeed form a kind of object lesson and reference library in the solid to students in design and its value and influence could hardly be over-estimated.[23]

In October 1907 the School of Art gallery hosted one of the first major exhibitions in England devoted to the work of Walter Crane. Crane loaned about 170 of his designs for display, including a number for textiles.

Over a period of fifty years, the School of Art amassed an impressive teaching collection of printed, woven and embroidered textiles. For the most part the collection of ancient and contemporary fabrics was the result of generous donations; some from local benefactors with a strong interest in Indian designs. Outstanding amongst these were a wide range of Oriental, Coptic and ancient European examples given by C.P. Scott, proprietor of the *Manchester Guardian*; the L.F. Day collection of Indian embroideries; donations by Jane Morris, and T.C. Horsfall of the Manchester Art Museum and contemporary designs by William Morris and C.F.A. Voysey. Ultimately the collection contained one of the most complete displays of Arts and Crafts workmanship in the country and was considered to be a great asset to the cultural life of Manchester. There was a purchase fund for items and donations were augmented by loan collections from the South Kensington Museum. In 1966 the textile collection of 2,500 items was deposited on permanent loan to the Whitworth Art Gallery, Manchester.

The Indian silk textiles that have survived can be briefly summarised as an assortment of embroidered woven and printed pieces mostly from the nineteenth century, although some pieces were from the seventeenth and eighteenth centuries. The collection consists mainly of small pieces although one large shawl is complete. Some are crudely executed while others display sophisticated techniques. The printed cottons demonstrate the traditional Indian motifs that were widely known at that time. This collection contains a number of distinctive fabrics from the Lewis Forman Day Bequest, including the collection of Mrs L.F. Day, which forms a sub-group, chiefly of Indian embroideries. The characteristics of this small embroidery collection demonstrate an interest in strong colour contrast rather than fine technique. Bold patterns are typical; and examples of different stitches are evident.

The School of Art collection also included woven and printed Indian silks. These are not of the highest order, although one piece is an early nineteenth-century gold and silk *kincob*. Other silk fragments include brocades, satins, tissue and a piece of cotton towelling with a silk stripe. On the whole, the designs are of small repeated floral motifs, including some recognisably Indian *buti* motifs. It is likely that these textiles were used to demonstrate the use of colour, motif or a particular example of embroidery stitch, rather than to teach the complex techniques necessary to weave silk cloth.

In addition to the college collections, students in Manchester, Macclesfield and Bradford had access to John Forbes Watson's *Collection of Specimens and Illustrations of the Textile Manufactures of India*. This was a primary source of huge importance, containing as it did, over 700 fabric samples for designers and manufacturers to study. A text accompanied the samples and was illustrated with images of Indian people wearing garments made from textiles of the types represented in the sample books. The Science and Art Department circulated books on various subjects to the provincial art schools. In 1869 the Manchester School of Art acquired the illustrated publication *Fifty Etchings of Objects of Art in the South Kensington Museum*.[24]

The *Collection of Specimens and Illustrations of the Textile Manufactures of India* had been assembled by John Forbes Watson (1827–92), a Reporter on the products of India for the East India Company. Like a number of other doctors in service in India, he may have become interested in the classification of plants because of their use as *materia medica*. From this background Forbes Watson developed a broad knowledge of textiles and dyes, working tirelessly to collect and identify specimens for the India Museum and a series of international

exhibitions where Indian goods were featured. Forbes Watson anticipated the problems that would face Indian crafts and began a method-
ical study of Indian textiles in the India Museum, which proved to be
a lifetime's work. He organised the purchase of a comprehensive range
of textiles in India, including many made for indigenous use. This
collection provides us with valuable evidence of the fine skills that
were still in existence in the mid-nineteenth century.[25]

Forbes Watson was aware of the great surplus of Indian textiles
following major exhibitions, notably the Paris Exhibition of 1855, and
devised a project that would make use of them. He formed a collection of 700 different textiles from the stores – an almost complete
range of India's textile products. They were arranged into eighteen
volumes, each dedicated to a different textile type and classified as
they would be in a permanent museum. Specimens of a uniform size
were cut from lengths of silks, cottons, wools, etc., in a manner that
allowed the whole design, including border, to be seen. The specimens were mounted into bound volumes in such a way that they
allowed a physical examination of the cloth's texture and weight.
Each sample of cloth had detailed information attached related to
its original use, finished dimensions and, sometimes, cost. He thereby
fulfilled a long-standing ambition to establish a (portable) trade
museum of textiles, which would encourage commerce between India
and the West. Each eighteen-volume set was accompanied by a lavishly
illustrated book *The Textile Manufactures and Costumes of the
People of India.*[26]

Thirteen sets of the first series were distributed to British manufacturing towns and ports in 1866, and a number of volumes were sent
to India.[27] The town halls in the textile-producing centres of Manchester, Salford, Preston, Macclesfield in the North-west region, and
Bradford, Halifax and Huddersfield in Yorkshire, all received complete
sets. They were made available to manufacturers and were favourably
received. Forbes Watson was sufficiently encouraged to assemble a
second series, which appeared at intervals between 1873 and 1880.
This series contained samples of surplus cloth from the Paris exhibitions of 1855 and 1867. Throughout this period, English textile
manufacturers were repeatedly calling for trade museums to be established in manufacturing regions. They were quick to point out the
disadvantages they suffered compared to continental industrialists –
French and German manufacturers benefited from local museums
stocked with ancient foreign and contemporary items selected for
their connection with regional industries.

Although we know that manufacturers regularly visited the South
Kensington Museum and the East India Company Museum (known

as the India Museum after 1858), the usefulness of a London museum to the artisanal classes in the North and Midlands was minimal. The sets of Indian textiles assembled by Forbes Watson were the only archival resource locally available to artisans working in the textile trades in the Manchester region, until the founding of the Manchester Museum of Art by Charles Coglan Horsfall in 1884.

The Manchester Museum of Art, in Great Ancoats – a grim, polluted, industrial area of Manchester – was an unparalleled project in art and design education. The proposals which led to the formation of the museum were first made public in Horsfall's letter to the *Manchester Guardian*, in 1877. Shortly afterwards John Ruskin commented on the project in his seminal publication *Fors Clavigera*, reprinting several extracts from Horsfall's letter and referring to it as 'the most valuable passage I have seen published in a public journal on the subject of the Arts'.[28] Horsfall and Ruskin corresponded thereafter and their mutual interests are evident in Horsfall's publications: *An Art Gallery for Manchester* (1877), *Art in Towns and Villages* (1878), *The Study of Beauty and Art in Large Towns* (1883); *The Manchester Art Museum* (1891); *the Need for Art in Manchester* (1910) and the *Place of Admiration, Hope and Love in Town Life* (1910).

Horsfall was a philanthropic Mancunian, a wealthy manufacturer with a hatred of slums. He was fundamentally committed to improving the lot of the working classes and totally convinced of the benefits of cultivating a sense of beauty and good design. His visionary plans hoped to improve the moral and physical environment of those condemned to work and live in the heavily polluted atmosphere of Manchester and Salford. A supporter of Ruskin and Morris, he utilised both of the greatest art and design theorists of the time to bring his ideas to realisation. The Manchester Art Museum was conceived and developed by Horsfall to provide a counterpoint to its squalid surroundings. The *Journal of Decorative Art* reporting on the museum, depicted it as: 'thronged with human beings to whom the sweets of life are, in the great majority of cases unknown, and who pass their life in an atmosphere of shadowy grey without the brightness and variety which falls to the lot of their more favoured brothers and sisters'.[29]

The museum was planned to cultivate a sense of the beauty of well-made everyday things, providing a form of visual stimulus to those working in the decorative trades, who might otherwise have none. In particular, Horsfall aimed to expose schoolchildren to fine and decorative arts in an attempt to counteract the unrelieved bricks and mortar of their surroundings. As someone based in the major centre of textile production, Horsfall was aware that successful design was a vital component of a trade that gave employment to so many. In order to produce excellent designs and gain competitive advantage, some input from beautiful objects was felt to be necessary. The museum contained furnished rooms that demonstrated 'good' decorative and industrial products in a familiar domestic setting. Displays were planned to allow the public, children and adults to walk freely through them, inspecting the furnishings and ceramics. A main component was the interpretive material. The written explanatory notes were simple, authoritative statements by acknowledged competent judges. They included prices and, where relevant, historical and cultural history. William Morris provided information on household furnishings and these were positioned next to the objects on display. Morris also provided notes on the principles of flat pattern design. Furthermore, two rooms were furnished, under Morris's supervision, specifically with low budgets in mind.

From the outset the museum had a loan scheme for schools and the staff actively encouraged elementary school children to visit. Indian silk textiles were some of the first things that the public encountered when they entered the building. A case in the entrance hall contained 'beautiful textile fabrics from India and Persia'. Room nine contained 'Scarves of silk, embroidery, brocades, robes and Indian carpets'.[30] Because of the pollution-laden atmosphere the textiles could not be exposed to the air and were placed behind protective glass. Despite the unfavourable conditions a number of the Indian silks have survived and it has been possible to assess what Horsfall and others meant by 'good' design. The Museum Committee requested Caspar Purdon Clarke, of the South Kensington Museum, to procure fine textiles for Manchester when he was on a tour of India in 1881/ 2 to purchase objects for the India Museum. The budget for the Manchester purchases was the considerable sum of £2,000. A list of the purchases provides us with evidence that the textiles were some of the costliest fabrics then in production in India. The few surviving pieces are mainly complex woven silks, most with gold and silver incorporated. They were luxurious, handmade items and would have fulfilled the remit to show the finest products: textiles of excellent quality that demonstrated the finest technical expertise. Some of the items were large, including one sari, two large shawls and one emerald green silk satin coat, thickly embroidered with gold and silver. The *Journal of Decorative Art* featured the Indian brocades on display, describing them as showing the 'exquisite taste, which distinguished India's work'.[31]

Taken as whole, Manchester's textile collections at the end of the nineteenth century bore very little relationship to the printed calicoes for which the city was widely known. Manchester concerned with much more than the production of printed cottons, however. There was also a silk trade and numerous other 'Art' industries for the most part dependent on hand techniques, for which the School of Art was educating a workforce. Moreover, most contemporary design theories stressed the point that design principles could be learnt and then applied to different media. An understanding of colour harmonies was, however, considered to be a fundamental element of successful design and Manchester's textile collections demonstrated this in numerous ways.

Case study: Bradford Technical College 1878–1930s

Bradford was a major centre of textile production and an important city in economic terms. Its technical college (1878–1999), the Society of Dyers and Colourists (1885–1999), along with Bradford Textile Society and its journal (1893–1999), were major influences on England's textile development, yet historians have largely ignored them. Although noted as the centre of the woollen industries Bradford was also a centre of silk manufacture with long-established connections with India.

The archive of the current Bradford and Ilkley Community College (BICC), (formerly the Technical College), contains material in the form of students' notebooks, their designs and finished textile samples, along with documentary evidence, which reveals how artisans were trained for the woven textiles industry. In addition, there are various publications on textile design and technology by Bradford tutors. The archive also holds a complete set of eighteen volumes of Forbes Watson's *Collection of Specimens and Illustrations of the Textile Manufactures of India* (first series), given to the city in 1866. They were obviously considered to be a valuable resource as the city subsequently purchased a further nine volumes of the second series in 1872, 1873 and 1874. The Indian volumes are still in their original glazed wooden bookcase, with a gilded inscription. The Bradford textile archive was officially opened in 2004.

The Bradford Mechanics' Institute was established in 1825 for the advancement of the working classes. By the mid-nineteenth century it became apparent that Bradford needed a better system of technical instruction if the city's textile manufacturers were to keep abreast of their continental competitors. The need for change was further stimulated by the capricious nature of fashionable taste. The fashions of the 1870s demanded softer draping fabrics and rejected many of the heavier 'lustre' cloths, for which Bradford was famous. Lustre fabrics used alpaca and mohair fibres to produce a cloth of great softness and brilliance. As there was a pressing need to diversify textile production, a school of design was organised in 1865 by local textile manufacturers. This evolved into the Technical School in 1883 with a separate Department of Art.

Early in 1877 local industrialists met to consider the establishment of a weaving school and made donations of the necessary looms and appliances. Shortly after its opening (1883), the new Bradford Technical School changed its name to Bradford Technical College. The institution was conceived and maintained by public effort in the conviction that commercial supremacy came from technical education. The college founders were far-sighted and took financial risks. Opportunities for self-improvement for thousands of young people was, to a large extent, provided by local benefactors and a generous donation of £3,000 from the Clothworkers' Company of London. There was no financial support from the public purse until the Technical Instruction Act (1889). Bradford County Council then raised grants to subsidise technical education. The new college was comprised of a Trade school and an Art Department, which was one of the most comprehensively organised art schools in the country. There were departments of chemistry, dyeing and maths and, in addition, French, German and Latin were taught by able teachers. No institution in the country related so directly to the local textile and mechanical industries. The Textile Department evolved to include textile industries, engineering, dyeing and art. Ultimately, that which began as a weaving school adapted to change and grew into a technical college of the first order; it went on to make a major contribution to the prosperity of the city.

Textile journals

The Bradford Textile Society, allied to the college, made a major contribution to the city's business. It became the '. . . largest and most influential organisation of its kind in the world'.[32] The society's journal provided samples of cloth, design sheets and lists of monthly patents. Published monthly, it served a commercial as well as an educational purpose; it had an investigative role and was not afraid to comment on topics that were sensitive issues in the city. Close attention was paid to global design developments and critical articles discussed the poor state of English design compared to that in Europe. The importance of understanding the underlying principles of textile design was a conspicuous feature of the early editions.

Other textile trade journals reveal similar preoccupations. The *Textile Society Journal* and the *Textile Recorder* both highlighted design education as a major concern, along with competition from foreign markets. The journals had a global perspective: correspondents based abroad informed readers on world matters. Every issue offered details of fashionable fabrics from all over Europe. Manufacturers were urged to cast aside their own preferences and study consumers' requirements. As the market for luxury silk textiles was consumer led, sound commercial judgement had to be based on accurate observations of fashionable trends. The *Textile Recorder* aimed to assist manufacturers by reporting on developments and regularly quoted major fashion journals. By inserting designs and diagrams for textile production its clearly stated aim was to promote textiles that satisfied the public's taste. There were constant references to India and its textiles including: aspects of design, use of labour, trade figures and the Europeans' use of Indian fabrics to satisfy fashionable demands.

Professor Roberts Beaumont, of the Yorkshire College, Leeds (later Leeds University), a noted author of technical textile books, contributed a series of major articles on design and colour to the *Textile Recorder* over a three-month period in 1888. The majority of his illustrations featured Indian textiles as models of excellence. In his 'Design and Colour for Fancy Vestings', referring to the most popular motifs utilised by designers, he stated:

> Foremost of all is what is technically called the pine, a figure that largely enters into the decoration of Paisley and Indian shawls. It is not an exaggeration to say that thousands of patterns have been constructed on this ingenious base. Being capable of such elaborate modifications and diversity of structure there is no limit to its application to textile design.[33]

The Roberts Beaumont articles clearly defined fundamental laws and principles necessary to achieve commercially successful textile designs. A thoroughly trained designer-weaver was central and the author outlined the necessary weaving skills thus: knowledge of the technicalities of weaving, knowledge of form and colour, but above all the ability to combine these when formulating a design. The ability to construct a suitable texture, which developed the pattern and fitted the purpose for which it was intended, was fundamental. The options inherent in various weaving techniques, even when taking account of the laws that governed patterning, along with the many variables in the type of yarn, design and colouring, meant that the designer's ingenuity was rarely exhausted.

Roberts Beaumont stressed the point that a good design could be completely ruined by a lack of understanding of colour. Colour played a primary role in the pattern. He gave examples of a 'Turkey carpet and Indian shawl, unique and gorgeous in colouring. Invariably the shades employed are bright and lustrous, but combined with such taste as to form soft and charming contrasts.'[34] The author defined the fundamental laws that these examples demonstrated as the appropriate distribution of rich, fresh shades. The quantity of colour used was dictated entirely by the position it occupied in the pattern and the degree of colour intensity and quality. Following well-understood principles, the colours were so blended that when the pattern was seen in its entirety it would possess an overall harmony. Designs containing a number of pronounced colours would not achieve such a balance and the result would be discordant. Bright and powerful colours could be used, but in such a way that no single or pair of colours overpowered the others. Great care was needed, for example, when five colours were commonly employed in the production of fancy silk vestings. Each colour should relate to specific areas of the design where it would be most effective, contributing to the overall effect through combinations and juxtapositions. The most effective woven pattern needed to demonstrate 'the greatest ingenuity of structural arrangement, in combination of form and in harmony of colouring'.[35] Clearly designers needed to be inventors of new patterns, practical colourists and skilled weavers. Roberts Beaumont illustrated the lengthy articles with his drawings of designs chosen to convey the principles he promoted. Four of the eleven illustrations were patterns derived from Indian textiles, four were 'Modern' styles, the remaining three were universal patterns.

The textile department

From an analysis of the documents in the college archive, textbooks published by Bradford author-educators, student's notebooks and their woven examples, it is possible to draw some interesting conclusions about the education of artisans for the woven textile trade in Bradford. The archival material clearly demonstrates that technical college education differed in its perception of textile design from that promoted by schools of art. The aims of the curricula in technical colleges such as those in Bradford and Macclesfield were to make the student proficient in the conception of designs and in taking those designs through the various stages necessary to realise them in cloth. In the first instance, designs grew from the possibilities and limitations of technology and utility. Although drawing classes and aesthetic considerations were important, they were not the primary concern, and the designer needed also to consider the function of the cloth. This was in contrast to the schools of art in the later nineteenth century.

Although modern technology had mechanised aspects of the silk industry, silk weaving, particularly of ornamented cloth, continued by hand well into the twentieth century. As will be seen, this was a demanding process requiring complex skills from those involved with dyeing, designing the patterns and the weaving. Far from being deskilled by the rise of mechanisation, some artisans training for the silk trade needed to be multi-skilled. Before textile training was formalised, weavers in the silk trade followed an apprenticeship system specialising in specific aspects of production. The college course of weaving instruction (up to seven years in duration) was of a more comprehensive nature, arranged specifically to meet the requirements of the Bradford trade. As the curricula at Bradford and Macclesfield demonstrate, with more formal education, operatives became skilled in most aspects of production, including the theory and practice of spinning, weaving and of pattern-designing for plain and figured cloth. In addition, technical drawing and pure chemistry, applied to bleaching, dyeing and printing, were included. Technical college students needed to acquire complex skills, and undertake a number of preparatory stages, before their designs could be realised in cloth.

A number of Bradford College tutors published textbooks on designs for woven fabrics. These were held in high regard and became authoritative texts. They continued as standard textbooks for students nationwide up to the 1950s – T.R. Ashenhurst's texts still had currency in the 1990s.[36] The texts were based on, and informed, the curriculum at Bradford; the dates of the publications coincide with the dates of surviving samples of students' work. Therefore, through an examination of both the objects (textiles) and the texts we can observe the aims and contents of the weaving course and the tangible results of its teaching.

T.R. Ashenhurst, already a well-known author of standard textbooks for textile design and manufacture, became the first head of the Textiles Department at Bradford (1883). By securing his services, the Bradford Textile Department was destined to reach a very high standard. His leading texts were: *Weaving and Designing of Textile Fabrics* (1882) and *Design in Textile Fabrics* (1883). C. Stephenson, a Master at Bradford Technical College, and F. Suddards, Master at the Yorkshire College, Leeds, co-authored *Ornamental Design for Woven Fabric* (1897), and *Dealing With Ornamental Art for Woven Fabric* (1897). These key textbooks by Bradford tutors provide a comprehensive view of the curriculum that weaving students followed. The texts varied little in their aims – this is hardly surprising, as the college tutors were focused on producing technically efficient workers for the local industry. However, the texts differed in their emphasis.

Ashenhurst's texts concentrated on aspects of designing related to the construction of cloth. All of the classes of woven fabrics that were discussed, including plain and twilled weave, satins, double cloths, brocades, gauze cloths and velvets, had an Indian equivalent in the Forbes Watson collection in Bradford, to which students could refer.[37] Ashenhurst immediately made the theoretical basis of designs for woven fabrics clear to the reader. This can be summarised as follows: Knowledge of appropriate design was founded on the knowledge of the end to be achieved and the means by which that end had been achicvcd by others. There was, of necessity, a close relationship between the structure of the cloth and the ornament that decorated it. The fundamental principles governing the design of woven ornamental fabrics rested on patterns produced by structure, patterns produced by colour, or both. Although colour would not usually detract from utility, the numerous ways of constructing a fabric might. Designers needed to consider the limitations or possibilities inherent in the looms, the yarns and the purpose for which the cloth was intended. The first and main object when designing woven cloth was utility. Ornamentation of the structure could only take place if it did not detract from, or compromise, its end use. The two elements could be combined, with the further aim of producing an article economically.

Ashenhurst, like Roberts Beaumont, considered consumer satisfaction to be a factor in the design process. He acknowledged that consumers demanded beauty as well as utility and that demand must be satisfied. 'We must ornament wherever we can, but in introducing ornament we must be careful that we do not do it at the cost of utility. It is in these considerations that we have the groundwork of our theory.'[38] The sound principles were clearly laid down in the texts, along with illustrations; nothing was left to chance. Students were advised to visit museums, to experience examples from the past, or from other cultures.

The type of cloth (fine or coarse) dictated design features to some degree. When designing fabrics with an open texture, the designer needed to avoid curved motifs that ran for great lengths in the direction of either the warp or the weft. Curves that did so would lose their value as curves and would appear as stepped straight lines. The most satisfactory curves were those that ran diagonally across a surface. However, if all curves were placed in that manner then the result would be less aesthetically interesting. Nevertheless, as it was an important technical consideration, as many diagonals as possible needed to be incorporated into a design, to gain a better relative tension. The successful designer produced a balance between the curves with more movement and beauty and those with utilitarian benefits.

Although the jacquard loom had mechanised the action of raising the warp threads, 'fancy' silk weaving was, for the most part, still done by hand. Extensive weaving skills were necessary to control the thread's tension throughout the weaving process. Even plain weaves demanded total control over the tension of the warp and weft yarns. Intricate figured cloths also demanded close attention to the pattern details. Moreover, each colour in a design required the weaver to throw a separate shuttle of yarn whenever that colour appeared in the design. To aid students' understanding of the laws of pattern design, observation and drawing classes were considered to be fundamental. Many of the points made could be exemplified from the Indian cloths available to the Bradford students.

In Stephenson and Suddards's publications, design was of necessity subservient to structure, much as Ashenhurst described. However, the authors demonstrated further refinements in the laws of repeat patterning. They promoted additional theories, the structural basis of which was geometry. Geometrical laws governed designs based on forms such as the ogee, diamond, wave-line, rectangle, etc., which were commonly utilised in Indian textile design. Examples of this form could be clearly observed in the Forbes Watson First and Second Series. A *Kincob* (No. 483) is a satin weave construction with figured gold flowers from Trichinopoly, Madras. It was woven using an all-over geometrical trellis or net format, repeated along horizontal, vertical and diagonal axes. Each symmetrical ogival shape in the design contained the same floral motif, woven in contrasting colours and texture. A *Kincob* (No. 429) from Ahmedabad, in the Second Series uses the same format but with diamond shapes containing a repeat floral motif. These patterns also demonstrate a fundamental law; they are so arranged as to be continuous, joined on all sides and are perfectly recurring if extended or repeated in any direction.

Although seemingly simple, figured checks were very difficult for beginners to handle; the precise alignment of horizontal and vertical elements was crucial as mistakes would be glaringly obvious. Other decorative elements such as the treatment of plant forms in textile design, 'traditional' or abstract ornament, and animate forms had separate sections devoted to them in the publications. The desirable characteristics of abstract or 'traditional' textile ornaments were characterised as an arrangement of forms, which carefully considered the overall relationship of individual design elements. Each separate element was in itself complete and related to all other elements in such a way that they formed an overall coherence. Harmony was achieved when varying densities of shapes were balanced and forms were arranged symmetrically, thereby creating contrasts between large and small masses and contrasting directional lines. Forbes Watson Second Series, No. 422, a *Kincob* from Benares, shows a strong diagonal meander, which anchors elements of the design together. Meandering tendrils and petals of a smaller scale balance the diagonal emphasis. The use of colour (white and black) emphasises the movement while strong outlines accentuate individual floral shapes. Students were advised by the authors to study past examples and to make numerous notebook studies in order to familiarise themselves with their details. Illustrations in the key texts and trade journals constantly referred to examples of cloth from other cultures and eras that displayed the theories being promoted. Alongside the constant references to Indian exemplars, Italian, Spanish and Sicilian woven fabrics from between the twelfth and seventeenth centuries were used to illustrate the correct use of 'Traditional or Abstract' ornament. Japanese silk textile designs of the nineteenth century illustrated animate forms.

Stephenson and Studdards went into great detail about the most useful application of pattern elements for ornamental purposes. Mass and outline needed to be balanced in order that visual and literal 'weight' was evenly distributed across the surface of a cloth. Contrast could be obtained in three ways: firstly, in the use of colour where gold is placed against dark tones of red, green and blue; secondly, through the use of light and shade created by the juxtaposition of smooth silk satin and the shine of figured precious metal threads; thirdly, through texture where a smooth plain ground provides a foil for the more textured motif.

The use of the complex 'turn-over' or 'mirror image' occurs when the design is bisected either horizontally, vertically or both and one half of the motif mirrors the other. This effect can be seen in Forbes Watson Second Series No. 508. The example is an *Imroo* from Aurungabad, Deccan. The design of peacocks and flowers in an ogival format is woven in gold against a black ground. It is formed from one mirror image repeated on the horizontal axis and a reverse of the image, which is repeated on the vertical axis.

Stephenson and Studdards concentrated on the special use of sateen arrangements in detail. Examples of this technique can be seen in Forbes Watson First Series No. 487, a satin *Mushroo* with a silk surface and cotton back, from Hyderabad, Deccan. The satin ground provides a smooth foil for the texture of the figured design described as 'loom embroidered flowers'. Successful patterns utilised the inherent qualities of yarn. Beautiful effects could be obtained simply by using the different properties of the yarns, silk being more lustrous than wool.

The important role of colour in designing was given a great deal of thought by the technical authors. Ashenhurst's publications dealt with the subject of colour as it related to cloth structure. As with other decorative devices this was governed by principles. Figured weaving, using supplementary weft or warp threads or both, enabled very rich and elaborate patterns to be formed, allowing the use of many colours. Even one extra colour gave good scope. Designers could aim for mild, tame effects or striking ones. Kashmir shawls were thought to exemplify the best use of different pattern elements allied to the use of colour; British versions of the shawls were also respected. From its inauguration (1854), the *Journal of Design* promoted the same colour harmonies seen as inherent in the Kashmir designs. Ashenhurst considered that there was a place for ingenuity in the use of colour as long as harmony and balance were maintained. He referred to the designs of Kashmir shawls as the most successful use of colour known:

> One striking feature of this design, as indeed of many of the Patterns for this class of shawl, is that there is not at any point a great quantity of one colour either on the face or back of the cloth at once. . . . Although we may not bring any of the colours to the surface in large quantities at once, yet there is no difficulty in making predominate sufficiently at any part of the design to give character to it.[39]

The steps taken by the Bradford Society of Dyers and Colourists indicate the importance given to the role of colour in textile production. The society promoted colour research, and there were dyeing schools at Bradford and Leeds technical colleges. All three institutions proceeded to develop expertise through scientific methods. The aim was to encourage dyers to undertake their own research and be less dependent on developments in competing countries. Thomas Wardle gave the inaugural lecture at the society's opening in 1885. Speaking at length on the importance of understanding the principles of colouring in textiles, he described how Bradford was a leading centre in technical instruction in the dyeing schools. Colour played a vital part in decorative textile production and the range of available dyes was extensive. However, there was no room for complacency and further research was needed if local firms were to compete with French manufacturers. French textiles were known to exhibit a superior knowledge of colour and many English consumers preferred them. Wardle was convinced that this was because the laws of harmony and contrast were better understood in French design education, along with the tonal properties of the colours themselves. He rigorously argued his point, using objective data. He was adamant that dyeing success would only grow from experimental observation and research. He advocated a scientific approach, which used pooled talent, and started from first principles, not competitors' products. For this purpose he recommended the study of Indian textiles, which would give dyers a firm basis from which they could develop a healthy competitiveness.[40]

Reading from another paper at the Bradford Municipal Technical College in 1903, eight years later, his focus was once again on the importance of colour. In his opinion special education was still necessary in order to understand the application of colour to textiles. The late William Morris was the person who best understood colour; his understanding was not intuitive, but the result of years studying the best textiles and artwork. Although Bradford was the home of decorative textiles, the application of colour could be improved. Wardle was convinced that although English pattern designing was then superior to the French, the knowledge of colour was still inferior in England. He admired the French designers' exquisite use of harmony, contrast, and the relationship of shading in colour effects. He remained convinced that if colouring was better understood in Britain the consumer would cease to purchase French silks. He recommended the creation of a separate Chair for colour and colouring at the School of Design in South Kensington where he was an examiner and attended the annual prize giving. Although drawing and designs were both admirable there, as a rule, colouring was weak, often crude and not suitable for its purpose. At that point there was not one teacher of colour in the whole country. Masters at schools of art did not have the scientific knowledge of colour, which was essential for textile production. He recommended the appointment of a separate colour-master at Bradford, to bring about reform in technical and aesthetic teaching. This he considered to be the most important, although difficult, priority for the school.[41]

The role of Indian textile design in Bradford at the end of the nineteenth century and the beginning of the twentieth century was a highly influential one. All of the essential aesthetic and technical principles referred to by educators of designers and weavers were displayed in India's textile designs. Furthermore, in Indian textiles they were combined with the requirements of utility and expressed with an exceptional command of colouring. It was the unique combination of these elements in India's textiles that made them the most suitable exemplars for hand or machine production. It therefore becomes obvious why India's designs are so strongly represented in the archival material in Bradford: key textbooks, students' work, trade journals, products of the textile industries and the fashion journals. It is quite apparent that the Bradford author-tutors had much in common with the teaching staff at Manchester College of Art and Macclesfield School of Art. Their aims were cognate and their methods of achieving them were similar, although the Manchester Art School students were not expected to grapple with the intricacies of technology.

The Bradford authors, Ashenhurst (1883) and Stephenson (1897), like the Manchester authors Crane, Day and Glazier, and Ward at Macclesfield, strongly recommended students to draw from good examples of textile ornament in museum collections. This was intended to develop a feeling for the beauty of line and form and an understanding of good principles as applied to design. The Forbes Watson First and Second Series of Indian textile samples, which acted as a portable museum, contained samples of patterns consistent with these principles. The samples, ranging from the finest gauze to heavy velvets, exhibited the principles of repeat pattern designing, which authors, trade journals, manufacturers and institutions, considered to be fundamental. The same samples were available to students in Manchester and Macclesfield; surviving material evidence shows that students' designs from these textile towns were remarkably similar.

The woven silk samples produced by the Bradford and Macclesfield students represent in a tangible form the abstract theories relating to technical skill, utilitarian considerations and contemporary aesthetic preferences taught in the art and technical colleges. They combine the expectations of South Kensington with current fashionable taste. Although students were following principles evident in Indian textiles, they were not slavish copiers. Their colour schemes indicate that there was a melding of Arts and Crafts influences with India's design heritage.

Many of the students' designs demonstrate colour schemes favoured by William Morris and other leading contemporary designers. In this they were following theorists' advice, and interpreting Indian designs with a contemporary, English sensibility. The contemporary influence of Art Nouveau design is also evident and is complimentary to the theories promoted. Art Nouveau textile designs often follow the same principles evident in Indian designs. In addition, the examination system, including the City and Guilds awards, South Kensington and Owen Jones prizes, promoted the same ideals, obviously influenced by examiners such as Walter Crane, Lewis F. Day, Owen Jones and William Morris.

The principles that were promoted during this period were maintained, as subsequent textile tutors continued with extensive research on pattern analysis. This demonstrates that design theory was far more than fleetingly fashionable, or subject to conditions of taste during the period under review. It is clear from the evidence of surviving textiles and publications that the successful structure of figured cloth in any era or culture was predicated on a set of principles concerning symmetry. The Bradford evidence undeniably demonstrates the close fit between principles advocated by the Bradford tutors and the collection of Indian textiles available to them and their students.

Case study: Macclesfield School of Art[42]

Macclesfield, Cheshire was an important centre of silk production for over 300 years. Throughout the nineteenth century the town was as a prominent centre for the throwing, weaving and printing of silk. A broad range of silk products and designs for fashion and furnishings were produced for internal and external markets; and a diversity of production methods allowed old and new technologies to coexist well into the twentieth century.

The archives at Macclesfield Silk Museum[43] contain material relating to the training of textile designers in the town, an aspect of textile history that has hitherto escaped attention. Evidence from the School of Art has survived in the form of student notebooks, paper designs, woven silk samples and documents. Over 800 manufacturers' pattern books dating from circa 1840, containing thousands of woven and printed silk samples, demonstrate the huge variety of designs in silk that the town produced.[44] A complete set of Forbes Watson's *Textile Manufactures of India* (First Series), given to the town in 1866, has also survived. This was an important source of reference, used by manufacturers, artisans and anyone involved in the textile trades at the time[45] as the town then had no museum.[46]

After Macclesfield silks had been poorly received at the Great Exhibition of 1851, concern over design education in the town intensified, although not all local manufacturers were immediately willing to change their design practice. When the new school of art opened in November 1851 expectations were raised over improvement in the town's designs. The school reached its full quota of pupils within two months of opening; the more skilled artisans such as weavers and designers were well represented. Design was the occupation best represented between 1851 and 1873. The pupils were those already employed in the local silk industry, and who attended evening classes – a balance which reflected the wishes of the school's founders. The courses were, to some extent, governed by the Department of Science and Art's guidelines and its examination system. They also reflected the abilities of the masters and concerns of local industries. Manufacturers wanted to see more designs for local production as early as possible, and under their influence special classes in design and colour for silk were introduced.

Under the guidance of the first Headmaster, the fine artist George Stewart, students produced designs for silk before reaching the department's recommended stages of training.[47] Manufacturers introduced monetary prizes in 1855, in local competitions that were of a lower standard than for national prizes. They were attempts to resolve the evident tension between the dictates of South Kensington, the national competitions and the requirements of local industries. The main problem seemed to be the unsuitability of designs produced at the time under the 'High Art' philosophy of the Museum of Manufactures at Marlborough House (a disused royal palace used for temporary exhibitions), as they did not relate closely enough to local production. Local opinion favoured the reduction of the initial course, with its bias towards painting and drawing skills, advocating instead a more technical education to ensure that designs could be practically executed. The Headmaster, however, defended the course by comparing it to the French system of design education. His aim was to develop talents in a more general way. Changes were needed as Macclesfield, more than any other town, had suffered the consequences of free trade. It was thought with some justification, that Macclesfield had been deliberately sacrificed to the French, due to the Cobden-Chevalier Treaty of 1860.

James Ford, who followed Stewart as Headmaster, gave greater emphasis to instruction in colour and design for the silk trade. Thereafter, many designs for silk goods were sent to national competitions. Local money prizes were still used as the major stimulus for silk design projects within the school. The emphasis on local industries' immediate use was, conversely, stifling creativity. Designs became simplified to accommodate commercial considerations and the relatively unsophisticated technology of the town's looms. Ford, however, continued to emphasise the importance of good design, and by the end of his career he claimed to have filled the mills of Macclesfield with locally educated designers. After 1867, more designers were employed in the town as the silk industry was less depressed. In 1868 local manufacturers purchased sixty 'sketches' or designs from the School. In 1879 the art school was extended; and the opening exhibition displayed a large number of fine Indian textiles from the India Museum at South Kensington.

The art school went on to achieve great success in national examinations. Its position in national competitions steadily improved and it was rated first in design in both 1882 and 1883, and fifth in the country for many years. By 1888 it was considered to be one of the leading art schools in the country with a strong emphasis on textile design. Increasingly the Department of Science and Art encouraged a more practical approach, judging designs on the products made from them, rather than as concepts on paper. In 1887 Macclesfield School of Art was one of the first to submit a design realised in woven silk to the national examinations.

James Ward became one of the best-known artist/author/educators of the time. He was an artist with a national reputation, but it was as an educator that he was particularly respected. His lectures at Macclesfield on the 'Principles of Ornament' became the basis of his first publications: *Elementary Principles of Ornament* (1890), *Principle of Ornament* (1892), and *Historic Ornament* (1897). Ward's publications promoted the history and theory of design; all received favourable reviews and sold well, helped in part by the fact that the Science and Art Department recommended some of them as set texts.[48] Ward studied chemistry to fully understand pigments, eventually gaining an international reputation for his knowledge of colour.[49] When William Morris spoke at the School's Annual General Meeting, his focus was on the need for designers to gain a general art education, something with which Ward concurred. Moreover, Ward, like Morris, Crane, Day and Wardle encouraged the study of nature as the basis of successful decorative design.

Between 1909 and 1914 the school achieved highly successful results in government examinations, along with success in the national and Owen Jones competitions, as long as they lasted. The Owen Jones Prizes for the best designs for hangings of damasks, chintzes, etc., were awarded annually from 1872. Designs were regulated by the principles laid down by Owen Jones in his publications. Awards were given to students of the schools of art on the basis of an annual competition, run by the Science and Art Department. Each prize consisted of a bound copy of Owen Jones's *The Principles of Design* and a bronze medal. Students could not receive more than one award.

A series of Macclesfield students' samples, woven between 1899 and 1920, provides clear evidence that weaving skills were of a high standard as many of the designs were complex figured silks. Many examples of Macclesfield students' work can, moreover, be connected to designs in Indian cloth. One design for a complex woven silk was awarded the Owen Jones Bronze Medal in 1910. The design has a graceful, curvilinear floral motif placed within a diamond-shaped, arched framework, alternating in horizontal rows. Colour plate 1 shows the original design on paper. This relates closely to the naturalistic floral imagery depicted in Mughal decorative arts of the seventeenth and eighteenth centuries, which would seem to be the principal design source. Versions of this form were illustrated in Owen Jones's *Grammar of Ornament*.[50] This student's design also has an affinity with a Forbes Watson example of a satin *mushroo*, First Series, No. 486. Further comparisons can be made with a woven silk collected by Thomas Wardle in India and displayed in London in 1886, Manchester in 1887 and thereafter in the Whitworth Institute Manchester (Museum No. T9939). It also bears close comparison with many examples of Mughal embroidery.

Another Macclesfield student's design shows a trellis format of ogival shapes enclosing an ornate floral motif. Colour plate 2 shows the design woven in silk. The design closely relates to many Indian textiles as embroidered, printed and woven cloths have all adopted this format. One example of such was a white and gold *kincob* purchased by Horsfall for the Manchester Art Museum. In this example the ogival trellis is formed from intertwining leaves, in much the same way as the Macclesfield example. In both cases the leaves break the outline of the frame. Each component of this particular design has a different type of weave construction producing a variety of textures, along with strong colour contrasts.

The school's achievements peaked between 1910 and 1930. In 1914 there was great confidence in the school's standard of work and in its future. His Majesty's Inspectors found it to be well organised and the teaching staff suited to the needs of the students. At that stage the school was fully focused on training designers and weavers for the local silk industry. By August 1922 the results for Macclesfield School of Art surpassed any previously recorded.[51] Designing was by then integrated with the practical and theoretical study of silk weaving classes at the Technical School. By the 1930s, however, it was clear that the school was failing to adapt to new situations in the global silk industry. Standards declined, especially among the advanced students.

The diversification of the industry during the inter-war period had lessened the emphasis on the weaving of fine silks and there was less need for designers to be highly trained. Jacquard designing required five years' training, with three to four nights' attendance per week at Macclesfield School of Art, for City and Guilds qualifications. There was, nevertheless, an attempt to develop a full-time course in handloom weaving in the late 1920s. At that time all the handloom weavers were of alarmingly advanced years and the town was still producing handwoven and hand block-printed silks and continuity was a concern. However, this proposal was not approved by the Board of Education.

Macclesfield's designs

The surviving evidence from Macclesfield School of Art and local companies reveals abundant evidence of an Indian influence, often in the form of clearly derived motifs or colour combinations. Manufacturers' sample books demonstrate just how many Indian-inspired designs were produced from at least 1842 onwards. The woven and printed samples cover a range of pattern types and colour schemes that are observable in Indian textiles. The all-over designs include ogival forms enclosing floral figures, net formations, stripes, repeated *buti* motifs and floral forms in different colourways. They clearly demonstrate the variety evident in just a small number selected from among the many hundreds of samples produced by Macclesfield manufacturers in the mid-nineteenth century.

Archival evidence clearly demonstrates the many ways in which Indian textile motifs had been interpreted quite closely, although the occasional use of soft tones of colour is more typically European. Although these silk samples are from known Macclesfield manufacturers it is not always possible to state the exact provenance of the original designs. Manufacturers obtained designs and fabric samples from many sources, including India and France, as well as from other English companies. Textile samples and pattern books had always been a major source of reference and many kinds of design literature were available, including illustrated articles in trade journals. There was a lively market in source books such as Friedrich Fischbach's (1839–1908) *Ornament der Gewebe* (1874–78?), which was used by manufacturers throughout Europe,[52] alongside pattern services from French firms such as Bilbille and J. Claude Freres, which Macclesfield manufactures were known to have used.

Before the Great Exhibition (1851) it is doubtful whether any manufacturer would have been aware of the full extent of India's silk products, particularly the variety of cloth produced for its internal market. We know, however, that Macclesfield manufacturers exhibited in the Great Exhibition[53] and at Manchester's Royal Jubilee Exhibition (1887); so it is reasonable to conclude that they would have viewed Indian textiles at both events, as well as those in the Art Treasures Exhibition (1858).

From 1884, the Manchester Art Museum displayed the Horsfall collection of costly Indian brocades, and from 1888 the Whitworth Institute had a teaching collection of Indian silks formed by Thomas Wardle of Leek. Many silk manufacturers who were well travelled would have visited European cities with major textile collections. In the second half of the nineteenth century there were, therefore, opportunities for manufacturers to observe the finest examples of India's silks.

Despite numerous recommendations, Macclesfield never gained a trade museum. The Forbes Watson volumes, therefore, must have been an invaluable work of reference. They served as a miniature version of the India Museum at South Kensington, but were accessible locally. Loan collections and exhibitions from the circulation department of South Kensington were extremely popular; Macclesfield was one of the first venues to receive a loan exhibition of the finest specimens of Indian silks, which attracted thousands of visitors.[54] There is enough evidence to indicate clearly that in Macclesfield the positive influence from India's textiles was strong. Some manufacturers even emulated Indian processes as well as designs. One manufacturer trained workers to produce tie-dyed designs by hand, following the traditional Indian techniques, as early as 1820. A series of printed designs, inspired by the tie and dye techniques, was produced in 1903 and again in the 1930s.

Figure 2 shows an employee using traditional Indian tie-dye methods in 1948. The illustration shows the technique in progress, and finished cloth can be seen in the background.[55] Although it had been possible to mechanically produce the effect of this fabric for some time, one particular manufacturer preferred the original methods, although this was more time-consuming and, therefore, expensive. The process of wax resist is a further traditional Indian technique, which was also used in Macclesfield. Ikat was another complex Indian dyeing technique that was inspiring for designers although not practised in the town.

The use of Indian *tasar* silk took various forms in Macclesfield. A number of surviving examples have a strong affinity with the Forbes Watson examples from Bhaugulpore and Benares. Both are simple weave constructions, one of which shows the natural colour of the undyed silk contrasted with a deep blue check pattern (No. 637). The Macclesfield samples also show the natural colour of *tasar* silk contrasted with either deep red (manufacturer's No. 5706B) or blue (manufacturer's No. 5705B) – both are simple check designs. The red check has a more pronounced texture. The dates of production coincide with the period that Thomas Wardle was experimenting with Indian *tasar* silk dyeing in order to promote its greater use. Colour plate 3 shows examples of brocaded designs woven in undyed 'tussore' silk (1885–88). One length has a number of different designs woven into it.

It is quite apparent that many of the English silk designs inspired by Indian motifs were executed in a colour palette that probably owed more to the Arts and Crafts movement than it did to India. This is true of many examples of Macclesfield students' work. In this, the students achieved what Morris, Crane, Owen Jones, Wardle and their contemporaries hoped for. Their work demonstrated an awareness of

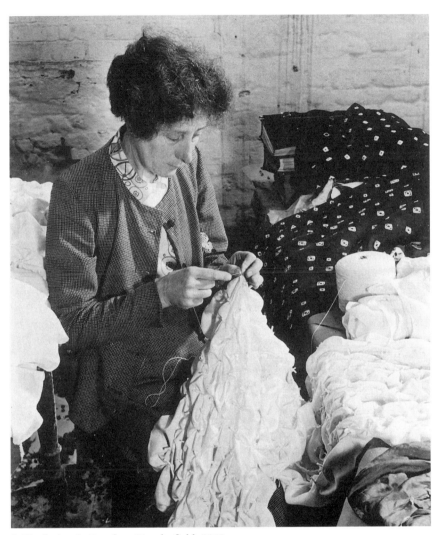

2 Tie-dyeing in Langley, Macclesfield, 1948.

sound principles, interpreted with an English sensibility. Furthermore, the dominant stylistic influence during this period was that of Art Nouveau, the features of which had an affinity with the curvilinear aspect of many Eastern designs. Students' work was, therefore, simultaneously following sound principles and was eminently fashionable. It is clear that many local manufacturers employed Macclesfield designers because the school was producing what local industry and English consumers required.[56]

[49]

As the evidence from Manchester, Bradford and Macclesfield shows, those who committed themselves to design education – students, staff and industrialists – all responded to Indian textiles as well as to the national guidelines of government and the stimulation of prizes, grants, etc. However, what individual designers or manufacturers could achieve was also obviously affected by other, more general factors. The demands of the consumer and international economics were also determinants that affected design.

The particular problems of the global silk industry eventually reduced the chance of Macclesfield developing design education any further. From the 1920s the overriding concern became the reintroduction of protection from foreign imports, while the superiority of foreign technical schools became of less importance. By the mid-1930s the English silk industry was at a comparative disadvantage as synthetic yarn production rose alarmingly. However, what is certain is that Indian design remained a constant source of inspiration. Indeed, when Modernism, which rejected ornament, was well established in the late 1920s and 1930s, and even when artificial fibres were replacing silk, there is evidence that Indian designs were still a powerful source of inspiration. Figure 3 shows James Warmsley, a Macclesfield designer preparing a *buti*-inspired design for hand-block printing on to silk in the 1920s. Colour plate 4 shows two striking example of Indian-inspired designs printed onto Macclesfield woven silk using a typically Indian colour scheme of strongly contrasting red and yellow. Colour plate 5 shows printed silk from the 1930s–1940s, the designs show both tie-dyeing and woven Kashmir shawl influences. However, the colour schemes are of a softer European palette. Manufacturers continued to use designs inspired by Indian textiles when artificial fibres came into production. Although there is no concrete evidence to support this, it is possible that manufacturers were using tried and tested designs in order to offset the unknown aspect of the new fibres by providing them with a respected design pedigree.

Conclusion

Over a period of a hundred years there were, naturally, many changes in design education both in the form of its central organisation and the administration of individual institutions. However, the frequent changes should not be allowed to obscure patterns of continuity over much of the period. Educational developments in leading institutions in Manchester, Bradford and Macclesfield followed similar lines. Their objectives, moreover, were consistent with the theories of leading practitioners of design education. Furthermore, India's textile designs supplied examples that were consistent with these aims.

Manchester's author-tutors had much in common with those at Bradford and Macclesfield. Authors from all three institutions referred to India's designs as exemplary, and their publications became standard works of reference for students of design, remaining so well into the twentieth century. Although other cultures provided exemplary designs, it was only Indian silk textiles that offered such a wide range of construction types, designs and, in particular, outstanding expertise

3 James Warmsley, block print designer, working on Indian-inspired pattern, 1920s.

in the technology and aesthetic use of colour. Indian textiles offered so much that they could be referred to in any type of publication that dealt with textiles. Technology, aesthetics and ideologies were meshed in the cloth and any aspect could be drawn upon. Furthermore, students and tutors at Manchester, Bradford and Macclesfield had opportunities to study a broad range of Indian textiles at first hand. Indian textiles displayed a number of features that rested on principles that were clearly understood by the educators in both art and technical schools.

Although the fashionable market for silks was always subject to changing whims, which seriously affected patterns of consumption during the mid- to later nineteenth century, there was a growth in consumer demand for Indian textiles, designs and colours. As fashion and trade journals indicate, over a considerable period of time, the Kashmir shawl and its British equivalent from Paisley and Norwich were an indispensable item of fashionable dress.[57] There was, therefore, a consistency between the ideas advocated by the leading designers, practitioners and theorists of design education and certain consumers. Design educators never needed to compromise themselves when it came to promoting designs that needed to be commercially viable. Indian silks demonstrated many of the principles that lay behind their design teaching. The same designs and colourings were those demanded by consumers. It was possible, therefore, for manufacturers to employ designers who could supply what wealthy consumers considered to be fashionable and well designed. As a result, neither fashionable taste nor serious design education acquired a profile that rested on its difference to industry; on the contrary they were linked.

Notes

1 William Ewart, MP for Liverpool.
2 Due to a slump in the trade of British goods, the Board of Trade appointed the Gorrell Committee in 1932.
3 For example Manchester Municipal School of Art, Bradford Technical College and Macclesfield School of Art.
4 Manchester School of Art, Report Proceedings, at the Annual General Meeting in the Council Room of the Royal Manchester Institute, 7 May 1855.
5 This should not be confused with the current Central School of Art, London.
6 Manchester's School of Design was established in 1825 and Macclesfield's in 1835.
7 Bell, 1963, p. 224.
8 Rifkin, 1988, pp. 89–102.
9 The Manchester Mechanics' Institute was founded in 1825, the art courses were very popular and students were encouraged to progress to the School of Design (renamed the School of Art in 1853). They were mainly female students destined to be art teachers, not artisans aiming to work as designers in industry.

10 Macdonald, 1970, p. 86.
11 *Journal of Design and Manufactures*, Vol. II, 1849, pp. 89–191.
12 *Journal of Decorative Art*, 1888, pp. 181–5.
13 The article acknowledged the city to be an art-loving one having hosted two major exhibitions: the Art Treasures Exhibition (1857) and the Royal Jubilee Exhibition (1887) – testimonies to the fine and discriminating taste of the local community.
14 He was previously Head Master at Manchester's Technical School.
15 Walter Crane, Principal of the Royal College of Art, South Kensington (1898). He was previously an external examiner at Birmingham School of Art. He sold his textile designs to Thomas Wardle, Edmund Potter, Stead McAlpin, Birch, Gibson & Co., J. Wilson and A.H. Lee.
16 Macdonald, p. 294.
17 Crane, 1900, pp. 246–51.
18 It would seem that he referred to the *Boteh* or 'pine' motif here.
19 Crane, London, 1898, pp. 210–12.
20 A part of the L.F. Day embroidery collection is now situated in the Whitworth Art Gallery, Manchester, and a part at the Platt Hall Museum of Costume, Manchester.
21 Manchester Metropolitan University Archive.
22 *Catalogue of the Silk Section of the Royal Jubilee Exhibition, Manchester*, 1886.
23 Crane, *Recommendations and Suggestions*, 1893.
24 This was a series of photographs sent on loan; it is still in the University archive. Commercial publishers were also a source of images.
25 Irwin and Hall, *Indian Painted and Printed Fabrics*, Ahmedabad, India, 1971, p. 100.
26 Dr John Forbes Watson, The India Office, G.E. Eyre and W. Spottiswoode, London, 1866.
27 Swallow, 1999, pp. 29–45.
28 Ruskin, *Fors Clavigera*, 1877, pp. 181–204.
29 *Journal of Decorative Arts*, September 1884, p. 572.
30 Horsfall, *Handbook to the Art Museum*, May 1888, p. 21.
31 *Journal of Decorative Arts*, September 1884, p. 575.
32 Keighley, *Woven With Wisdom and Skill*, 1993, p. 51.
33 'Design and Colour in Fancy Vestings', *Textile Recorder*, 1889, p. 212.
34 Ibid., Nov. 1889, p. 158.
35 Ibid., Oct. 1889, p. 135.
36 Emery, *The Primary Structure of Fabrics*, 1994, repeatedly refers to Ashenhurst's theories.
37 For example: First Series: Brocade No. 485; Satin No. 483; Satin *Mushroo* double-cloth, No. 486/7.
38 Ashenhurst, 1883.
39 Ibid., p. 153.
40 Wardle, *On Several Species of Silk Fibre, and on the Silk Industry*: read before the Society of Dyers and Colourists, the Technical College Bradford, 8 May 1885.
41 Wardle, Sir T., Address, read at Bradford Municipal Technical College, December 1903.
42 Developments in design education in Macclesfield were similar to those in Bradford. Where training of designers in Macclesfield, including the process of designing and weaving figured silks and the laws of repeat pattern design, duplicate those in Bradford, they will not be repeated here.
43 Macclesfield Museums Trust, The Heritage Centre, Roe Street, Macclesfield, Cheshire, SK11 6UT.
44 The pattern books are stored in the archive of the silk museum.
45 The Chamber of Commerce placed a large notice in the *Macclesfield Courier and Herald* to announce the arrival of the Indian collection.
46 The current museum and archive is a recent development, instituted after the silk industry had virtually disappeared.

47 Directives stated that students should reach stage 15 or 16, out of 23, before applied designs were produced. Stewart allowed such designs at stage 10, a situation of which many manufacturers approved.
48 *Progressive Design for Students* (1902); *Colour, Harmony, and Contrasts* (1903); *Floral Studies* (1903).
49 His books were in demand in French, German, Japanese and American universities. Furthermore, while still at Macclesfield he was commissioned to report on the art and technical schools of France, Germany, Switzerland and Italy.
50 Jones, The Grammar of Ornament, Indian No. 3 (2, 9, 19) and No. 4 (5, 10, 11, 16, 17, 18).
51 Collins and Stevenson, 1994, p. 24.
52 Thomas Wardle was a known subscriber to these French pattern distribution services.
53 *Macclesfield Courier and Herald*, July 1851, p. 55 and 18 October 1851, p. 4.
54 Loan collections were intended to influence local manufactures.
55 Collins, and Stevenson, 1994, p. 38. The illustration shows an employee of BWA, Langley, Macclesfield, tie-dyeing cloth prior to dyeing, 1948.
56 According to Collins and Stevenson, in 1877/88 thirty independent designers were employed by six firms; by 1888, 100 were employed by eighteen firms. Statistics taken from the Royal Commission on the Depression of Trade and Industry.
57 Genuine Kashmir shawls imported from India were highly prized from the mid-eighteenth century. Byrd, 1992; Reilly, 1989, p. 8.

CHAPTER THREE

Perspectives on Indian silk

The silk textiles of India were and still are, some of the most widely admired and skilfully produced in the world. Although other nations produced excellent silks, the expertise of Indian makers lay in all fields of textile production; the weaves, prints and embroideries could all attain the same extraordinarily high standard. Professional makers catered for a diverse internal market and for the export trade and there was also production for personal use at village level. This short overview of textile production in India briefly indicates why these textiles had such an enormous impact in Europe providing as they did beautiful, practical cloth with inspirational designs.

A huge demand for fine Indian textiles in Europe arose during the seventeenth century. India, a highly sophisticated nation, was the source of the many different cloths that were needed to satisfy Europe's increasing demands. India's crafts skills, technologies and wide range of textiles, particularly cotton cloth, were ahead of the rest. The European market was almost inexhaustible, the demand for cotton textiles particularly appeared to have no limits. By that time Indian craftspeople were used to adapting their products to the demands of different markets. Astute Indian merchants were aware that product definition was crucial if exports were to be maintained. As trade between East and West increased, so did the specificity of the orders placed by Europeans. Through overseas trade there was an aesthetic cross-fertilisation, which had an effect on textile designs for export.

Throughout the nineteenth century and beyond, India's fine quality fabrics provided England's manufacturers, designers and consumers with inspiration and potential solutions to their production and design problems. During a period of intense debate over suitable designs for English textiles they were models of excellence in every respect. The Indian silk industry was experiencing huge production problems, however, and the number of workers employed was severely reduced.

Indian silk goods were often manufactured from raw silks imported from Afghanistan, Bokhara, Burma and China. In the latter half of the nineteenth century India looked to England for solutions to remedy its declining silk industry. A symbiotic relationship developed as each country gained inspiration from the other.

The production of silk cloth in India, from the preparation of the yarn before weaving or sewing, to the final embellishment, involved a number of highly specialised craft skills. As different social groups developed different expertise, cloth could be moved from village to village or region to region, depending on where the many processes were undertaken. Weaving techniques, for example, varied according to the type of fabric under construction. In the case of more expensive elaborate fabrics the setting up of the loom alone was a matter of considerable skill.

Design characteristics of Indian silks

There has been a great deal of continuity in the aesthetics of Indian textiles as most designs are handed down from generation to generation and many are still in use. Buddhism, Hinduism and Islam have all contributed different elements of pattern over time and played a large part in the design repertoire. The differences may be small to the casual observer, but function and fashion account for some subtle and significant differences. Textiles for ritual purposes had designs and colours of clear symbolic importance and some motifs were deemed auspicious. For example, the peacock was, among other things, an emblem of Sarasvati, the Hindu goddess of wisdom.

Islamic patterns, along with new forms of embroidery and other textile crafts, were introduced from the medieval period. Decorative elements included intricate flowing calligraphy, plant forms, especially the rose, lily, carnation and cypress tree, which were added to the existing floral motifs, fabulous birds and beasts. When Europeans began trading with India, the pattern repertoire was extended with floral and figurative forms from Europe. Influences from west and central Asia, Persia and China were also integrated over time. The Mughal dynasty significantly developed art and craft forms under court patronage.

The most perfectly prepared and costly cloths were produced for sacred purposes and were also a central part of courtly life. Textiles had a role in customs and festive activities throughout the sub-continent and ritual dictated by whom, when and where they were worn or hung.[1] Techniques, fibres, colours and motifs varied, however, as they were connected to the local culture, topography, plants and climate.

Textiles that were part of everyday life – were frequently worn and often recycled into appliqué, patchwork and then oblivion – usually had designs that reflected familiar forms connected to the home or village.

Broadly speaking, the juxtaposing of flowers, birds, fruit and animals, which were intertwined and layered, gave India's textile designs an overall decorative complexity. Abstract elements were used frequently. Barnes's work on printed cotton textiles broadly separates the designs for that particular type alone into two groups. Those that are successfully combined to form a pattern over a continuous field, and those 'that are especially suited to be contained in bands'.[2] The two groups of designs may be combined in one cloth. One of the simplest pattern devices is the stripe, which can run along the length, breadth, or diagonal of a fabric. Different lines and stripe combinations have indigenous names.

It is believed that the *kalga* or *buti*[3] was one of the most widely used and distinctive decorative motifs in the design repertoire of Northern India from the eighteenth century onwards, and over time its form has undergone changes. This floral or foliate motif allowed endless possibilities for designers of woven, embroidered and printed textiles. It was an essential design element of the Kashmir shawl and is still widely popular.[4] It is in the development of the *buti* and the creation of its new forms that the Indian designer of textiles generally spent his inventiveness; the fashions in *butis* varied every year. The outline alone contained sinuous movement. When multiple versions were placed in a pattern repeat an effect of movement across a whole design was created. The effect of dense patterning was intensified when the motif had its own elaborate infilling of intricate smaller motifs, often multi-coloured. When the *buti* is enclosed in a network of geometrical patterns, in compartments, it is known as a *jal*.

The crafts of dyeing and printing reached the highest standard in India, distinguishing its cloths and yarns from those produced elsewhere and making them sought after abroad. The knowledge of colour and the proliferation of designs reflect a civilisation that had evolved complex dyeing technology over more than 5,000 years. The use of natural dyes was one of India's ancient craft traditions. Over time, outside influences, particularly from Persia, resulted in the addition of new colours to the original range. Indian dyers were famed particularly for the practice of fast dyeing, a complicated procedure that depended on a detailed knowledge of fixative agents or mordants; usually metal oxides, as not all dyes were fast. Mordants enabled dyestuffs to be absorbed by cloth, where they remained fixed throughout repeated washings and exposure to light. Until the importation of

[57]

synthetic dyes from Europe, towards the end of the nineteenth century, Indian dyes were derived from natural sources. Regional variations existed, as geographical, agricultural and climatic conditions all affected the dyeing and printing processes. The cost of different dyes varied greatly as each colour, even different shades of red, used a variety of plants and minerals.[5]

Cultivated silk was known and valued universally for its many properties, not least for its ability to take dyes particularly well. Dyeing techniques for silks ranged from the simple resist technique to the more complex process of mordant printing and dyeing and tic-dye techniques. The natural products used to dye silk were often similar to those used in dyeing cotton, although there were some differences. All dyes other than indigo were boiled before the silk was steeped in them. Before skeins of silk were ready for weaving they were soaked in a starch mixture composed of ghee, poppy seeds, buffalos' milk and treacle. This was partly to strengthen the threads and partly to give them a gloss.[6]

Dyeing, printing, weaving and embroidery were all used to vary the aesthetics of cloth production. The dominant visual characteristic of all the traditional textiles in India, however, was the use of colour. The importance of colour to Indian society was unparalleled; different colours were symbolic and almost every ceremonial occasion had an appropriate colour and garment that was worn. Depth and mass throughout a design could be expressed by using colour in varying depths and combinations. The objective, as far as the role of colour in design was concerned, was not to follow nature but to produce pleasing effects from the harmony of colour combinations; although these were not studied on fixed, definable principles. A common device that was often used for harmonising a contrast of brilliant colours was to introduce paler, linking colours; a practice that accords with one of the principles laid down by Owen Jones in his *Grammar of Ornament*.

The techniques of imparting a pattern on the surface of a cloth using dyes – block printing, tie-dye and *ikat* were all developed and perfected in India. From at least the second millennium AD dyed textiles specifically for export were traded to the Middle East, South-East Asia and the Far East, from western India. Later, this trade included Europe and America.[7] However, local communities maintained their textile traditions alongside those produced for external markets.

Block-printed designs usually reflected the various rural and ethnic group cultures in their motifs and colourings. Although most block printing was done on cotton fabric, silk was occasionally patterned using this technique. The technique allowed multi-coloured designs to be produced relatively quickly. Colours were applied to the cloth with carved wooden blocks. The pattern to be printed was left raised on the surface of the wood in order to carry the dye to the cloth's surface. Each colour in the design had a separate wood block. The dyes were fixed, or made fast, to the cloth, through the use of mordants, which were applied before the dyes. A wide range of different shades could be obtained from one dye bath if different mordants were applied, by painting or printing onto the cloth, following the demands of the design. They usually required heat to 'fix' them permanently to the fibres. Block printing was occasionally combined with hand painting, sometimes known as pencilling, to produce very finely detailed patterns.

The technique of tie-dyeing cloth to produce a resist pattern was known as *bandhani* in Gujarat; it was also the name given to the cloth itself. According to Buhler[8] and more recently Crill[9] the technique was known in India since the early centuries AD. Many different social groups were involved with traditional *bandhani* production. The important centres of excellence for *bandhani* were Jamnagar (Saurashtra), noted for the production of bright red cloth, a result of local water conditions; Bhuj (Kutch), an area which produced the finest knots; and Ahmedabad (Gujarat), which was a major centre of textile production, along with many centres in Rajasthan. There are numerous categories of the tie-dye technique from the region.

Patolu (singular) and *patola* (plural) are Gujarati terms for silk textiles with designs produced by the double-ikat technique; the most complex and costly tie-dye procedure practised in the western region of India. These valuable and prestigious textiles were only affordable by the wealthy and have always had auspicious associations. Colour plate 6 shows a *patolu* sari that was collected in India in 1886 by Thomas Wardle and exhibited at the Colonial and Indian Exhibition in the same year. *Patolu* saris were worn for weddings or other auspicious occasions and were considered by some the noblest products of Indian dyeing. All stages of production required the combined extraordinary skills from the best dyers and weavers. Despite this being one of the 'most interesting of all Indian textiles',[10] very little was written about the technique until Thomas Wardle produced the first description in English in 1886.[11] This particular skill was practised at several centres including Alwar and Kota, where it was unsurpassed. Although the process varies in different regions the basic principles of production are the same. Prior to weaving, the warp or weft yarns (or both in the case of a double *ikat*), are tied in bundles and immersed in dye vats. The yarns are tied tightly to prevent unwanted colour penetrating the yarns and re-tied and re-dyed, according to the colour and pattern required. When warp and weft yarns are combined on the loom, the desired pattern is formed; this requires great skill on the part of the weaver. Red, green, yellow, brown, blue, black are the main colours used in the symbolic designs.[12]

Woven silks

Possibly no other country produced so many varieties of woven textiles over such a prolonged period of time as India.[13] Dhamija states that many groups of silk weavers can trace their origins back to Gujarat, from where weavers migrated throughout the sub-continent, transporting designs, and technical influences with them from one region to another.[14] Bühler is more circumspect, however. He argues that the 'traditional and historical accounts of the origin and migration of Indian weavers, especially *patolu* weavers, yield a confusing picture with a multiplicity of contradictory information. This is probably due to the unreliability of the sources.'[15]

Because silk was accepted as an auspicious and pure material by Hindus, costly woven silk cloth for ritual purposes has always played a prominent part in their textile traditions. Muslims, in contrast, curtailed its use and under certain circumstances pure silk could not be worn next to the skin. The practice of weaving silk with cotton to form *mashru*, a warp-faced satin weave construction, woven with a cotton weft, which lay next to the skin, overcame the prohibition. Silk was also woven in conjunction with other fibres to form numerous types of cloth.

The figured silks of India were often known in the West by the generic term, brocades, broadly indicating a richly patterned silk in which the designs were woven in on the loom by means of supplementary weft threads.[16] Silk brocades for export were woven in the *karkhanas* or workshops of the Sultanate period. These cloths were an important aspect of trade and were exported widely. All fine silks were popular, however, and of the woven silk textiles, it was probably the *kinkobs*,[17] with their lavish use of gold and silver threads (*zari*) woven with silk, which had the greatest impact in Europe in the nineteenth century. Colour plate 7 is a detail of a crimson silk satin with a 'net' pattern, formed from four prancing tigers woven in gold thread, enclosing an eight-petalled gold flower. The *kinkobs* were produced using a complex weaving technique that had specific structural features.[18]

The weave type used in the brocades of the eighteenth and early nineteenth centuries was usually a plain weave, although in some cases twill was used.[19] Before the arrival of the Jacquard loom, teams of weavers used the traditional draw looms[20] a complicated mechanism that created multi-warp and multi-weft figured silks.[21] Extra-weft brocade weaving was a highly demanding skill, possibly developed due to Central Asian influence. A number of categories of cloth are included in the term brocade, including those produced in pure silk known as *amrus*,[22] or *kimkhabs* (cloth of gold or silver). *Baftas* or *potthans*, are brocades where the major portion of the ground is closely woven silk, a certain portion of the pattern is in precious metal thread.[23]

The surface treatment of cloth could make it gleam, shimmer and glint as different yarns and types of weave created different effects. Their poetic names are descriptive of the effects achieved: *chandtara* (moon and stars), *dhoop chaon* (sunshine and shade), *mazhar* (ripples of silver), *mayurkanthi* (peacock's neck), etc. . . .[24] Silk gauzes or muslins with certain portions of the design in gold or silver thread, or gold borders and end pieces sewn on to them, were often called *abrawans* or flowing water.[25]

Centres of excellence in Ahmedabad and Surat, in the west, and Varanasi in the east were acknowledged as important for their fine brocade weaving traditions. In 1903 George Watt wrote of both Ahmedabad and Surat still being flourishing centres of brocade manufacture.[26] Ahmedabad, with its imperial *karkhana*, was famed for its fine gold and silver brocades and velvet cloths, which were major exports to the Persian Gulf, Arabian ports, Southern Asia, other parts of India and Europe.

A characteristic feature of Gujarati brocaded saris was an all-over field of '*butis*' placed sideways; the end piece would contain a panel of floral motifs which bore a striking resemblance to the inlaid stone motifs used in Mughal architecture. The famed Asavali saris had a distinctive enamelled appearance (*minakari*). This specialised technique involves the inlaying of an extra coloured silk weft into the ground fabric, which is then outlined by a thread of contrasting colour. The lively colour schemes, both in the main body of the cloth and the floral motifs, were executed in rich tones. Panchromatic colours such as red, pink, green, blue and purple were common, however the colour scheme was dependent on current fashionable taste.[27]

Gujarati designs showed a definite preference for animal and bird motifs such as the parrot, peacock and lion. The motifs, which are part of the folk textiles of Gujarat, are a distinctive feature and present in most textiles from the region. Agra was a centre for the production of 'cloth of gold'. Watt states that they were of such superb quality that they could be washed without being either torn or tarnished.[28]

The celebrated Banaras (Eastern region) figured silks varied tremendously as the weavers responded to market forces, regional preferences and changing fashionable taste. However, certain technical and design features distinguished them from other brocades. Weavers produced dense elegant patterns by using some of the finest threads available, creating designs with a three-dimensional quality. Generally the designs such as complex intertwining plant motifs, with *kalga* and *bel* show a marked Mughal influence. A characteristic motif *jhaalar* (frill) was used on borders and resembled a strip of upright leaves.[29] Banaras brocades can be classified into four types, all acknowledged as the finest of that type: opaque *zari* brocades, woven using thread of flattened gold wrapped around a silk core; *Kincobs*, *baftas* or *pothans*; *Amrus* which were woven with a coloured, figured silk without *zari* threads and *Abrawans*.

Elaborately figured silk brocades were also made in the villages around Baluchar in Murshidabad district in the eastern region, from at least mid-eighteenth century.[30] Watt wrote of the 'hundreds of villages throughout the district where pierced cocoons are employed for obtaining a coarse thread used in making *mathas*'.[31] The intricate Baluchar saris were created using similar techniques to the Banaras brocades and have a similar appearance, but never contained *zari* thread. Baluchar *butidars* (flowered *saris*) typically contained elaborate floral borders and end pieces, the colours of which contrasted with the main body of the cloth. The grounds of these sari fabrics were invariably of deep colours, often shot through with a differently coloured warp or weft; purple (dark red shot with blue) and dark brown, were common. The motifs were usually *buti* for field patterns and a row of large floral *kalga* placed in the centre of the sari's end piece. Simpler and less expensive versions of these cloths were also made.

By the sixteenth century, the reputation of Bengal's luxury fabrics was already widely known.[32] Bengal was the main producer of lightweight silks called 'taffeties', or 'taffeta', a generic term for fine silk fabrics used by the English in the seventeenth century.[33] However, Bengal hand-weavers were famous for various kinds of textiles: silk, pure cotton and cotton and silk mixtures.[34] The colour palette of eastern Indian cloth was often based on the natural colours of the fibres; the golden shades of wild silks were impervious to dyestuffs.[35] In parts of West Bengal, undyed saris were wore on a daily basis. Of the three 'wild' types of silk *eri* and *atlas* were too heavy to be woven into saris and were usually worn as a *chadar* (shawl or blanket). The patterns, formed on simple looms, were usually of tribal derivation or were mainstream Indian designs.[36]

Embroidered textiles

Indian embroidery has a long and rich tradition, demonstrates the highest skills and allows for diverse creative expression. The standard of work throughout the country has clearly been remarkable and maximum standards were achieved both in professional workshops and the home. Professional embroiderers were men, mainly in the north and north-west.[37] The system of apprenticeship was often from father to son, which helped maintain traditions and standards. Professional workshops in Kutch – Gujarat, in particular – produced exquisite pieces. Although a high standard of embroidery was in use everywhere, the finest examples were made for the courts and temples.[38] Domestic producers, nearly always women, produced work that was closely associated with family life and social customs, using designs that were handed down over generations.[39] Embroidery was found in many forms, and some of the techniques were unique to India. The term embroidery in India includes appliqué, cut-work, drawn-thread work, patchwork and quilting – frequently embellished with mirrors, beads, sequins and beetle wings. There were different types of silk threads, both floss (untwisted) and twisted, some were covered with precious metal to form *zari*. They may have been worked on a silk ground or other fabrics.

Embroidered objects were exported from India from at least the tenth century AD. The first reference to Bengal embroideries in English trade documents appear in East India Company records of 1618. In the seventeenth and eighteenth centuries, European influences were evident and a distinctive, localised Chinese influence was apparent in the nineteenth century. It was the high quality of the chain-stitch embroidery from the Cambay region of Gujarat, however, that was most sought after by the traders. Embroidered goods were among the principle exports of the region, which became the most renowned source of commercial embroideries in the world during the seventeenth and eighteenth centuries. Merchants were instructed by the East India Company to purchase quilts made in Cambay, and records of 1641 show sales of silk-embroidered quilts and hangings. Craftsmen in Gujarat were sent pattern tracings from England to be worked in silks.[40]

During the eighteenth century, silk appliqué was practised in Bihar and silk on muslin embroideries were commercially produced throughout the region. During the nineteenth century a number of collections of fine embroideries were formed in European from the many international exhibitions. The Forbes Watson volumes of Indian textile samples (1866–72), contain a number of embroidered pieces.[41]

They include a variety of techniques, mainly from Dacca, Bengal, Hyderabad and Madras. When fashionable taste changed in the early part of the twentieth century there was a subsequent decline in demand.

Embroidery designs had a great deal in common with woven and printed textiles, often sharing the same motifs and colouring. Some designs were worked directly onto the cloth from the worker's memory, or copied from existing pieces. Stitches created overall designs, negative forms and infill shapes.[42] Some work used one stitch only, while other pieces combined a range of stitches. Not all embroidery in India was executed with needles. Over time the *ari* (a hooked awl), originally developed for stitching on to leather, was adapted to embroider cloth held tautly on a frame, or hand-held. Usually chain and zigzag stitches were produced by this implement and were worked onto a variety of base fabrics including silk.[43]

Some techniques were localised; for example, the *phulkari* (flowering work) work of the Punjab. It is a form of counted-thread work produced by women, who often worked in groups. Fine examples of *phulkari* work were acquired in the nineteenth century for English collections. The brilliant floss silks (*pat*) were closely worked in a darning stitch, entirely from the reverse of the coarse base cloth.[44] The traditional colour palette included white, gold, orange, green and crimson, and designs are mainly geometric forms, which were passed down through generations. While the famed, woven shawls from Kashmir are probably its best-known textile product, the area also produced fine embroideries, developed as an off-shoot of the shawl industry. Late nineteenth-century examples demonstrate great expertise. Men, working in small groups, produced this embroidery with an ari or hook. Kashmiri hookwork used different stitches worked in silk thread onto wool or cotton cloth.

Notes

1 Riboud (ed.), 1989.
2 Barnes, 1997, p. 63.
3 Also known as the mango (*aam*), *konia* or 'Paisley', or pine motif.
4 It is not clear when the first Kashmir shawls entered Europe, but by the 1770s they were ubiquitous. See Irwin, *The Kashmir Shawl*.
5 T. Wardle prepared a fifteen-volume *Specimens of Fabrics Dyed With Indian Dyes* (1885), also known as the *Dyes and Tans of India*, containing 3,500 samples of dyes from Indian plants, insects, shellfish and minerals.
6 Cookson, 1886–87.
7 Bean, 1990.
8 Bühler, Alfred, 1980.
9 Crill, 1998, p. 93.
10 Watt, 1979 (first published 1908), p. 259.

11 Wardle, 1886, 1887.
12 Designs were divided into three categories: geometrical forms related to Islamic architecture; plant motifs, such as *paan bhat* (paan leaf); figures such as dancers, parrots and elephants.
13 Several first-millennium Buddhist texts refer to Banaras (Varanasi) cloth, and Varanasi retained a reputation as the undisputed centre of India's *zari* silk-weaving industry. Classical Indian texts, the *Arthashastra* and *Harshacharitamanas*, refer to sericulture (silk rearing and weaving), and the silk weaver's guild was an ancient, prestigious institution.
14 Dhamija, 1995, p. 6.
15 Bühler and Fischer, 1980, p. 333.
16 Controversy surrounds the inconsistent use of the term brocade.
17 Also known as *kamkhab* (which literally means *kam*-little and *khwab*-dream), *kincob* and *kinca*.
18 Patni-Bhowmick and de Jhala, 1992, p. 56. A pattern is formed using the extra weft technique with a twill binding, the ground is satin or satinette weave. The width of the twill varies according to the number of warp threads passed over by the weft threads each time. The *Silk and Rayon User's Association*, 1951, pp. 41–2.
19 Patni-Bhowmick and de Jala, 1992, p. 9.
20 Lynton, 1995, p. 54.
21 It is thought that this loom was first developed in Persia c. AD 300 possibly arriving in India with waves of Islamic immigrants between 700 and 1200.
22 In 1904 *amrus* were produced in Benaras, Murshidabad, Bhawalpur, Multan, Ahmedabad, Surat, Yeola, Poona and Aurangabad. Watt, 1979, p. 320.
23 Patni-Bhowmick and de Jala, 1992, p. 4.
24 Dhamija, 1995, p. 82.
25 Patni-Bhowmick and de Jala, 1992, p. 4.
26 Watt, 1979, p. 311.
27 Patni-Bhowmick and de Jala, 1992, p. 49.
28 Watt, 1979, p. 321.
29 Lynton, L., p. 18. During the late nineteenth and early twentieth centuries, Banaras weavers were influenced by Western wallpaper sample books. Weavers introduced these patterns voluntarily into their repertoire, they ranged from Victorian naturalistic motifs through to Modernist designs.
30 Lynton, 1995, p. 47.
31 Watt, D., 1979, p. 303.
32 Chaudhuri, 1997, p. 193.
33 Scott, 1993, p. 76.
34 Including: *Baftas* and *Mulmuls* of cotton, *Soosies* (cotton and silk); *Gurrahs*, *Muga Saries*, *Muga Dhuties* (silk).
35 Lynton, 1995, p. 47. Saris known as *gorad* (white-undyed) traditionally had undyed ground with coloured borders.
36 Although many woven wild silks were relatively plain, some early Assamese silks for sacred use had complex designs. Crill, 1995, p. 37.
37 Morrell, 1994, p. 16.
38 Ibid.
39 Items were dowry pieces for the home, wedding garments, clothing for everyday use and animal trappings.
40 Hall, 1986, p. 4.
41 These are mainly from Dacca, Bengal (now Dhaka, Bangladesh), Hyderabad (Deccan) and Madras.
42 Although most Indian embroidery was worked on single layers of cloth, some techniques used multiple layers of fabric. Furthermore, embroidery was worked on both plain and patterned cloth and on different types of fabric which were stitched together.
43 Morrell, 1994, p. 115.
44 Ibid., p. 55.

CHAPTER FOUR

Indian sericulture: an industry in decline

For centuries Indian artisans produced luxurious silk cloths for both the external and internal markets. Sadly, many have been lost over time, as the Indian climate and culture is not conducive to the preservation of fabric. The earliest silk textiles to have come to light so far date from around the fifteenth to the sixteenth centuries.[1] However, other surviving documents have assisted historians to form a detailed picture of the early Indian Ocean trade. The sacred *Rig Veda* texts (1500–1200 BC), refer to cloth of gold and *Kinkhabs*. Barnes, when discussing the early Indian cloth trade states:

> [T]he production of fabrics was already well documented by writers of Mediterranean antiquity, and references to the cloth trade can be found in Chinese, South East Asian and Islamic sources, all of which predate the arrival of Europeans as participants in the maritime Asian economy by centuries.[2]

Sir George Watt refers to Greek texts that have details of Indian cloth:

> Megasthenes, speaking of the costumes of the princes of India, remarks that their robes were worked in pure gold. The rich stuffs of Babylon, brought from India, were in all probability gold brocades from Ahmedabad, Benares or Murshidabad. It would appear that the *Kinkhabs* were originally woven of pure gold and that silk was added both to give a body to the textile and to afford a means of colour illumination.[3]

During the pre-modern period (up to the mid-seventeenth century), the trade routes of Asia were part of a highly managed system of production and distribution. The Indian Ocean trade stretched from the South China Sea to the eastern Mediterranean. Within this network, the position of the Indian sub-continent differed from the rest of Asia. Its diversified economy and climatic variations generated a wide spectrum of commercial goods and the sub-continent remained, from the medieval period to the mid-nineteenth century, the primary textile exporting nation of Asia. As Gittinger states: 'before the arrival of Europeans, Indian and Arab traders had made Indian piece goods a major trade item in the Middle East, in the Mediterranean, and on the coast of Africa, and a principal currency in the spice trade of the East Indies and other parts of Asia'.[4] Indian merchants traded in bulk in South-East Asia; Gujarati silk textiles, including the superb *patolas*, were traded widely, never disappearing from long-distance trade.[5] From the tenth or eleventh century the trajectory was more to the west, towards the Red Sea and the Persian Gulf, where Indian merchants would market their goods and load up their ships with Middle Eastern and European exports. The most important destinations were the great entrepots of Malacca, in present-day Malaysia, the leading commercial emporium of the Eastern Sea, and Hormuz in the Persian Gulf.[6] In 1518 Malacca was known as 'the richest seaport ... in the whole world' and functioned as the 'interface between the east and west of Asia'.[7]

The significance of this early period is that it clearly demonstrates how the large-scale, artisan production of Indian textiles was flexible and capable of responding to the demands of varied and distant markets, well before the arrival of European traders. Indeed, certain areas of trade were always deeply dependent on external markets. India developed many different kinds of cloth as a response to specific market preferences.[8] The level of international demand was, however, unpredictable being subject to periodic depression and boom conditions. Nevertheless, from at least the tenth century, patterns of product specialisation and the basic structure of markets were in place. Three different market sectors and their related categories of commodities were in operation; the distance over which goods were transported serving to define each sector. The most important factor was the ability of a local economy to create a surfeit of goods over and above subsistence demand and to maintain that level of surplus productivity over a sufficiently long period.[9]

Throughout the sub-continent there were both surplus and deficit areas at different times. In all but the most sparsely populated areas of India there was a local exchange economy, where items of daily consumption such as agricultural produce or textiles were traded. The second level was inter-regional trade, which, for the most part, supplied wholesale merchants and markets. The third level was the premodern, long-distance trade, which was intercontinental and mainly concerned with luxury goods. The link between long-distance trade, capitalism and production for the export market was a fact of daily life for the Asian artisan and farmer alike. Silk, nevertheless, was an integral part of the local economy and despite the importance of the export sector it continued to depend on internal demand.[10] Textiles, moreover, became the main currency of exchange in the spice trade. These conditions prevailed throughout the nineteenth century, although other factors were also present.

The English East India Company and trade with Asia

In 1600 a royal charter incorporated the English East India Company and Britain began to trade directly with India. The Dutch East India Company, the *Vereenigde Uosindische Compagnie* (VOC) of 1602, and the French *Compagnie des Indes Orientales*, 1664, discovered within a decade that the Indian Ocean had a vast, structured, commercial unity, involving an economic interdependence between regions.[11] Das Gupta argues that although this was a period when Europeans were participants in the Indian Ocean trade, they failed to exert any supremacy over the Asian merchant communities.[12] The East India Companies were obliged to follow the established network, otherwise trade would not have developed so quickly, and as a result, it was some time before they made an economic impact.[13] Much of the trade was under the control of Gujarati merchants (independent entrepreneurs), whose ships were larger and valued at up to five times the amount of European vessels.[14] The situation was summed up thus: 'The Europeans were poor relations. Nor in the seventeenth century, were they capable of teaching new commercial or manufacturing techniques to the locals. The two seem to have been on much the same level of development.'[15] The Indian traders remained as the dominant force; in the early eighteenth century over 80 per cent of the Red Sea trade of Surat was carried in Gujarati ships. Asian merchants only yielded to European trade demands from the mid-eighteenth century, and only then because of changes in the Asian world.[16] The European companies did, however, introduce another dimension to the trading structure: they carried goods all the way to Northern Europe and laid the foundation of the nineteenth-century trade in commodities and raw material.[17]

The value of raw silk as an article of trade was recognised by the English East India Company at an early stage of its existence. It was, however, the silks of China, Japan, Siam and above all Persia, that were held in greater esteem than the silk of Bengal. Raw silk trading with India always had its problems as both supplies and qualities were unpredictable.[18] The cause of the problems with Bengal silk was that only the so-called 'country-wound' silk could then be obtained from India. The main fault, which was out of the company's control, was that this silk thread was wound from the cocoons in a rudimentary manner, the defective reeling technique lead to inequality in the same skein, which could range through many thicknesses throughout its length.

The East India Company, however, realised the commercial potential of Indian silk yarn as the English silk industry needed raw material for its weavers. The company, therefore, sought to address some of the production problems in India and experts were sent out to the sub-continent to improve matters. Different methods of mulberry cultivation, silkworm rearing and comparative methods of reeling were tried, and by the first half of the seventeenth century trading began in Bengal raw silk. It was not until 1775, however, that the better yarns resulted in an increase in exports and demand in London was generally better.[19] At this time there was an increasing demand in Europe for high quality silk textiles, particularly those from the Kasimbazar district, which were soon 'competing favourably with the high quality silk goods made in France and Italy'.[20] Although the importing of Indian piece goods alarmed the English silk weavers, raw silk yarn from India was needed and did became a staple commodity for the company during the seventeenth and eighteenth centuries.[21]

In 1830 evidence from company managers and London silk brokers was taken before a select committee of the House of Lords and it was very clear about the still poor state of Bengal silk. Although reeling methods had improved, exports of silk from Bengal remained almost stationary.[22] The export of silk from China, and from 1859 from Japan, however, increased enormously, which meant that, comparatively, Bengal silk was in decline. By the 1870s the trade in Bengal silk was languishing, although exports of waste silk had increased. The general result of the English East India Company's connection with the silk culture of Bengal was to improve aspects of reeling silk yarn, which allowed the yarn to have some place in the European market place. The breeding and rearing of silkworms were still left entirely to the Indian citizens.

Indian silk textiles: production and consumption

Production in India's silk trade was smaller than in cotton. Nevertheless, the internal market for silk textiles in the form of saris, stitched and unstitched clothes and decorative hangings alone was huge. The nature of Indian culture meant that textiles have always been more than items of fashion, frequently relating to beliefs and customs, which often demanded the specific use of cloth. Silk was not, however, a homogenous product; it was distinguished by many variables such as methods of production and yarn types. There were two distinct types of Indian silk products: those made from the domesticated, or mulberry-feeding silkworms *Bombycidae*, and those from the 'wild', non-mulberry-feeding silkworm *Saturnidae*. Each type had its particular physical properties that influenced its potential use; silk being more suitable than other fibres for specific cloths or threads, which invariably affected demand.

Mulberry, or cultivated, silk from the domesticated silkworm (the *Bombyx mori* moth) was the finest; the thread was a continuous filament, which could be reeled directly from the cocoon. Cultivated silk came from those areas of India where mulberry trees could be grown, usually at higher altitudes. The process of production was labour intensive, but the thread could be wound in a continuous length; it was white, lustrous and smooth. Periodically, however, production problems affected the predictability of the yarn supply. The mulberry plant was itself prone to disease as was the silkworm, and both needed careful management.

Wild silk thread in contrast was broken by the silkworm escaping from the cocoon; it needed to be spun, combed or carded to make a continuous filament, which meant that the thread was often uneven, although harder-wearing. It varied in colour from cream to light brown, with many golden shades in between – one of the reasons that made it difficult to dye. India produced a wide range of silk cloth, and was the only nation with such a variety of wild silks, which were highly developed all over the sub-continent. The north-east region of India produced the most varieties of wild silk. This area contained the Ganga plain and includes what are now Bangladesh and the states of Bengal, Bihar and eastern Uttar Pradesh. Silk reeling and spinning took place there and many women knew how to reel, spin and weave silk. It was an important aspect of their life. The weaving of wild silk, which took place in villages and towns, was usually done for family use. However, surplus thread was sold to weavers.

Wild silk was of various types including *atlas, eri, muga* and *tasar*. Variations in the yarns were to some extent determined by the moth and were less dependent on human intervention in the initial processing stages. *Tasar* silk (from the *antheroea paphia* moth) was known by various entomological and vernacular names in different parts of the country.[23] It was the most commercially viable and was widely distributed all over India. Traditionally, *tasar* cultivation was a tribal activity; the bulk of India's early *tasar* production came from the hills of southern and eastern Bihar. In the eighteenth century, the East India Company listed five types of *tasar* silk cloth as being woven in the region. According to Thomas Wardle the most striking feature of *tasar* silk yarn was its flatness; this reflected light from its angled surface and gave it a characteristic lustre. Cloth made from *tasar* was generally very durable. Plain, undyed *tasar* silk cloth was judged by the fineness of the weave, which depended on the quality of the thread. In the late nineteenth century, *tasar* was generally woven to form mixed fabrics of cotton warp and *tasar* weft.

Muga (from the *Antheroea Assama* moth) silk was produced in Assam; the *muga* silkworm fed on a tree known as champa. Although this silk was at its best when fed in the open air on trees, tribal people also cultivated it in their homes. *Muga* had a more lustrous appearance than other wild silks, its rich golden colour meant it was much sought after and always costly. The thread was exported from Assam. Some of the famed *Jamdani* muslins contained brocaded designs that utilised the natural golden colour of *muga* silk. They were also embroidered with *muga* floss silks. Golden *muga* thread was also incorporated into white-work (*Chikankari*) embroidery. The result was a subtle, understated aesthetic. Examples of woven *muga* silk fabrics were included in the Forbes Watson collection of Indian textiles (1866). They were generally of crudely reeled threads and were not the higher quality fabrics.

The *Eria* (*Attacus ricini*) silkworm fed on the castor oil plant, native to Assam. The thread varied between white and brown shades and as it was difficult to reel it was spun like cotton. It was mainly used for domestic clothing and was seldom exported from the area. *Eria* cloth was exceptionally durable and passed down from generation to generation. Poorer people wore it in all seasons, and richer people in the winter.

During the Mughal period[24] sericulture was encouraged by patronage and royal workshops in all the imperial capitals ensured that high standards of craft skills were maintained. Fine textiles were a major feature of court life, valued as prestigious items, and given as badges of honour to nobles and coveted gifts to foreigners. Although different styles were evident, a Mughal aesthetic developed. Floral motifs were prolific and were executed in a distinctive manner in woven and embroidered silks. They were characterised by finely drawn details of single plants, often with multiple flower heads in profile. The colour schemes were more delicate than previously, although they were still richly toned.

The range of silk products in India differed according to quality and texture, which in turn were predicated on types of yarn, numbers of thread per square inch, the type of design and colouring. Furthermore, these could change from year to year.[25] Only an expert in the trade could judge whether the prices asked by weavers, or intermediate dealers, were appropriate. The high cost of luxury products such as silk piece goods meant it was a decidedly speculative operation to finance the materials for weaving. The element of risk was reduced on both sides through the operation of commercial agreements between the wholesale merchants who were the lynchpins of the system, in touch with both the consuming markets and weavers.[26] This could take the form of a cash advance for the weavers to enable them to purchase the necessary and costly raw materials. The need for pre-planning and a considerable amount of organisation meant that merchants also assumed an entrepreneurial role.

The production of fine Indian textiles needed careful management as Indian craft workers provided for the vast domestic market as well as the export trade. Production was fragmented into many stages, each requiring specialist expertise. When discussing seventeenth- and eighteenth-century cloth production, Chaudhuri stated that 'the technology of production involved many intermediate stages, and the separation of function was social as well as technical'. He emphasises that 'the textile industries required the combined skills of several separate groups of craftsmen before the finished cloth could reach the consumer in a usable form'.[27] For example, the production of gold thread or *zari*, which was only one of many ancillary industries for the silk trade, was divided into seven discrete processes, each performed by a different set of artisans.

Large-scale operations were in place for the production of both luxury articles and basic goods.[28] The degree of specialisation in the export market was often so great that if the contracting merchants failed to take delivery, goods could not be sold locally.[29] The different types of textiles destined for the overseas market in South-East Asia were completely specific as to their designs, colours and textures. Although many weavers were independent makers, the export market was seldom accessible to small producers.

Even though the sub-continent was the source of the widest range of silk yarns, sericulture in all its forms was depressed in the latter half of the nineteenth century. The province of Bengal, famed throughout India and abroad for the quality of its cultivated raw silk, once supplied the looms over a vast area of the country, including all the great silk weaving centres. Due to its unpredictable quality, demand for Bengal silk yarn had gradually fallen away until there was hardly any international market left. Indian weavers would not use it and manufacturers were obliged to import silk thread from China, Bokhara, Afghanistan and Burma.

The scale of India's silk operations was much reduced due to; *inter alia*, the lack of systematic sericulture, diseased silkworms and a poor understanding of modern technology. Methods of producing and preparing silk yarn had not kept pace with improved production methods in other countries. The 1870s and 1880s marked a period of crisis for both English and Indian silk production, and this was a matter of considerable debate and serious concern. It was nevertheless believed, by both Indian and British authorities, that of all the products in India silk held the most potential and was worth investigation and support.

Thomas Wardle, who had, as we shall see, established a reputation as a progressive businessman with a great deal of knowledge of Indian silk yarns, was despatched to India by the government of India in November 1885. He was expected to provide solutions to serious problems and thereby help India's silk producers overcome their severe difficulties. His principle remit was to reinstate Bengal to its former position as the main provider of silk yarn throughout India. A further goal was to increase demand for Indian 'wild' silk yarn and facilitate its export. Constructing a better system of silk yarn production would help stabilise Indian sericulture; it would create a foundation for a system of manufacture that would leave India independent of imports and, therefore, less vulnerable to external market forces.

When he was in India, Wardle reported his findings to the government; he found that upwards of 60 per cent of the silkworms died of disease before making cocoons. This was due to a lack of scientific knowledge and management. One of his solutions was to recommend that someone from the Indian silk industry should be given the opportunity of studying in Europe in order to understand the latest sericulture methods then being practised in France and Italy. The knowledge gained could then be taken back to India and could be used to establish an Imperial government institution, where every branch of scientific sericulture could be conducted and taught to the local people. In other words a government-run silk school, either in Calcutta or another important centre, with highly qualified teachers, who could instruct on disease prevention and the annual improvement of the stock of silkworms and the growth of mulberry. In the event, Nitya Gopal Mukerji travelled to Europe. There he studied first in Padua, Italy, then in France at Montpelier, and lastly at Paris under Pasteur, who had succeeded in eradicating pebrine and other silkworm disease, which had once devastated the sericulture of France and Italy.

Kashmir

Because of its obvious potential for raw silk production, Thomas Wardle also turned his attention to Kashmir. He had been interested in the possibilities since 1886, and this was reactivated in 1889, when he was in correspondence with John Lockwood Kipling, then director of the art school at Lahore, who described the potential for increased productivity in Kashmir. Wardle raised the subject of developing a useful industry dedicated to the production of raw silk with officials. He became deeply interested in the silk future of Kashmir as its geography and climate indicated great potential. In summer the climate in Kashmir was similar to that of Italy and therefore considered to be suitable for the cultivation of the mulberry and of the univoltine silkworm of commerce, the *Bombyx mori*. Kashmir, therefore, had the potential to become one of the most important centres of sericulture. It was the only country that Wardle knew where the *Bombyx mori* was found in the wild in sufficient numbers to be harvested.

Although it had an ancient history, sericulture in Kashmir had been disorganised and erratic for centuries. The silk industry had been closely connected with developments in Bokhara, with which it had an interchange of silkworm, seeds and silk. In 1869, the Maharaja Ranbir Singh enthusiastically set about modernising production on a large scale. The cost of buildings and equipment was enormous, but owing to the scattered nature of the rearing houses, production was not closely supervised, and there was no one with sufficient technical knowledge to manage larger-scale production, although some improvements were made in reeling. In 1878 disaster struck when nearly all of the silkworms were killed by disease. Although the industry lingered on, due to great efforts made by Babu Nilambar Mukerji, the Chief Justice of Kashmir, who did improve silk reeling, by 1890 sericulture was virtually finished.

Wardle was convinced that the decline was due to lack of knowledge of modern scientific method relating to the work of Pasteur on silkworm disease and disease prevention. He offered to do anything to assist the progress of Kashmiri sericulture, including making a visit there to report on its capabilities. He felt it was a great pity that Europe, and especially England, did not obtain more silk from the sub-continent, and that the bulk of its raw material was chiefly supplied by China and Japan. Wardle asked for the cooperation of the Indian government in this matter, and, as a result, his suggestions were enthusiastically taken up.

In 1891 Thomas Wardle discussed with the government of India, the possibility of installing systematic sericulture in Kashmir. His primary motive was that famine and disease were widespread in the State, and that many people were dying from lack of food and employment. He had other incentives, realising that the repeal of the regulations connected with the cultivation of opium in the country would result in poverty. The increased volume in production and subsequent prosperity to be derived from a revived silk cultivation and industry would be sufficient to recover the losses from reduced opium crops.

He openly stated his deep conviction that the future of the silk industry would be of great importance if the Maharaja of Kashmir thought the idea was worthwhile and would give it the necessary encouragement. Over the ensuing years Wardle actively encouraged sericulture in Kashmir by conducting experiments on samples of its raw silk yarn in Leek, and advising on types and prices for the European markets, particularly those in England and France. He was most encouraged by the quality of the samples sent to him and he distributed these to manufacturers and London silk brokers, requesting them to report independently on the potential. Wardle visited France and Italy at the request of the Indian government. He made exhaustive tours of the major silk centres in both countries, from where he ordered the latest cocoon reeling machinery and disease-free silkworm eggs, the latter at a cost of more than £600. Wardle took full responsibility for what was considered to be an extravagant purchase, as he was utterly convinced that the time was right for developments in India to take place.

The purchases were completely successful and he was ordered to more than double the purchase of eggs for the next season. Under the management of a Mr C.B. Walton, whom Wardle engaged for the purpose, new filatures were established in the Valley of Kashmir in 1897, in order that silk reeling could take place in a controlled environment. A considerable profit was made and the raw silk, which was sent to England in 1899–1900, commanded a good price. Success proved so great that orders amounting to £4,000 arrived for the silk in 1900. In 1901 more than 25,000 people were employed in rearing the silkworm crop in the Srinagar Valley alone. The purchase of European seeds was entirely justified and Wardle earnestly recommended the continuation of the system he established.

The production of silk was essentially a cottage industry, as far as silkworm rearing was concerned; the reeling of cocoons was, by then, managed entirely by Srinagar men and boys in the new filatures. He also continued to promote the idea of a government-backed institution, such as those in France and Italy, to conduct research and thoroughly train local workers in all matters relating to scientific and commercial sericulture. Much to his regret this was not done, although better management of silk production following his advice, resulted in year-on-year improvements in output. Wardle went on to recommend improvements in the management of the black mulberry tree, which was native to Kashmir, and recommended the systematic planting and cultivation of the white mulberry, which was the variety grown in France and Italy, and which could extend the production of raw silk.

In 1903 Wardle visited Kashmir to assess the sericulture situation at first hand. By that time 44,245 people were engaged in silk production.[30] Although many of the workers were comparatively inexperienced, their dextrous manner of cocoon reeling was thought to be a considerable advantage. On his return from Kashmir in May 1903, Wardle visited Lyons in France to see one of the largest distributors of raw silk on the continent. He received very favourable reports of Kashmir silk, which was quickly becoming sought after by some of the principle manufacturers in France. He was assured that any quantities of Kashmir silk would readily be purchased. He also received very encouraging reports in England. By 1904 he conveyed much pleasure in the fact that, mainly due to his unstinting efforts, the Kashmir silk industry was reinvigorated and enormous numbers of people had gained employment.

As part of the promotion of Kashmir silk, a number of high profile exhibitions were organised in London by the British and Irish Silk Association. One aim was to bring the attention of Indian and Kashmir silks to English women, in order to encourage their purchase in preference to French-made silk. In 1901 displays of Indian and Kashmir raw silks and varieties of woven textiles were highlighted at the Women's exhibition at Earls Court, in a display that demonstrated the versatility of the yarn. Plain and figured silks for upholstery and dress purposes were featured: silks dyed by Wardle in Leek and woven by Warners of Braintree and Spitalfields.

At considerable personal expense and with some anxiety, Wardle visited most of the silk users in England with samples, as well as several large continental manufacturers. Although this took a great deal of his time, eventually he succeeded in overcoming prejudices and obtaining a favourable reception for the new silks of Kashmir. The silks were tried on their merits and demand followed; and French silk merchants went on to import the silk directly from Kashmiri producers.

Wardle was adamant that the Kashmir silk industry should not fall into private enterprise. He agreed with Lord Curzon, the Viceroy of India who emphatically argued thus: 'There is no spectacle which finds less favour in my eyes, or which I have done more to discourage, than that of a cluster of Europeans settling down on a Native State and suckering from it the moisture which ought to give sustenance to its own people.'[31] Wardle's efforts had always been to benefit the

4 Thomas Wardle on an elephant, Jammu, Kashmir, 1903.

Kashmiri people and the profits of the improved silk industry were intended for the good of the State not for private enterprise. The question of employment of thousands of Kashmiri people who were on the verge of starvation carried more weight with him than profit making.[32]

Thomas Wardle was 72 years of age when he decided to visit Kashmir. He felt a moral responsibility to ensure personally that no losses were incurred and that sericulture was continuing to employ many people. He also wanted to investigate the possibility of introducing weaving to the State. His difficult journey to this far-flung region is worth recording here as it clearly indicates the strength of his commitment to Kashmiri sericulture. On his way out to India he spent a week in Lyon and the south of France gathering the opinions of silk merchants and manufacturers on Kashmir silk and studying up-to-date methods of cocoon reeling. Due to the kindness of two of the best filature owners at Alais in the Cevennes, he was able to experiment with Kashmiri yarn. His lengthy report on his progress took up much of the voyage time to India. He journeyed alone from Bombay on 9 March, travelling night and day by express train; he was met by the Resident Mr Colville in Kashmir.

After a day's discussions he was off to Jammu where he stayed several days and where he had the use of an elephant and a horse-drawn carriage, he attended a Hindu festival and met local rulers. Figure 4 shows Wardle and the elephant outside the Residency at Jammu. He left for Rawal Pindi (*sic*) en route for Srinagar, the nearest railway station to the Kashmir Valley 200 miles away. The route through the Kashmir Valley was still blocked by snow and would not be open for another ten days. On learning that the snows were at last beginning to melt, Wardle again tried to travel to Kashmir and set out alone to tackle the dangerous mountainous journey with a tonga (a light two-wheeled carriage) and pair of horses, changing horses every five or six miles. A huge fall of snow stopped him at one point and he was forced to leap out of the tonga to avoid a fall of rocks; the river Jhelum was foaming in a flood 1,000 feet below him. Four days later he arrived at Srinagar at noon, where he was given every comfort; by the afternoon he had clearly recovered as he was out visiting silk filatures. Undoubtedly, the sight of the new silk industry and its workers was enough to make the arduous journey worth while. In Srinagar, Wardle learnt from the Chief Judge of Kashmir and the State Medical Officer that had it not been for the successful introduction of sericulture, Srinagar would have been famine stricken; there were still people in the city who were all but starving and in need of employment. His suggestion of introducing silk weaving was welcomed as having great employment possibilities.

In an article he sent from India to his local Field Club in Leek, Wardle described:

> driving through the length of this valley of wondrous beauty, about 80 miles long and 35 miles wide. It seems full of mulberry trees and secures the home of an industry, which even after its present marvellous expansion is yet but the nucleus of an immense future development, if it can be retained and managed by the state, and so preserved from commercial rivalries.[33]

His mission had several aspects as far as he was concerned. First, he wanted to show the great advantage to the State of retaining the industry and keeping it from private hands and company promotion; second, he hoped to provide employment for a large population greatly in need of it and to help them to be trained. He had no doubt that it could work on every count; his admiration for the Kashmiri people was transparent:

> I have never seen a people so marvellously clever with their fingers as the Kashmiris. It is a sight to go down to the bassines in the filatures and see the beautiful way the men and boys can handle the fine threads of the cocoons, even those who have been engaged in it for a few weeks only. They do it with a readiness and skill, which compares favourably with the south of Europe filatures, who have gone through an apprenticeship to learn cocoon-reeling.[34] (see Figure 5)

He had further ambitions though; he wanted to help perfect the raw silk so that it could hold its own against that of France and Italy. It was nearly at that point and he hoped to see his aims accomplished before too long; when that was achieved he felt that the future was secured.

Thomas Wardle was warmly welcomed in Jammu by both His Highness the Maharaja of Jammu and Kashmir and his brother General Raja Sir Amar Singh at the palace at Jammu, where a durbar was held to greet him, and many members of the local nobility attended. Wardle discussed French developments in reeling and showed examples of Kashmir silk which he had had woven by Warner & Sons into magnificent black-figured brocades. They were ultimately presented to the Queen. The Maharaja of Jammu and Kashmir agreed that the local silk industry should not be taken over by private enterprise; as far as possible it was to be retained and developed by the State.

Wardle went on to tour other districts and attend conferences held to discuss the development of the silk industry in Kashmir. Figure 6 shows Thomas Wardle on the horse he used as transport. In Srinagar he strongly advocated the commencement of fine silk weaving and discussed its desirability as a cottage industry, capable of giving employment to those women who needed to work at home. The idea was entirely his own, and as he was solely responsible he gave it a

Silk filatures in operation in Srinagar, Kashmir, 1903.

great deal of consideration before mentioning it to anyone else. At that time no silk weaving existed in Kashmir or Jammu. As the production of cocoons had been brought to such a point of perfection it made sense to Wardle that local people should gain the advantage of turning it into cloth for the internal and external markets. There was still considerable poverty in the region and the prospect of increased employment was greeted with much approval. For some time Wardle had been concerned about the hard lot of Kashmiri women, realising that they were bearing the burden of the lowest and most laborious daily work. A cottage weaving industry would, he felt, enable a great improvement in the material condition of local women. The Hindu widows, in particular, were living in a state of pitiable degradation. In due course 1,350 women were employed in the silk industry The establishment of such a system was, however, fraught with practical problems. Regretfully, Wardle agreed that a small weaving factory might be a more practical solution and on his return to England set about ordering the necessary looms and other equipment. With the help of a friend, a woven silks manufacturer of Macclesfield, he set about drawing up detailed plans for the factory. He sent out a highly skilled weaver with equipment and for some months he was kept employed perfecting the looms. Only one problem remained: How

6 Sir Thomas Wardle on horseback, with Indian bearers, Kashmir, 1903.

cheaply and quickly could the Kashmiris, once they were trained to use the loom, compete with the Chinese and Japanese?

On his journey home Wardle wrote to his local Leek newspaper describing another great interest, the natural history and geology of Kashmir. He was already known as a geological expert in Stafford-shire, and he made time to use his visit to report on what he said was a most interesting part of the world.

Notes

1 A Jain silk embroidery from Gujarat dated fifteenth to sixteenth century is now in the Calico Museum, Ahmedabad, India. A late sixteenth-century Bengal embroi-dery is in Hardwick Hall, Derbyshire, the Victoria and Albert Museum holds some sixteenth and seventeenth century pieces and the Embroiderers' Guild has a late seventeenth-century Mughal hanging.
2 Barnes, 1997, pp. 1–2.
3 Watt, 1904, p. 320.
4 Gittinger, 1982, p. 13.
5 Guy, 1998, p. 26.
6 Chaudhuri, 1985, p. 37.
7 Gittinger, 1982, p. 137.
8 Ibid.
9 Chaudhuri, 1985, p. 182.
10 Bag, 1989, pp. 74–5.
11 Chaudhuri, 1978, p. 83.
12 Das Gupta, 1979, pp. 10–12.
13 Gittinger, 1982, p. 13.
14 Goody, 1996, p. 128.
15 Pearson, 1976, p. 10. Quoted in Goody, 1996, p. 128.
16 Das Gupta, 1979.
17 Chaudhuri, 1985, p. 82.
18 Bag, 1989, pp. 36–40.
19 Chaudhuri, 1978, p. 352.
20 Ibid., p. 352.
21 Ibid., p. 343.
22 Geoghegan, 1872.
23 Also known as tasar, tussar, tussah, etc.
24 The Mughals were from a Muslim dynasty of Central Asia who ruled most of India from 1526 to 1858.
25 Arasaratnam, in Mazzaoui (ed.), 1998, p. 181.
26 Ibid.
27 Chaudhuri, in Roy (ed.), 1996, p. 49.
28 Dhamija, 1995, p. 13.
29 By 1904 this had risen to 50,000–60,000 people in employment in silk production.
30 Curzon, Lord, Jaipur, April 1902.
31 Wardle, 1904, p. 45.
32 Ibid., p. 279.
33 Ibid., p. 280.

PART II

Thomas Wardle

CHAPTER FIVE

Background influences

The history of Thomas Wardle's company highlights factors common to many of the small firms that made up the English silk industry. Many developments in the industry in the latter half of the nineteenth century were down to the efforts of owners of individual companies, their concern for good design and their anxiety over the fluctuating fortunes of the English and Indian silk industries. Small and medium-sized companies were a feature of the silk textile industries; they contributed extensively to a nation's economy and provided employment for many people. There is, however, a wider significance to these activities. There is a clear need for a comprehensive charting of manufacturers' contribution to the English silk industry and the inspiration that underpinned their actions during the era of empire. The histories of individuals' efforts demonstrate that businessmen in regional industries in different countries sometimes had more in common with each other, through the mutually dependent demands of a shared trade, than they had with their fellow citizens operating in other spheres of interest. Business networks, with their interlinked supply chains, the range of individuals' knowledge and entrepreneurial skills often crossed imperial boundaries.

Although not a leader of a large enterprise, Wardle, like other silk manufacturers, made a significant contribution to the global silk textile industry during the sixty years that he was in business. He became the spokesman for the English silk industry and earned a reputation as one of the most expert dyers and printers in England. He was acknowledged as the leading authority on India's wide range of silks. Some of his greatest achievements include a greater understanding and use of India's wild silks and the revival of the Kashmir silk industry, alongside the production of beautiful textiles. He was driven by far more than the profit motive – common humanity, understanding nature and how to use it for the benefit of mankind, the desire to make beautiful things and to make them well, were all strong driving forces. He saw and sympathised with the people of textile regions in England, who had suffered acutely from the rapid decline of the industry and its transfer under adverse conditions to other countries. He had equal regard for the losses, which for various reasons had fallen on his fellow subjects in India in connection with the decay of the trade and crafts of that country.[1] His many-pronged approach to problem solving played a key role in helping both the English and Indian silk industries to survive. An all-encompassing outlook took account of education for the textile industries, international trading conditions, sericulture particularly in India, dye chemistry, collecting and exhibiting Indian silk textiles, the role of museums in industry, craftsmanship, tradition and the role of the consumer.

Thomas Wardle was born in 1831 into a region of England dominated by the silk industry. For a period of ten years he worked in all the branches of his father's silk dyeing firm in Macclesfield, Cheshire; there he developed an interest in chemistry, which remained with him throughout his life.[2] In 1866 he moved from Macclesfield to nearby Leek in Staffordshire, setting up a silk dyeing business with his brother at Leekbrook. Six years later he purchased the Hencroft Works on the banks of the River Churnet in Leek. The water of the Churnet was known locally as being particularly good for dyeing purposes. This site was used initially for hand-block printing of fabric; within a few years it was the centre of some of the company's most outstanding achievements. It was at the Hencroft Works that Wardle's and William Morris's experiments with natural dyeing took place. After this period the site reverted to hand-block printing. The Churnet Works was also acquired some years later. Initially a dye works, it became known as 'Sir Thomas and Arthur Wardle'[3] and was advertised as a finishing, printing and dyeing company.

From childhood, Wardle had experience of his father's silk dyeing processes with vegetable dyes. As he was dissatisfied with many of the results from artificial aniline dyes he became interested in reviving traditional, natural dyestuffs in Leek. The more a textile company could control the various stages of production the greater their lead over quality and complexity of designs and colours. The raw materials involved were constantly monitored as any variation in their condition could affect the final result. Inter-company factors were also important; the ability to control aspects of the supply chain and communicate with suppliers was vital. At any one time Wardle's company was both receiving and supplying goods and commissions and a great deal of tacit knowledge was exchanged in the process. The specialised knowledge exchanged between supplier and customer

was embedded in the workforce through the daily routines of research, development, design and production, which were constantly
turning grey cloth and undyed yarn into beautiful goods. All of this
was time-consuming and contributed to the high cost of the finished
item, which made it a luxury product. But, as consumer demand
indicated, the results were worth the effort; there was a wide range of
silk fabrics required and silk thread had many uses.

The silk trade was a labour intensive business. Many different,
lengthy processes were involved in turning the different types of silk
yarn into cloth, ribbons, trimmings, embroidery and sewing silks.
Equally, there were a number of varieties of silk cloth – each with
different considerations, which required appropriate procedures. The
dyeing and printing of silk was a notoriously unpredictable process
dependent as it was on such variables as timing, temperature, combinations of dyeing, fixing and finishing agents and the physical properties of the items to be dyed. The dyeing of 'Blue Black', for example,
was a two-day process, which involved soaping and softening stages
and much washing and drying in alternate cold and warm baths containing logwood[4] and black iron. There were many different blacks
to choose from, for example Raven Black and Glacé Black, and each
needed a different recipe.

Numerous calculations were essential for each vat of dye before a
satisfactory result could be obtained. A number of dye vats could be
in operation in the dye house with different colours in production
simultaneously. Moreover, separate types of silk yarn and cloth needed
individual monitoring. Figure 7 shows silk dyeing by hand at Leek,
during the 1920s.[5] An experienced workforce with embedded knowledge was vital, as consistency of colour depended on accuracy and
strict timing. An inattentive or inexperienced operative could ruin a
batch of yarn or cloth. Even a good sense of smell was important in
some cases. Too much or too little time, or heat, or ingredients, and
the colours would be entirely different. The translation of a design or
a desired shade of colour into production was, therefore, an arena of
particular complexity. It required careful management to maintain a
balance between production-driven compromises on the one hand and
the maintenance of the original artistic concept on the other.

Communication between those responsible for the design concept
and those carrying out the dyeing and printing needed to be clear. As
a client's or a designer's knowledge of technical requirements, and
the artisan's knowledge of aesthetics, might be seriously incomplete,
it was a stage of production that depended on the combined understanding of both art and science. Thomas Wardle was able to bridge
the gap; as a chemist he understood the difficult processes involved in

7 Hand dyeing silk yarn in Leek, Staffordshire, c.1920s.

dyeing and printing, he also had a deep interest in aesthetics and took great trouble to understand the principles that lay behind successful design and colouring. This was crucial, as many designers and other manufacturers depended on accurate dyeing and printing to realise their concepts; it was the basis of successful woven, printed and embroidered textiles.

The dyeing and printing of textiles used copious amounts of water. The Leek silk trade, therefore, required several reliable sources of both river and well water. The River Churnet was considered to be particularly suitable for silk dyeing and had considerable advantages, possibly due to the local mineral content. A number of manufacturers used the same source, however, and the possibility of pollution was high. Wardle & Company records show just how vital a clean water supply was; the testing of river and well sources was a constant task and the cause of some serious concern at times. Local expertise was crucial to the efficiency of the supply and water diviners were called upon to search for new sources. Water was continually monitored for natural and synthetic pollutants as contaminated dye baths could change the depth or evenness of a colour and ruin expensive silk yarn and cloth.

Wardle & Company quickly rose above local and national competition and gained a high reputation. Using in-house designs for its own finished goods, the company also responded to external demands and took on a number of other roles. On the whole, the firm acted as commission printers and dyers for a number of clients. They converted skeins of raw silk, wool and cotton yarns, and unfinished 'grey' cloths, using diverse printing, dyeing and finishing processes. Some of the orders were for small batches, but large, important bulk orders for the supply of sewing silks and black silk handkerchiefs to the Admiralty were catered for. Plain and figured English woven silks were usually dyed in the piece for other manufacturers. Plain and figured Indian silk fabric was dyed and printed for the retail market through Liberty & Co. of London and other outlets. A different, specialist knowledge, however, was called into play on occasion – for example the testing of ancient blue yarns for Flinders Petrie, the Egyptologist.

A highly committed personal drive for quality on both sides brought William Morris to work with Thomas Wardle to conduct experimental dyeing and printing (see Chapter 7). As well as Morris, a number of leading designers had their designs printed by Wardle at the Leek works. Furthermore, within a very short period of time of A.L. Liberty opening his Regent Street store in 1875, Wardle & Co. became the main supplier of his dyed and printed cloth, particularly Indian silks. Liberty imported large quantities of silk cloth from India but found the dyes were inconsistent and not always fast. Wardle, after prolonged experimentation with vegetable dyes, produced a fast, distinctive range of soft delicate shades, with which he successfully printed and dyed the Indian silks for the London retailer.[6]

The need to maintain high standards meant that Wardle constantly monitored his supply chain and experimented to expand his supply of raw materials and improve dyeing techniques. Product development was part of the company's ongoing activities and constantly reviewed. He was not against modern technology for its own sake, nor did he believe that modern methods were incompatible with good design. He utilised what was appropriate for his business: the production of luxury goods for the higher end of the market. Wardle continued to hand print silk with wood blocks as they gave him maximum control over production, but used roller printing when appropriate. One example, a cotton velvet, was roller-printed with an all-over poppy motif designed by Thomas Wardle junior. It was one of a large group of printed cotton velvets known as 'Manchester' on the continent. A version of the velvet was regarded as good enough to exhibit at the Centennial International Exhibition at Melbourne in 1880, the Arts and Crafts Exhibition, London 1889–90, and London City Exhibition of 1890.[7] In 1902 it was also produced for the Aesthetic Gallery, New Bond Street, London, which specialised in retailing 'artistic silken fabrics of English manufacture'.[8] Roller printing in this case was clearly used because it was the best technique for that particular cloth and not for economies of scale. A modern synthetic dye such as Prussian blue was also used for sound commercial reasons; principles and market awareness were not incompatible.[9]

The textile industries generally were changing rapidly and responding to different needs at this time. New developments in production processes, dyeing technologies and yarn preparation produced new classes of goods; the price of cotton goods fell and this alone had a huge impact on silk production. Hand-block printing and the use of natural dyes were highly expensive compared to the mechanised processes of mass production. However, they distinguished Wardle's products from his competitors and were an important aspect of the company's identity. They were some of the few areas left in textile production that required artisans to exercise a degree of skilled expertise. The majority of the mainstream textile workforce, concerned with mass production, however, consisted of mere machine minders who had no input into technique, designs or colouring. As Wardle stated:

> The absence of a proper motif has robbed the work of so much artistic value, in so doing has robbed it of its commercial importance. More than this has robbed the worker of the proper pleasure in his or her own work and has made life a drudgery because it has not been possible to enjoy the doing of it and so we have descended to a position of mediocrity from which it is the intention of art teaching and technical training to raise us.[10]

The continuation of traditional methods was important not just for its own sake but because there were tried and tested methods of doing things which, if done well, using well thought-out principles, were timeless. Traditional craft skills, with the individual worker's understanding of materials and idiosyncrasies, gave more life to a fabric than machine production did. The expertise and tacit knowledge gained from a time-honoured method added to the pleasure of the artisan's task and dispensed with the need to constantly update production methods. Wardle was at one with William Morris in this respect, who cogently argued the case for the continuation of tradition in the decorative arts:

> So strong is the bond between history and decoration, that in the practice of the latter we cannot, if we would, wholly shake off the influence of past times over what we do at present. I do not think it is too much to say that no man, however original he may be, can sit down to-day and draw the ornament of a cloth, or the form of an ordinary vessel or piece of furniture, that will be other than a development or a degradation of forms used hundreds of years ago.[11]

[90]

Throughout the second half of the nineteenth century, and into the first third of the twentieth century, the production of luxury goods, particularly fashionable clothing, remained comparatively unaffected by mechanisation. Generally there was a considerable demand for handmade goods at this time as the elitist value of the handmade grew. Many of the growing number of department stores offered bespoke products and emphasised the individuality and craftsmanship of their goods. Their product differentiation was in direct contrast to the uniformity and cheaper nature of the mass-produced items, which were increasingly associated with the working classes. Luxurious English silk textiles were also gradually more in demand throughout Europe.

This was concurrent with significant developments in the more specialised sectors of English silk production, particularly the weaving, printing and dyeing branches of the industry, which enabled many leading designers to achieve the results they desired. The meretricious was giving way to more subtle hues and colour combinations partly owing to the Arts and Crafts Movement, partly as a result of research and development in the silk industry. A number of silk manufacturers developed suitable dyestuffs for the preferred softer aesthetic, surmounting the difficulties of production associated with vegetable dyes, and produced deep and muted tones.[12] Others revived ancient block printing and discharge-printing techniques, which complimented the flat, design format and facilitated the designs into production. Although these methods were less commercially viable than mechanised production methods, they enhanced the products and were in demand. The textiles were distinctive, interesting, and therefore, appealing to a particular, discerning consumer group.

Throughout these developments Indian textiles were the touchstone. They were constantly referred to as excellent examples of their type whether they were woven or printed, silk or cotton, embroidery or carpets. Throughout his working life Wardle studied them in order to understand both techniques and principles of design. He specifically admired the Indian use of colour. Natural dyestuffs were ingeniously used and colour combinations never went far wrong. India was the place where the best dyeing had been done for thousands of years; both fugitive and permanent dyes were used as each had its merits. To strengthen his case he frequently took his collection of Indian textiles to his lectures in order that the audience could see these principles for themselves. This was not simply advancing personal preference – the public's taste was changing and the harsh tones of aniline dyes were being replaced. Less gaudy colours were increasingly preferred in all decorative fields and the truer principles of colour combinations were more understood and liked. There can be no doubt this change had been brought about in the general public by painting, for instance, by modern pre-Raphaelite thought and work.[13]

Wardle became a pivotal figure in English silk production as he tackled numerous problems that regularly bedevilled silk manufacturing in Europe and India. His admiration for Indian fabrics had a wide application; they influenced many of his thoughts and activities and provided a continuous source of inspiration. To Wardle, whose judgement in this field was impeccable, they represented a complete range of excellence in silk textile production and he held them in high regard for their technical and aesthetic brilliance. His travels in India reinforced his opinions. Furthermore, Wardle's involvement with India's raw silk production when he visited the sub-continent in 1885–86 and 1903, proved to be of crucial importance to the survival of India's sericulture (see Chapter Four).

Wardle experienced the hard actuality of running a textile company with responsibility for a labour force. He also had a sense of the broader picture, with a good grasp of international events. He was totally in step with the times in which he lived and was only too aware that the survival of his firm depended on the survival of the English silk industry as a whole. The success of his own business was always perceived within the framework of the international silk trade and its uncertainties continually haunted him. He regularly travelled to France, Italy and Germany and knew the economic realities of the global textile market and what it needed to survive. His actions and recommendations were evidence based, reflecting his experiences, and on this basis he stressed the need for long-term strategies. There was no denying his growing concerns; he persistently emphasised the dangers of ignoring the growing threat from Far East silk exports.

He encouraged cooperation between manufacturers believing that this would strengthen the industry as a whole. Experimental work in collaboration with German industrialists helped him to develop 'Sealcloth' and thereby introduce a new silk product to the silk manufacturing tradition. First-hand knowledge of the latest Italian reeling technology allowed him to give a fresh impetus to India's potential as a silk exporting nation. Over the years, Wardle could count a number of French silk manufacturers as his friends and they constantly exchanged information. France may have been a fierce commercial competitor for Britain, but this was less important than a sharing of expertise. As someone driven by humanitarian needs, Wardle recognised the dangerous deprivation that would follow a declining and defensive world silk industry.

Indian silk and Thomas Wardle

The Indian sub-continent was the source of the widest range of silk types. However, its sericulture in all its forms was depressed in the latter half of the nineteenth century.[14] The cultivated silk for commercial use was then mainly produced in the Bengal region. This silk was suitable for all types of silk cloth and yarn production and was transported to silk producing regions throughout India. Bengal silk had, however, gained a poor reputation in Europe due to the irregular nature of the thread (see Chapter Four). The methods of preparing yarn in India had not kept pace with production methods in other countries and Indian silk had fallen behind so much that it had almost no place in the global market; even Indian manufacturers would not buy it and were reduced to importing raw silk.

The wild or semi-domesticated silks such as *eria, muga* and *atlas* were little known in Europe and only used locally in India, mainly for domestic production. *Tasar* was a wild silk, plentiful in the forests of India where it had been known and used for centuries. It was never used commercially in the West, however, for three reasons: the natural colour was an unfashionable deep beige; it had proved resistant to bleaching and dyeing and it was slubbed in texture, a characteristic which in Europe was regarded as an imperfection resulting from poor workmanship.

A number of silk manufacturers, including Thomas Wardle's father, had experimented for about 40 years with dyeing *tasar* silk in Macclesfield. Wardle make continued these efforts to try and discover why *tasar* fibres were so impervious to dyestuffs. His persistence meant that *tasar* silk gained a greatly extended use than was at first imagined. Science provided him with the key as through microscopic examination he discovered that a natural, protective gum coated the silk fibres and prevented dyes from penetrating evenly. Raw *tasar* was also exported from India in a very unclean state, which contributed to its resistance to dyes. Although a French scientist had previously experimented with *tasar* silk along similar lines, it was Wardle who made the crucial breakthrough and learnt to dissolve the protective gum that surrounded the yarn. Once *tasar* was more skilfully reeled and prepared, the fibres were then able to 'bite' the dye and he could make progress. Only shades of grey were available at first, but they were quickly followed by weak tones of primary colours. By 1872 he could dye *tasar* to any subtle shade required, and the years of struggle had paid off. In another major breakthrough Wardle also became the first person to block-print fast colours onto *tasar* cloth. Both developments greatly extended the market for *tasar* yarn in Europe. As a direct result of his involvement the cultivation and marketing of India's *tasar* silk improved. This increased the range of silk thread available in Europe for both weaving and embroidery, changing the course of Indian silk production.[15]

Over a period of seven years, Wardle experimented at Leek with indigenous Indian dyes sent to him for that purpose by the government of India. He worked under the direction of Sir Louis Mallett, the Under Secretary of State for India, who took a great interest in the developments in order that 'a new and very profitable industry may be founded in India'.[16] It was a long and unbroken course of investigation and experimentation, which led to the first work of reference of its type: *The Dyes and Tans of India*, finished in 1882. Also known as the *Blue Book*, it consisted of 3,500 dye samples, produced from 181 varieties of Indian dyestuffs, plus copious notes. The findings were sent back to India in order that Indian dyers could learn to colour *tasar* with their native plants and minerals and thereby increase the value and importance of the yarn. Copies of the results were also sent to the Science and Art Department of the South Kensington Museum.

Thomas Wardle barely recovered his expenses for this major project; nevertheless he continued to add to this research, working voluntarily in order to complete the investigation.[17] He firmly believed that the plentiful natural resources that were readily available in India should be understood and used beneficially, but there were other compelling motives. The increased use of synthetic dyes from Europe, with their crude colours and fugitive tendencies, was a worrying trend in Indian dyeing, one which Wardle and others felt was in danger of ruining traditional dyeing skills.[18] Indigenous dyestuffs, which India had in abundance, had, for thousands of years, been used to great effect. Traditional methods, although very time consuming, gave more permanent results than the mainly fugitive aniline dyes. Examples of old specimens of Indian silks in South Kensington Museum confirmed this. Wardle's experiments on *tasar* silk were promising and opened up greater possibilities for the use of India's natural products within India and throughout the world. The natural dyes, moreover, gave more 'refined and therefore more artistic tones . . . hence they are preferred by those whose tastes and insight are more artistic'.[19]

Largely due to Wardle's efforts, demand in Europe grew for India's little-known *tasar* silk.[20] From 1873 a sample of dyed *tasar* silk had been displayed at South Kensington Museum; but it was the Paris Exhibition of 1878, however, which was the catalyst for the greater European use of Indian silks. Woven and printed *tasar* silk cloth, some block printed in Leek with designs by William Morris, were

[94]

displayed by Wardle along with dyed and undyed yarns and 'Sealcloth'. This was done with the support of Sir Philip Cunliffe Owen of South Kensington Museum. The display was awarded a coveted Gold Medal, which Wardle passed to the Secretary of State for India. Thereafter many samples of the silk were conspicuously displayed in the Indian Section of South Kensington Museum, in order to aid its promotion. Wardle & Co. also produced the printed Indian silks in Liberty's much admired display for the same exhibition.

It was not simply the new dyeing technology that enhanced the properties of *tasar* silk, it was Wardle's experiments with new reeling equipment which also widened its application. Although not a manufacturer of silk yarn he had conducted extensive reeling tests in France and Italy and the result was a finer and more even thread. These improvements also contributed to better and more even colour application. He was justifiably proud of this breakthrough as it was not his area of expertise and he had not expected to find untrodden ground in this unfamiliar domain.

Wardle energetically promoted Indian silk in Paris, as at that time India's *tasar* silk was virtually unknown on the continent. He succeed in attracting the attention of French silk manufacturers during the Paris exhibition, and the French response was positive. Invited to submit a chapter on India's silks to *L'art de la soie*, published in association with the Exhibition, he produced thirty-eight pages, in French. As a result of this high-profile activity, Lyons' silk manufacturers requested their own collection of Indian wild silks for research purposes. Research on behalf of the Lyons Chamber of Commerce, the centre of French silk production, resulted in a valuable resource for France. Wardle compiled a collection of a hundred specimens, including cocoons, moths, dyed silks and other materials from a dozen species of Indian silkworms; he also wrote an accompanying catalogue containing a large amount of scientific data. This work was done at his own expense as he failed to obtain backing from the government of India. He made a gift of it to the Lyons *Chambre de Commerce*. A special showcase was ordered for the Indian silk collection in order that it could be studied. It was displayed for many years in the Bourse and was known as the Wardle Collection. This major contribution to the French silk industry was recognised as very valuable.[21] The President of Lyons *Chambre de Commerce* assured Wardle that the Indian silks would be in great use since he had increased their commercial possibilities. In recognition of his work for the silk industry in 1879 he was awarded France's highest honour, the prestigious *Chevalier de la Legion d'Honneur* and was made an *Officier de l'Academie Français*.[22]

[95]

Undoubtedly the Paris Exhibition focused the attention of French manufacturers on to the increased possibilities of India's silk products. M. David, the largest ribbon manufacturer in St Etienne, saw the improved manufacture and dyeing at the Paris Exposition and offered to buy all the *tasar* cocoons produced in India if he could negotiate the right price. He applied to the Indian government for 2,000 kilograms of cocoons for experimentation at his own cost. Ultimately French silk agents traded directly with India and imported their own supplies so that India benefited enormously. By 1900 Lyons' manufacturers were processing an average of 405,000 lbs of raw *tasar* silk weekly, importing more than British manufacturers.[23] Silk fabric made of *tasar* was very strong, durable and possessed an attractive lustre. It was also between three and four times stronger than cultivated silk. Printed *tasar* silk quickly became very fashionable in France and England and was used for furnishings and fashionable dress. Using his personal contacts, Wardle also persuaded Italian manufacturers to take an interest in Indian *tasar* after the Paris Exposition. One manufacturer in Milan was able to produce fine threads for weaving and reported back to Wardle on his success.

When Indian *tasar* thread was tested as a sewing silk in England it was given a full trial by manufacturers, one of whom described it as 'simply perfection' and a 'serious influence on the China and Canton trade'. One major Macclesfield manufacturer, who tested the silk for weaving, declared it 'a good substitute for Italian silk and cheaper'. Surviving woven *tasar* silk samples from another Macclesfield manufacturer's sample book of 1887–88 reveal that a wide range of woven designs were produced from very small and finely textured weaves to a range of small floral repeat patterns.[24]

As part of his campaign to promote the use of Indian silk, Wardle's experiments in Germany in the 1870s led to the production of Sealcloth. This was made from previously unusable *tasar* silk waste and proved to be a huge boost to the Indian economy.[25] This new cloth utilised the short fibres of waste silk, which, when dyed, were woven into a short-pile plush fabric with a cotton backing, which proved to be a most useful material with a number of advantages. It was porous, washable, hardwearing, soft and glossy. The new fabric received positive reviews in fashion journals. The following was typical: '[Sealcloth] has a very handsome and rich appearance, and recovers any injury from either wet or pressure by being put before the fire and then brushed.'[26] Eventually it was available in a range of colours and figured patterns. It was particularly suitable for women's capes and other outdoor garments and was quickly in demand. *Tasar* silk was particularly suitable for this type of product as it was three times the

[96]

thickness of cultivated silk and produced a lustrous long fibre, which resisted pressure. It was soon adapted for the production of travel rugs, floor rugs, carpets, fringes, pompoms for millinery, tassels and cords for curtains, chenille for upholstery, and silks for embroidery purposes – it was found to have a 'brightening' effect when it was inserted into tailoring cloths. The new product also helped to fill a widening gap in English textile production. As Yorkshire wool manufacturing was in decline Bradford and Huddersfield, textile manufacturers produced the new fabric in great quantities. Lister's Manningham Mill in Bradford, the largest of its type in Europe, was given over to the production of Sealcloth. A new application for the waste yarn in India was found as it was discovered to be eminently suitable for carpet making. Intensive developments of the new product followed, which meant that India's silk producers experienced an enormous and yearly increasing demand for their waste silk, which eventually outstripped supplies of the raw material.

Thomas Wardle's publications

The evidence contained in Wardle's papers demonstrates that he was an articulate spokesman for his industry at home and abroad, whose ideas were convincing as they were based on his experience as a manufacturer. His publicly expressed observations were the result of personal experience as well as admiration for the theories of others. They were the foundation of his business practice and formulated precisely because, and not despite, the fact that he understood the intricacies of international trade. Because he never lost sight of this, his views carried weight. He operated from a broad knowledge base and from first-hand experience was able to compare and contrast silk manufacture in Britain, France, Italy, Germany and India.[27] There is also evidence that he had a working knowledge of French, German and Italian and suggested the study of Hindustani for those who did business with India.[28]

Through his writings and lectures Wardle made an enduring contribution to the design education debate. He was actively concerned to offer his experience to the next generation and was invited to lecture at leading art and design schools and learned societies. When occasion demanded he wrote official papers, contributing to the *Royal Commission on Technical Instruction* in 1884. An analysis of Wardle's papers reveals that a number of themes are continuously present throughout the period 1878–1908.[29] They provide a detailed examination of the English silk industry and demonstrate a deep understanding of the many intricacies of the international silk trade. All of the major themes in his papers can be directly linked in some way to the qualities he admired in Indian textiles. That he held such a wide range of informed views is interesting, and the fact that he was constantly invited to express them publicly was indicative of his status and the widespread application of his theories.

The first of these themes and a major issue throughout Wardle's papers was the precarious state of the English silk industry. It is possible to chart a change in his attitude towards government policies regarding the industry, over the period of time spanned by his lectures. He became increasingly embittered by the Government's refusal to offer assistance.

Wardle's recommendations to improve the British silk industry centred on the need for better art and technical schools and more museums (See Chapters Two and Four). He was a member of the Higher Education Committee and the Society of Arts Examinations in Silk Manufacture. He worked tirelessly to raise awareness of poor design and clearly defined what he felt good design education entailed and the importance this had for industry. Others had done this before, but as a manufacturer and scientist he could reach a different audience and carry a certain weight. Wardle was utterly convinced that the English workforce was just as capable as any in Europe, but lacked the type of technical and artistic training that was available in France and Germany. Wardle often cited the German and French systems with which he was familiar, and that considered design as necessary as weaving and dyeing instruction. At Crefeld's Art School in the silk-weaving area of Germany, the pupils' education was strictly related to the local industry. The syllabus was a combination of art and technical training. Furthermore, the town had a magnificent textile museum.

The essence of good design was one of Wardle's most important themes, and on this subject he was absolutely serious. He argued that design was not an innate gift but could be, and was, taught. The creation and development of form and pattern was at the heart of designing, therefore, training in drawing skills was essential. It was not simply a case of embellishing an object according to the dictates of the latest fashion, a practice of which many manufactures were guilty. His insistence that good design should always relate to the article concerned was continually impressed upon his audience. He increasingly advanced the case that industrial and art training depended on government support and the cultivation of young talent. He argued that suppression of the word 'design' (it was replaced by 'art') had caused it to become of third-rate importance. Design should be the main objective of students, he maintained, who should aim to express thought and culture and not simply imitate. He was adamant that an English industrial style should be expressive of national character and developed to be quite as distinctive as that of the French. Good design was one way to beat off foreign competition.

Clearly Wardle never intended that Indian textiles should simply be copied. New opportunities for development lay in technical schools and technical teaching was to be the bridge between schools of art and industry. Moreover, the success or failure of the textile industry had an immediate effect on many peoples' lives and Wardle always had this in mind as he fought to keep the industry alive. He knew clearly what should be done to end the sorry state of English silk manufacturing and, not unreasonably, was frustrated by the subsequent lack of action.

The promotion of *tasar* silk for the benefit of the English and Indian silk trades was a major preoccupation. Wardle wrote and lectured on the topic at every opportunity and persuaded English consumers to demand products made from Indian silk in preference to continental imports. After overcoming the dyeing problems, he visited leading European manufacturers with samples for them to test. Moreover, his ingenious method of using formerly discarded waste silk, to produce 'Sealcloth', proved to be a huge boost to the Indian economy. Both advancements were extensively discussed in his *Handbook of the Collection Illustrative of the Wild Silks of India* in the Collection of the South Kensington Museum (1881). The collection referred to was one that he had assembled.

A major theme in Wardle's lectures centred on the roles that museums and textile collections had for contemporary production (see Chapters Two and Six):

> A museum is, in my opinion, a most necessary appendage and Corollary to a technical as well as to an art school. It should contain the best examples of all the industrial work of that kind in which the locality is engaged, arranged chronologically, as well as technically described. It ought adequately to show both the outcome of all that has been done in the other localities of the world, which have been or are engaged in similar work.[30]

The train of thought above was prompted by the lack of museums in England's industrial towns. Along with educators and other members of the Arts and Crafts Movement, Wardle argued the value of having well-appointed museums close to centres of technical instruction, rich in their collections of specimens, both ancient and modern and chiefly relating to local trade. He made his own donations of textiles to major museums and his *Handbook of the Collection Illustrative of the Wild Silks of India*, written for South Kensington Museum, became a major work of reference.

In many of his documents, Wardle also considered it necessary to study contemporary products of competing countries as well as historical work. No matter how artistic past products were, they related to a past life either extinct or changed. It was essential therefore, for each industry to see what its competitors were doing there and then, to observe what was of vital importance, at what cost the goods were made and the prices at which they were sold. Such knowledge was felt to be critical to both capital and labour. He was convinced it was this that demonstrated the true nature of competition and prevented erroneous ideas, led to wiser actions and prevented strikes and lock-outs. Although the value of museums and their textile collections was widely acknowledged, museums needed to be accessible locally to all if they were to be effective. Crefeld's museum engendered a sense of pride in the achievements of its local silk industry and was of great benefit to the young workers there. Wardle wrote:

> It would be most desirable to have in Coventry, Macclesfield, Leek, and all the other silk centres permanent museums exhibiting silk yarns and fabrics, plain and decorated, of all periods, but especially contemporary type-specimens of the manufacturers of silk in Europe, Asia and America, showing their qualities and the prices at which they had to compete against both in workmanship and in price.[31]

The study of textiles from other cultures and eras was felt to be vital to the contemporary textile industry. The old natural dyes were far superior, particularly in respect of colourfastness, as the centuries-old samples kept at South Kensington Museum showed. Indian textiles always received a huge coverage in Wardle's lectures and writings. He explored just about every aspect of them with deep respect. Textiles were discussed in the context of everyday life; religion, history and their social role was observed and fully acknowledged. When visiting India in 1885–86, Wardle noted how the various textile techniques were practised. He talked to weavers, printers and dyers in their villages, even penetrating into the jungle to find out more about native practices. This was a formative experience and reinforced his conviction that European designers and makers had much to learn from India about weave and dyes in particular. Wardle's own collection of Indian textiles was rooted in his desire to understand appropriate pattern design. Furthermore, they provided him with models for his business and visual evidence to accompany his lectures.

The reasons for collecting Indian textiles, for his own and the public's benefit, can be summarised as follows. Firstly, it was the fine qualities of manufacture and design, which he felt to be superior. Secondly, India's textile manufacturers valued tradition, and a high standard of continuing craftsmanship was evident in all fields. He had learnt from Indian printers how they often worked with ancestral' designs up to 400 years old. This lack of development in form or colouring was not perceived as a drawback, rather, adherence to a tradition was a positive aspect of designing. Many textile designs carried ancient symbols, the significance of which gave them a valued place in society. His description of the demanding warp and weft dyed *patolu* a traditional 'bride's garment' purchased in Baroda, was the first known in English.[32] *Patolu* weaving was a speciality of the province that included the silk weaving areas of Ahmedabad, Surat and Baroda. Wardle remarked how the geometrical effect of the symbolic pattern is produced by first tying and dyeing the warp and weft yarns and then weaving the fabric (see colour plate 6). He acknowledged it as a 'wonderful example of patience and skill and is as costly as it is beautiful'.

Wardle was convinced that with official help India's silk trade could be restored, for its own benefit and for that of England. Wardle's expertise was sought and acknowledged by Indian officials. His lectures and publications were noted[33] and distributed to staff in England and India, particularly a major paper given to the Royal Society of Arts.[34] When Wardle, always an independent thinker, took the initiative officials monitored his activities, which did not always meet with the bureaucrats' approval. He was seen as a 'confounded nuisance' when he promoted independent action to the Bengal administrators in 1886 (See Chapter Six). British government officials were more guarded, preferring *laissez-faire* policies to prevail and the trade to be governed by competitive market forces.

Undaunted, Wardle voluntarily returned to India in 1903. He abandoned his own business for three months to help restore the Kashmir silk industry, which was experiencing great poverty. Wardle felt that anything that he could do would be worth while. This resulted in the detailed *Kashmir: Its New Silk Industry, With Some Account of its Natural History, Geology, Sport, Etc.*, which was published in 1904. In it he said of Kashmir, 'I feel quite sure from its physical geography and beautiful climate that it is destined to be a great silk-producing country'.[35] Reports of his sericulture operations, sent to the government of India and to the State of Kashmir, are reproduced in the publication and we can see that they 'contain a large amount of technical and practical information which cannot fail to be of service to those other parts of India and the Colonies desiring to establish and conduct Sericulture operations successfully'.[36] These reports were a record of the work he had undergone in, and for, Kashmir during the previous seven years; this work was highly successful and encouraged the reinvigoration of the Kashmir silk industry. The Governor of Kashmir, Pundit Man Mohan Nath Kaul Sahib gave Wardle every reassurance and support he needed. Shortly after he produced his reports and followed these up with the recommended action by instituting improvements – in one region alone there were 50,450 people working in sericulture. Whereas six years previously there was hardly any industry at all, the 80 reelers and turners alone had increased to 3,300.[37]

This new industry based on the reports had saved the Srinagar region from extreme poverty. In *Kashmir: Its New Silk Industry*, he takes the opportunity to make some uncomfortable observations public when he makes it quite clear that there were still repressed people in the region, which is why he then suggested the introduction of silk weaving into the area. The Maharaja, his brother and the Resident all agreed to introduce it. Wardle urged the authorities to keep the Kashmiri silk industry free from private enterprise, to keep it State managed in order that employment could be better provided for a large number of people who were greatly in need of it.[38] The publication also praised the Kashmiri people and their readiness to learn new skills. The profitability of the new industry gave them hope for Kashmir's future, which the author felt would be prosperous. He was proved to be right. In the event the Kashmir silk industry remained healthy for some years after Wardle's death in 1909. It reached a peak in 1915, thereafter was a gradual decline when in 1925, and 1935, the price of cocoons fell by almost half. This was in line with the general decline of the silk industry worldwide.

Conclusion

Although a traditionalist, Thomas Wardle was not against change – in fact he made many changes in his business, in keeping with the spirit of the age. As a practical industrialist his study of ancient techniques went beyond sentimentality. The past was not an ideal in itself – it needed to produce tangible results. Both Wardle and Morris, like other leading designers and manufacturers, studied ancient textiles for technical reasons, searching out their principles and believing that successful design rested on an understanding of a material's inherent qualities and utility. In fact, Wardle's belief in tried and tested methods was generated by a passion for progress. As his publications show he was open to innovation and used scientific reasoning and pragmatism to inform his opinions. It was this combination of approaches that made him a successful manufacturer, and which helped him to venture forth in India, recommending the latest Italian technology and using microscopic examinations to identify disease. He experienced no tension in this, much as he admired India's ancient methods of silk production. As a pragmatist, his path to success was predicated on exacting investigation and a respect for realities; his solutions were rooted in the precarious and practical considerations of employment within an unstable industry.

The history of English silk manufacturers reveals that a number were often visionary, possessed of a political and moral courage in unpropitious times, striving to advance and working towards alternative solutions for the good of the many. Their history demonstrates that, faced with the government's *laissez-faire* policies and global trading difficulties, individuals and small companies managed to exercise long-term change. Undoubtedly, Thomas Wardle gained the respect and admiration of a number of eminent people in England, Europe and India who sought his expertise and acted upon it. Despite these endeavours, however, time was running out for the English silk industry; the growth of India's silk industry was declining by the start of the twentieth century, although it remained viable. Despite the frantic efforts of industrialists to promote inter-imperial trade between the two world wars and to consolidate previous efforts, too many factors were stacked against them. In particular it was due to the increased production of synthetic fibres, coupled with the widespread effect of the expansion of the cheaper Japanese silk yarn production.

There were innumerable historical connections between England and India through the textile trades, which were open to creative enterprise and initiative. The dynamic networks of commerce interconnected both countries over centuries and mutual understandings were commonplace as there were many conjoint factors. However, where textile design was concerned, designers and manufacturers in England frequently and unambiguously acknowledged the long-standing superiority of India's textile tradition which, although built on the tradition of a unique culture, was informed by what many theorists in nineteenth-century Britain regarded as universal design principles.

Notes

1 *Journal of Indian Art & Industry*, Vol. 13 (1910), p. 3.
2 He had a German chemistry tutor and studied under the French chemist, Chevreul, who examined and improved dyes for the Gobelin tapestry works. He became a Fellow of the Geological Society in 1863, and elected a Fellow of the Chemical Society in 1875.

3   Thomas Wardle was knighted in 1897 for his work for the Indian silk industry.
4   Logwood from a South American tree *Haematoxylon campechianum*, gave a very good black.
5   The photograph shows hand dyeing c.1905, at William Tatton's dye works, Upper Hulme, Staffs.
6   Company records show that at one time he employed a team of six men to work on corah silks alone, for Liberty.
7   This piece, with a number of other textiles, was presented by Sir Thomas Wardle to South Kensington Museum in 1908.
8   The Aesthetic Gallery by Mr Goodyear, c.1890.
9   Prussian blue was the accidental invention of a German alchemist and colour maker. It was an immediate success and was widely used in the early eighteenth century. In 1749 a French academician discovered how to dye silk with it. Lowengard, in Berg and Clifford (eds), 1999, p. 108.
10 Wardle, Staffordshire, 6 January 1891.
11 Morris, *The Lesser Arts*, lecture given to The Trade Guild of Learning, London, 1877.
12 Alastair Morton endlessly experimented with commercial dyes, producing excellent results. Benjamin Warner also developed printing technology.
13 Wardle, *Handbook Illustrative of the Wild Silks of India*, South Kensington Museum, London, 1881, p. 41.
14 Wardle, *The Indian Silk Culture Court*, 1886, p. 4. The quantity of Bengal silk production exported to Europe in 1870 was 2.5 million lbs. This had fallen to 457,600 lbs in 1885.
15 Yusuf Ali, Allahabad, 1900, p. 17.
16 Wardle, 1881, p. 11.
17 After lengthy negotiations it was finally printed in 1885 and copies were sent out to India. It was some time before Wardle received official acknowledgement for this important work.
18 *The Lady's World*, 1887, p. 350.
19 Wardle, 1881, p. 41.
20 'The Silk Industries of India', *The Journal of Indian Art & Industry*: Textiles, 1907, p. 13.
21 The Archive, Chambre de Commerce et d'Industrie de Lyon, France.
22 Ibid.
23 'The Silk Industries of India', *The Journal of Indian Art & Industry*, 1909 (obituary for T. Wardle).
24 The manufacturer was Brocklehurst of Macclesfield, a leading silk company.
25 It was also known as plush, sealskin, sealette, etc. It became a fashionable fabric and commercially highly successful. The demand for waste *tasar* silk was so great that good silk threads were cut up to provide the short yarns for sealcloth.
26 *The Lady's World*, 1887, p. 350.
27 Wardle also displayed a learned interest in geology, railways, sewage, rare books, music, botany, art and classical history.
28 Wardle, 1905, p. 3.
29 More than fifty-two papers were produced. The themes can be summarised as follows: the international silk trade; design theory; the value of museums and exhibitions; craftsmanship and tradition and government intervention v laissez-faire policies.
30 Wardle, *A Report on the British Silk Industry* at the request of the Royal Commission on Technical Instruction, 1885.
31 Wardle, *The Relationship of Design to Such Craft Teaching as May Be Undertaken by Technical Schools*. Address to the Art Worker's Guild, London, February 1883, with illustrations.
32 The description first appeared in the Catalogue for the Royal Jubilee Exhibition, Manchester. The fabric described is now in the textile collections of the Whitworth Art Gallery.

33 Minute Paper on the subject of Tussur Silk, India Office Library Register No. RS and C 950/9. 'The lecture is an interesting one. It will be observed that on p. 618 Mr Wardle makes an appeal to pursue a certain line of policy. But I do not think that the Secretary of State, if he forwards the lecture, need be regarded as committing himself on the subject.' AG, 18 June 1891.
34 L/E7/247 (950) India Office Library: 'opportunity is taken to send to India copies of the lecture for such publication as the Government there might deem fit. On previous occasions the good service done by Mr Wardle to the cause of the silk industries in India have been brought to the notice of the Secretary of State.'
35 Wardle, 1904, p. 12.
36 Ibid., 1904.
37 Ibid., p. 277.
38 Ibid., p. 280.

CHAPTER SIX

Exhibiting India

The importance of international trade exhibitions in England, and overseas, during the late nineteenth and early twentieth centuries cannot be over-emphasised. Enormous energy was required to organize, manage and coordinate these huge events both in the host cities and abroad, where the exhibits for the displays were sourced. Corresponding activities, such as the production of detailed official catalogues and reports, were the result of deep pools of shared knowledge and were equally challenging. The challenges were met because the events were vital to all concerned. Although apparently transient and seemingly entertaining, serious long-term effects were the main objective.

Because international exhibitions were a valuable, and probably necessary extension of an integrated, global system of trading activity between nations, they embraced many needs and interests. They were not planned and executed in isolation and cannot be fully understood as separate events, sealed off from wider social, economic or political considerations; they were firmly connected to many different contexts and agendas. They were simultaneously local, regional, national, international and inter-colonial; knowingly constructed to promote the material culture and products of numerous communities. Before the objects in question became exhibits they were firstly products of a commercial system, which responded to the needs of the market; a great deal of exhibition planning revolved around the same requirements.

Exhibitions contrived to bring about a dynamic response in the public, with the practical result of improved trade. By highlighting aspects of supply-side economics they sought to increase demand-side responses for products and materials. To be fully effective they needed to be consensual not coercive events. The mutually beneficial aspect of these occasions, which actively included and encouraged a significant and continuous interchange of detailed information between members of participating cultures and between exhibitors and visitors, was an extensive and effective aspect throughout. Businessmen in the East and the West cooperated with each other, connecting large groups of workers in both cultures.

Displays

One role of the exhibition display was to make visible those activities that were usually invisible, thereby making tangible connections between one commercial activity and another. Manufacturers and those in commerce were seen as inextricably linked to others in the empire with similar interests. The displays also allowed participating producers and visiting consumers to compare the goods and relative economic strengths of a range of participating countries, often for the first time. In such a vast sub-continent as India it would have been almost impossible for its own citizens to be familiar with all the different types of Indian silk available, let alone visitors from other countries. These displays celebrated nations and empire; they also revealed and created tensions. They allowed producers and consumers to compare merchandise and the financial strength of the countries of the empire without the presence of unwelcome competition. But in the case of Indian silk textiles there were no competitors within the empire. However, it was necessary to reintroduce and promote items through exhibitions, so that the new and improved economic products and raw materials, such as an extended range of India's wild silks, became more widely known internationally. In the process, India's superior technical skills in weaving, dyeing and embroidery were also promoted. The demanding techniques that produced cloth and embroideries using India's silk yarns were viewed by the exhibition visitors who could clearly see what was technically possible in the finished products. This helped to overturn an entrenched negative view of Bengal silk yarn that had prevailed.

Experts

Ever since the Great Exhibition of 1851, objects on display in exhibitions had been classified; this system prevailed because it had an obvious logic. Each group or class of objects, for example, silk products, had a jury that awarded honours and produced detailed reports. Participation on a jury and the judging of exhibits required an enormous amount of time and was only undertaken by those with specialist knowledge. Jurors for the different classes of exhibits prepared countless valuable reports, which resulted from meetings between groups of experts who held analytical symposiums: important, behind-the-scenes activities of international exhibitions. International teams of experts in the different fields conducted lengthy tests on products and raw materials and discussed their problems and possibilities over long periods. The reports demonstrate the versatility of businessmen's expertise. It was not uncommon to find competing businessmen on the same team, confirming a sense of even-handedness that overrode individual business interests. These works of reference were often lengthy and detailed documents, which provided technical data relating to new technologies, materials, improved agricultural methods, etc. They were openly educative, produced with a view to increasing trade in particular goods both within the empire and beyond.

The Paris Universal Exposition of 1878

Experts were invited to sit on exhibition juries; in the process they might forge links between usually disparate sectors such as lepidoptery and textiles. This was the case in 1878 when the organisers of the Paris Universal Exposition invited Thomas Wardle to contribute his detailed knowledge of a wide range of India's silks. He became a member of the prestigious Silk Industries Jury and produced a revelatory appendix for the official exhibition catalogue; it was 38 pages long and a version in French was supplied. Appendix 'C' described and analysed the improved Indian silk yarns and Indian dye techniques in great detail for the first time. This became an influential work of reference that earned the respect of rival French silk manufacturers. The global silk industry always faced keen competition, yet there was a mutual interchange of knowledge during exhibitions, as European silk manufacturers came together on juries and produced publications to help fight off increasing competition from China and Japan.

Wardle's Monographs on the *Wild Silks and Dye Stuffs of India, Descriptive of the Objects and Specimens Exhibited in the India Section of Paris Exhibition,* and on *Dyestuffs and Tannin Matters of India and their Native Uses, Descriptive of the Collection in the India Section of the Paris Exhibition,* was a part of the eight-volume *Handbook to the British India Section,* produced for the Paris event. The appendix formed the basis for his publication, the *Handbook of the Collection Illustrative of The Wild Silks of India,* which acted as an illustrated catalogue for the museum. These authoritative works, with illustrations, and details of microscopic measurements, were planned to aid silk manufacturing by informing industrialists of the physical qualities of Indian silks and dyestuffs. They were a permanent legacy of the 1878 event, along with the collection of raw materials,

Indian silks and Sealcloth which South Kensington Museum acquired. They are still quoted documents, with an impact today.

The monographs, with their huge amounts of data relating to sericulture, accompanied the exhibition displays of the many types of Indian silk moths; many of the types were previously unknown to commerce. Silk cocoons, undyed samples of *tasar* silk in its natural golden colour, skeins of *tasar* silk dyed with natural dyes in a range of fifteen rich jewel colours by Wardle & Co., and *tasar* silk dyed with aniline dyes by Thomas Wardle, were all on public view for the first time at the Paris Exposition. They demonstrate that with the right treatment both delicate and deep shades could be obtained using natural and synthetic dyes. There were rival merits and demerits of aniline, napthalymine, and other kindred derivatives dyes, and those of an older and more permanent nature. Although dyes from aniline were used in the Paris displays to indicate the variety of shades possible, their increased use was much lamented by Wardle in his monographs. Although they were cheaper and much easier to use they were mainly fugitive, particularly when exposed to light; in his opinion native Indian dyestuffs, properly mordanted, generally gave more permanent colours. It was also stated that the dyes obtained from natural substances gave more 'refined' and 'artistic' tones and were preferred by those with a more artistic insight who rejected the meretricious and gaudy shades produced by chemical dyes. Analine and analogous dyes had, however, recently improved and less garish effects had proved possible.

In historical practice there had always been both kinds of dyeing, i.e. permanent and fugitive, and both were acknowledged as having their merits. In India, where the best dyeing had been done for thousands of years, fugitive dyes had also been used but to a limited extent. In the event the company's exhibition display clearly highlighted that whatever dyeing method was preferred, any colour and any shade could be obtained using the improved *tasar* silk from India.

The examples of hand-block printed Indian *tasar* silk cloth on display in Paris revealed another breakthrough, which added a further dimension to the use of the silk. They publicised the first successful attempt, either in Europe or the East, to print on wild silk cloth of any kind: all the printed colours were fast dyes. There had been many fruitless attempts to enrich the *tasar* silk cloths before a good range of colours could successfully be applied to the surface using wood blocks. Thinking that Indian designs were the most suitable for a cloth of this type of wild silk, Wardle obtained a series of Indian wood-printing blocks from Dr Forbes Watson of the India Museum. The blocks were of hardwood and skilfully cut and they were only used to print Indian

THOMAS WARDLE

colours. Those patterns in the display that were printed in blue were particularly important as they were the first successful application of indigo dye on silk as a wood block-print and not applied as a 'Pencil Blue'.[1] Indigo dyeing was particularly challenging, as it demanded tight control over numerous variables. The main problem was that it oxidized before it could be applied to the cloth; resist and discharge printing methods were commonly used to overcome the difficulties.

The Paris Exposition displays visibly demonstrated that Indian *tasar* silk could be used for sewing and embroidery thread, the weaving and dyeing of wall coverings, curtains, upholstery and clothing. As *tasar* was a particularly strong and durable yarn with a good lustre it was eminently suitable for broad silk manufacture. *Tasar* yarn could now be put to greatly extended use for a variety of purposes. *Muga* and *Eria* were less abundant varieties of Indian wild silks that were also displayed in the Paris exhibition. They had fibres that were fine and long and the waste silk was also seen to have great potential. Wardle had successfully dyed them in beautiful shades. Indian dyestuffs were also promoted at the exhibition and specimens of different native dyestuffs were displayed alongside the yarns and fabrics in order to extend their use in Europe. The monograph for this display used an Indian lexicon and described in detail how the dyes were used in an Indian context.

The success of his company at the Paris Exposition was the culmination of personal achievement for Thomas Wardle. He also fulfilled another personal objective by giving great impetus to the trade in Indian *tasar* silk, taking it beyond the confines of colonial interest. Official approval, in the form of awards from rival French silk manufacturers, gave independent value to the product, clearly confirming that Indian silks benefited from exposure in an international arena. Moreover, as a consequence of his work for the Silk Industries Jury in Paris, Wardle's level of authority with the French was raised. Increased respect for his opinion in France meant that Indian silk producers benefited from improved trade owing to his recommendations and experiments. French silk manufacturers reacted positively to the displays and lobbying; after the exposition they went on to trade directly with India and French imports of Indian silks rose dramatically. The French formally acknowledged Wardle's work on Indian silks by awarding him their highest honours. The collection of Indian silks deposited in Lyons Chamber of Commerce, the heart of French silk production, would never have happened had Wardle not exhibited in Paris, contributed to the catalogue, acted as a jury member and gained long-lasting respect from French manufacturers. The dynamics of the international silk trade now connected India, France and Britain.

Although his status was raised, it was not the case that the Exposition brought about any fundamental changes in Thomas Wardle. His ideas were already well developed and he had tested their viability through science. His mind was focused, his own successful industrial practice was based on sound principles and he thought globally; but he needed to make others aware of new possibilities.

The striking displays of Indian goods in the British India section at the Paris Universal Exposition of 1878 were the combined efforts of many people. The active contributions of the Indian manufacturers and rulers were essential; without their involvement the Indian government would not have been able to organise the magnificent displays. The Governor of Bombay, the India Office Reporter, Lord Lytton (Viceroy and Governor General in India), members of the Indian civil service, Sir Philip Cunliffe Owen and officers from South Kensington Museum, along with a number of Indian princes, were all active in selecting India's finest products.

During the planning stages of the Paris event demand grew for increased space for the Indian exhibits. It was towards the end of 1877, as objects from India began to arrive in Paris, that the Maharaja of Kashmir offered to contribute to the exhibits. Other members of the Indian nobility swiftly added to his offer and the Indian collections assumed a scale larger than first anticipated. The Prince of Wales appealed to the French authorities for a position no less important than the western half of the grand transept or vestibule for India's displays; this was granted and the Indian section obtained the position of honour among the foreign departments.

From 1876 lavish, palace-like structures were appearing on exhibition sites and exhibiting India became an increasingly elaborate exercise. The 1878 Paris Exposition included the architect Caspar Purdon Clark's design for an Indian court; this was a series of pavilions connected by an arcade and gallery (see figure 8). *The Times* considered the Indian contribution to be the most comprehensive and best-organised display of India's arts, manufactures and natural products ever seen – better even than 1851. Exhibition judges awarded this section many honours: a Diploma of Honour, 11 gold, 15 silver and 21 bronze medals, along with 10 honourable mentions.[2] The Prince of Wales's gifts from India were some of the most popular items in the Indian Court. In 1875 the Prince had made a royal tour of India where Indian nobility had given him a range of elaborate gifts, including many costly textiles. An exhibition of these had been held at South Kensington Museum in 1875 and had drawn large crowds. It was so splendid and opulent a display that the Prince remarked on the need for a great imperial museum of the industries of all India and the colonies.

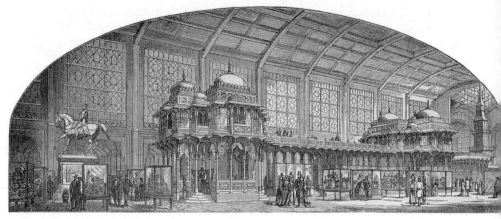

8 The Indian Court, International Exposition, Paris, 1878.

Dr C.M.G. Birdwood, a medical doctor, who went on to found the Victoria and Albert Museum in Bombay, wrote the handbook to the British India Section. He was publicly acknowledged for his 'independent and courageous criticism' of the government of India, for neglecting the traditional crafts.[3] Edward Burne Jones, John Millais and William Morris were some of the eminent artists who supported Birdwood's stance against the increasing industrialised production of goods in India. Birdwood was a great promoter of Indian crafts and viewed them as more than examples of well-made items; he took a wider perspective and always discussed them in the context of the society that produced them. His essay on the *Master Handcrafts of India*[4] was a paean to Indian artisan skills, which were still to be found in every village, but which he felt were in great danger of being lost. He contrasted an idealised version of Indian rural life with a critical judgement of Western industrialisation. Birdwood considered that there was a huge threat to this traditional way of life in India in the form of machinery for mass production. He was, however, at pains to point out that not all machinery should be banned from India, and that it was important to understand what tasks would benefit from mechanisation and what must still be done by hand. Economic forces needed to be balanced against the loss of skills and aesthetic principles, which had been learned through centuries of practice. The *Handbook to the British India Section* also included a lengthy section on the ancient history of Indian commerce and a very detailed section on India's textile history.

English manufacturers and retailers also took advantage of the prestigious Paris event to exhibit their goods to a huge international audience. Those in commerce were well aware that major exhibitions had become an essential aspect of trade and creative activity; international trade had always aided the two-way spread of ideas as well as the flow of goods. Awards were given to the official exhibitors of commercial goods and Wardle & Co. was awarded a gold medal for its display. The gold medal was donated to the Indian government; Wardle believed it was rightly theirs as the raw materials were sourced from the sub-continent. Liberty & Co. displayed a range of *tasar* silks dyed and printed by Wardle & Co., which also received wide acclaim. The silks were hand-block printed in Leek, using Indian designs or faithful imitations of these, in a range of beautiful 'art' colours. The display was purchased by the South Kensington Museum, as part of their dual role to promote trade and good design.

Throughout the duration of the Paris Exposition, Wardle was proactive and determined in his promotion of India's silk yarns. Acting on behalf of the English and Indian silk industries he targeted French manufacturers in particular, believing that they could make great use of India's raw silks; there was a lot at stake as he attempted to offset the strong competition, particularly from the Far East. Although France had its own sericulture industry it had been dealt a massive blow in the 1860s when disease decimated their stocks of silkworms. Since then French silk producers had turned their attention to their supply chain and the sourcing of alternative supplies of raw material. They also wished to avoid an over-dependency on Chinese and Japanese supplies, which were rapidly increasing. Improved materials from India also increased their options. French manufacturers were clearly impressed with the improved quality of India's raw silks; their newly revealed dyeing potential of *tasar* silk opened up wider uses for the French silk industry. In order to learn more of these Indian products manufacturers in Lyons demanded to have a range of Indian silks available locally for close study.

Examples of the new product, Sealcloth, which Wardle had developed using waste *tasar* silk, were also displayed at the Paris Exposition. The pile of the new cloth was made to lie like natural sealskin, but as it was waterproof and washable it had greater advantages. The yarn was three times the thickness of cultivated silk and very hard-wearing, which made it suitable for outdoor clothing such as capes. The exhibition displays demonstrated clearly how Indian *tasar* silk waste could be spun and used in the production of clothing, rugs, carpets, passementerie and upholstery. French manufacturers were equally interested in this aspect of the yarn and before too long were importing vast quantities of waste *tasar* directly from India to the extent that demand outstripped supply. In the event, longer *tasar* threads were cut into short lengths to supply this new branch of the European silk industry. Soon the French were also printing on *tasar* cloth and Parisian fashion houses were using *tasar* silk to make fashionable clothing in both its plush form and natural undyed cloth.[5]

Thomas Wardle used all his lobbying skills and mass of contacts to encourage a French market for the greater security of India's silk producers. As a result direct trading links were formed, which brought Indian producers associated economic freedom. Thus economic displays of silk in South Kensington and in international exhibitions had worked in the way envisaged. Although the French were commercial rivals for English silk manufacturers, India had a long-standing history of trading with other countries, and this was meant to continue. Indeed, exports of Indian textiles were extending to America, and there was no attempt on the part of imperial officials to curtail this.

After the Paris Exposition, the case for establishing a Colonial and Indian Museum continued to be debated, although any support from public funds was conspicuously lacking; by this time both Paris and Vienna had impressive Oriental museums. The Indian government, wishing to unburden itself from the costs of managing the Indian collections, formerly in the ownership of the East India Museum, reviewed a range of options but in the event dispersed them. The bulk of the textile collection was transferred to the South Kensington Museum in 1879. It continued to be housed separately and was known as the India Museum until after the Second World War, when its collections were absorbed into the Victoria and Albert Museum.

The Colonial and Indian Exhibition 1886

Ever since the Great Exhibition of 1851, India was celebrated at international exhibitions. Organisers of these shows were constantly pressurised to allocate more and more space to the sub-continent in succeeding events, and its goods were, thereafter, given the most prominent exhibition spaces to ensure maximum exposure. Members of a Royal Commission were appointed to organise and carry out the Colonial and India Exhibition, to be held in London, the capital of the British Empire, in 1886; the president was the Prince of Wales. The cooperation of the Indian government was sought and obtained as the impetus to trade was welcomed. The Royal Commission had the benefit of the services of Sir Philip Cunliffe-Owen, Director of South Kensington Museum, who acted as Secretary and dealt with all administrative arrangements, with Mr J.F. Royle as his assistant. As for previous events, the organisers also included private individuals and influential industrialists including Thomas Wardle, leading officials in the Deptartment of Revenue and Agriculture, Technical and Art School bureaucrats, and local government officers and Princes in India.

There was a long pre-history to this event. The government of India had reviewed various indigenous products to determine which would be the most likely to reward any investment to promote India's development. Of all the products of India it was thought that silk held the most potential, but of all India's industries it was silk that needed the greatest investigation and support. The Commissioners were anxious that the Exhibition should be used to bring the attention of Indian silk production before an international public. It was by mutual wish of the Commissioners and the government of India that Thomas Wardle had charge of the Indian Silk Court and this was proposed to the Bengal Silk Committee. The Bengal government readily agreed to the proposal and offered a collection of silks and their assistance to Wardle in his task. For these reasons a more substantial portion of the exhibition space was allotted to a complete collection of silks than to any other class of goods. The Royal Commission allocated the larger portion of the South Galleries of the exhibition site for the use of the Empire of India; exhibits covered 103,000 sq ft. The Secretary of State for India, who claimed to have the exhibition very much at heart, stated:

> There is perhaps, nothing more desirable for India than that its products and industries should be well known in this country, although we have much more to learn from them than to teach them. Their beautiful manufactures, which they have produced for so many ages, have proved that there is a knowledge of many branches of art, which it would be a thousand pities should be diminished under our rule. I have often been struck with the calamity of the introduction of our taste into eastern arts and manufactures, for their taste is far better than ours. Although we have no doubt engineering knowledge and skill and the command of capital; and I cannot conceive of any advantage greater than that the two countries should be brought together.
>
> The Government of India will undertake the collection and management to a great extent of what is sent to this country. You will see from the immense size of our Indian Empire and the position of the Government there that it is much better this should be taken in hand by the Government.[6]

Funding for major international exhibitions usually came from the Indian government, the British government and private sources. On this occasion the Indian Section of the 1886 Exhibition received all its financial support from government sources. From a total of £128,000, the government of India promised £20,000, the state of Bengal contributed the sum of £6,850 and donated many luxurious textiles in order that the Bengal silk industry would benefit from the European exposure in London. In addition, Bengali rulers and manufacturers actively sought expertise from England in order to overcome serious problems relating to silk production.

A number of Indian princes and other South Asian dignitaries usually participated in international exhibitions; they ensured that their local materials and manufactures were properly represented at home and abroad. The Indian sections were often indebted to their contributions of many of their most eye-catching exhibits. Those native princes and nobles who contributed to the Colonial and Indian Exhibition were: His Highness the Maharaja of Jaipur; His Highness the Maharaja of Jodhpur GCSI; Maharao Raja of Ulwar GCSI; His Highness the Maharaja of Kotah; His Highness the Maharaja of Bikanir; His Highness the Maharaja of Dholpur; His Highness the Maharaja of Bhartpur GCSI; His Highness the Maharaja of Meywar; His Highness the Maharaja of Jhallawar; His Highness the Nawab of Tonk; His Highness the Maharaja of Karauli; His Highness the Nizam of Hyderabad; His Highness the Gaekwar of Baroda; and from Kashmir: His Highness the Maharaja of Kashmir.

When Thomas Wardle was put in control of stocking India's Silk Court he was charged with collecting and displaying a representative collection of India's silk products then in production; this was a vital role that involved travelling to India to select the best silk products. The starting point for the collection of Indian silks was concern over the decline of India's silk industry; the selection of silks was, therefore, governed by an overarching concern to rescue a declining silk trade. Wardle was aware that, owing to the unpredictable nature of the yarn, Bengali silk production had gradually fallen out of favour in Europe, to the extent that there was hardly any international market left. India itself was importing more silk than it exported; clearly this serious state needed to change.[7] Indian silk producers had acknowledged the situation and requested help with the severe difficulties they were experiencing. While he was in India, Wardle was, therefore, expected to use his specialised knowledge to overcome pressing problems relating to disease and production. He had the ability to gauge the significance of the silk trade within India, where there was a huge demand for silk for weaving, embroidery and a range of other minor purposes. Bengal had the potential to supply all these domestic needs and service the export trade if its production problems were overcome. His intention was to reinstate Bengal silk to its former position. To do this it was necessary to consider the regional culture relating to silk production, including the local economy and education of artisans.

It was no coincidence that the collector of silks for the Silk Court was an industrialist and not an administrator. Wardle was able to supply a specialist expertise as a chemist and, moreover, he could advise on broader commercial matters arising from his experience as a manufacturer. He was also a man with vision who had invented new uses for a former waste product and predicted new markets for wild silks. He was convinced that collective action was needed, and he was only too aware that the international silk industry had its own agenda – albeit one which, if managed well, could operate with mutual benefits to India and England.

Although he was based in a small Staffordshire town, Wardle was a modern, cosmopolitan entrepreneur, who spent a great deal of time in London for commercial purposes, including the running of his own retail business; he also had membership of a number of London's learned societies. He had, moreover, been closely involved with other international exhibitions. He was international in his approach to business and regularly travelled to France, making lifelong friends with French silk manufacturers; he conducted research into aspects of the silk industry in Germany and Italy and knew manufacturers in both countries. Wardle was certainly someone with an acute sense of England's greatness but this was tempered by the knowledge that other nations also had their strengths. His judgements were, therefore, formed by his close proximity to events in other countries. Through an observant responsiveness which placed human agency at the centre of things, he could contrast developments relating, for instance, to industry, design education, technical education, in Europe with those in England, yet keep a critical distance from them. He had no illusions about himself or anybody else, his opinions were based on a pragmatic, first-hand experience of an international silk trade. Therefore, he knew what could be done in England with determination and hard work, and this was one of the most recurrent themes in his publications.

When Wardle played a prominent role on exhibition committees in Paris, he was called upon to use scientific skills to find answers to questions relating to India's industries. A further major undertaking was the writing of the official and descriptive catalogues of the Indian Silk Court. It was his commercial activities that fitted him for these roles; they were an extension of his working practice. In his capacity as silk dyer and promoter of good design principles, Wardle combined aspects of science and art along with the organisational skills necessary to run a successful company. But the tasks were also undertaken because he saw it as his duty as a citizen of the empire to use his expertise to help others.

His long-term contact with Indian officials, over many years of painstaking labour developing the use of Indian dyestuffs, meant that Wardle was well used to communicating with Indian officials. His experiments had promoted India's natural dye products in the face of increasing use of chemical dyes in India and Europe. As he was interested in India as a culture in its own right, he wished, therefore, to preserve what he knew was in danger of disappearing. His solutions were grounded in the practical requirements of a dyeing and printing company, including concern for the workforce and their families. His application of scientific knowledge was meant to benefit traditional forms of production, not remove them. Wardle did not reject industrial advances, nor was he a romantic who wished to hold on to ancient ways for their own sake. He somehow managed to be a thoughtful visionary as well as a pragmatist, using scientific knowledge to hold on to what worked best for a particular market. Nevertheless, he also queried some of the established underlying economic and traditional conditions.

Official bodies such as the Science and Art Department in England and the Revenue and Agriculture Department in India were established to oversee and bring together different sectors with a common aim. Involvement with exhibitions was part of their remit, along with the founding of public organizations and other important cultural events. For the purposes of the Colonial and India Exhibition, Wardle worked under the direction of Sir Edward C. Buck, who had scientific expertise and a strong interest in Indian silk production. Buck was the Executive Commissioner who coordinated activities for India at the Colonial and India Exhibition. He was a prominent Secretary for the Science and Art Department, and Secretary to the Government of India Revenue and Agriculture Department.

In his Preface to the catalogue for the Indian Silk Court, Buck outlined the complex scheme that was necessary for organising the collections of exhibits. At the same time he clearly demonstrated his knowledge of sericulture and the thinking behind the exhibition policy, a departure from previous events. He acknowledged 'the manner in which Thomas Wardle has devoted his time and labour and his funds towards promoting the cause of the revival of the silk industry in India'.[8] Earlier studies of silk were also included in the publication. While he was in London, for the duration of the exhibition, Buck organised related exhibits and lectures on sericulture and silk weaving in order to strengthen the promotion of Indian silk production and trade.

Wardle recorded that it was Buck who, with a Mr H.Z. Darrah Officiating Director of the Department of Agriculture, Assam, had discovered, whilst on a tour of inspection and search in the bazaars of Calcutta, that the embroidered turbans made in Dacca were worked in *muga* (*Antheroea Assama*) silk. This particular silk had engaged Thomas Wardle's attention for a number of years. Buck discovered that *muga* silk was used as embroidery thread in its undyed state, stitched onto a base cloth of *muga* silk mixed with cotton. This costly product was produced for a small niche market. It was in demand in Calcutta but also exported into Arabia and other parts of western Asia, but was kept in the hands of a very few merchants. Prior to Buck's discovery, the embroideries were thought to have been worked in *tasar* silk, as they closely resembled the fawn-like colour of that yarn. While he was in India, Wardle collected three *muga* silk embroidered turbans, each with a different design. Each was densely covered with subtle, self-coloured silk embroidery, worked in a very fine chain stitch along its entire length, approximately 9 feet by 3 feet. The general effect of the stitching was to produce a subtlely-textured surface with a soft sheen and patches of light and shade. The turbans were displayed in the Assam section of the silk courts at the Exhibition.

Collecting in India

Thomas Wardle spent a month in India visiting the major centres of silk production. His remit was to collect a range of silk goods that exemplified India's silk production at that time. He left England in December 1885 and returned in January 1886. En route to India he visited Italy to purchase a 'Tavelette Consono', the latest development in Italian silk reeling technology, hoping that this would resolve some of the problems he knew he would encounter.

Using his pass for the Indian railways, he travelled extensively in those regions noted for their excellence in silk production; even journeying for days into the jungle to track down a variety of wild silk. Throughout the duration of his stay he received encouragement and assistance from local people; they translated for him in order that he could understand the regional terminology and the social significance of designs. He developed a great knowledge of traditional pattern derivation and was able to investigate the regional skills of weaving, dyeing and embroidery, staying with villagers in order to better understand their way of life and observing techniques that had been practised since antiquity. He took many notes, gave advice, undertook experiments, assessed problems and made many contacts, appreciating all the differences to his usual existence; it was a galvanising experience. After observing silk weavers he stated: 'Although they have to weave with threads often much varying in regularity and thickness, yet they have down to to-day managed somehow or other, if they have had a pattern to weave, to put, so to speak, soul into it, and to raise it above the commonplace fabrics so often produced in modern Europe.'[9]

India had an extraordinary impact on Thomas Wardle; he thrived in the Indian climate and the signs of ill-health that had emerged in England, disappeared. It was clearly a fruitful and fulfilling stage in his life, which consolidated his admiration for India's textiles. His notes are full of incidental details which show his interest in other people and their different ways of life. Where possible, he discussed production methods and designs with artisans, clearly enjoying the experience. He witnessed the production of printed silks 'being printed on the squat tables of the Calcutta printers, with indescribable interest, who use their prettily sculptured little blocks with a dexterity and exactness marvellous to see, requiring no pin points to guide them in their repeats of patterns'.[10] Wardle, who particularly admired the use of colour in Indian textiles, expressed concern, however, at some recent changes he witnessed:

> For ages, and so long as they continued to use the natural colours which they obtained from their own beautiful dye-stuffs, coupled with an ingenious and traditional taste, they never could go very far wrong in colour. It is now impossible to observe without great regret in passing through India how the love of the modern brilliant European dyes has affected, to a serious degree, the products of the native Indian loom of today.[11]

His official task was to collect samples of wild and domesticated silk products; from silkworm eggs and cocoons to a range of finished silk cloth. He was also asked to rectify problems in silk production; particularly the important, long-established, but depressed silk industry of Bengal. He added a third reason, 'To stimulate and give encouragement to an extended production of *tusser* silk'.[12] He was successful on all counts.

The Department of Revenue and Agriculture employed knowledgeable Indian people within India to collect, analyse, organise and publicise those material displays, which were part of scientific and commercial projects. This included the sending of materials to Europe for exhibition and those materials permanently housed in the series of public museums in India. Local assistants were important links in the creation and diffusion of imperial cultural policy and the construction of knowledge about India at home and abroad. Silks were collected with the full cooperation of local people, as it was to

[120]

their collective advantage to have their wares on display in prestigious events. This was acknowledged as the best of way of gaining the
interest of an international audience. Wardle worked in collaboration
with Indian workers in order to learn from them, as well as to pass
on the knowledge he had gained across Europe. He needed to observe
methods of production in order to understand where the problems
lay. The local producers provided product information using local
knowledge of construction, location and often terminology: textile
terms could vary from village to village. The descriptive catalogues
for the Colonial and India Exhibition and the Royal Manchester
Jubilee Exhibition of 1887 used the local Indian terms for textiles
where they were known.

The completed collection of silks was composed of the cultivated,
semi-cultivated and wild-silk types that India produced. The silks
also demonstrated the finest textile skills in weaving, dyeing and
embroidery. All of the items were made for the domestic market
and many were in the form of complete garments. Wardle considered
the collection to be typical in both design and colouring and to give
an accurate account of all kinds of silk fabrics of which silk formed
the whole or a part.

Towards the end of his visit to India in January 1886, Thomas
Wardle addressed the Calcutta Silk Conference held in his honour.
The purpose of the conference was to discuss questions related to
India's silk production and the measures taken to equip the Indian
Silk Court at the forthcoming London exhibition. He was outspoken
about the deterioration of Indian silks and their reduced production.
While in India he had conducted a lengthy microscopic study of silk
fibres that were in use locally and uncovered a major problem. This,
he knew, could be speedily overcome. Over many years silk yarn
from Bengal had gained a poor reputation as the yarn was thought to
be inherently faulty. Wardle made a major advance when he found
that the silk itself was not the cause. He discovered that the difficulty
was in the reeling stage of production and the traditional methods
were producing an uneven thread. Using the newly acquired Italian
reeling technology, a selection of silk yarns was reeled under his supervision; and it was demonstrated that it was possible to obtain Bengali
silk of a uniform quality.

Thomas Wardle urged the State of Bengal to take immediate action
to improve silk production methods, although aware that the promotion of state intervention would prove unpopular with government
officials. England held *laissez-faire* policies, preferring to leave trade
matters to private enterprise; this outlook also prevailed among government officials in India. Nevertheless, Wardle knew how successful

government support was in France and Italy. He was not a government employee, but an independent manufacturer with specific expertise and significant authority that was greatly needed. His concern was with pragmatic solutions based on industrial experience rather than politics and he was not going to be compromised by government initiatives. Although India was part of the British Empire, and potentially a producer of silk yarn on an international scale, English manufacturers were importing silk yarn from China, Japan, Italy and France, as were Indian manufacturers themselves. This made no sense to Wardle and he saw how it could change; the timing was right and the mood was optimistic. He wanted people to take advantage of what lay in front of them and he encouraged local producers, knowing he would help develop a greater degree of self-regulation.

While in India, Wardle also tackled a disease that affected cultivated silkworm breeding, which wiped out the weak stock of silkworms. His final reports recommended a number of changes involving all that related to the production of a high standard of raw silk yarn. As it was pointless to overlook any aspect of the sericulture process which would weaken the system he suggested the introduction of new breeding methods, the improved growth and management of the essential mulberry trees along with the abolishment of the extortionate rental of mulberry lands. This last was because exploitative local landlords had constantly increased the rents on the land that grew the vital mulberry plants, forcing out small, individual producers. Finally, he recommended the further development of India's range of wild silks. He had done much to promote India's *tasar* silk, particularly during the Paris Exhibition of 1878, and demand had exceeded supply. He felt that there was still untapped potential.

Indian textile producers had been familiar with the demands of world markets for centuries, and it was only to be expected that they would want to build on previous progress and expand their markets. The Indian silk industry was, however, a complex system of local, often rural, traditional production and consumption, which had never fully been penetrated by overseas merchants. For the most part, local landowners and middlemen had managed it. Part of Wardle's solution was to expand traditional local knowledge with new knowledge from Europe. This would benefit the nation eventually, as the subsequent development would lead to greater financial independence. His observations of the established economic situation were intended to provoke changes for the benefit of India; they also provoked controversy with government officials. He was, however, able to advise local silk producers on effective measures so that their best products could be displayed at the forthcoming Colonial and India Exhibition, in London later that year. The Calcutta audience was promised that the best examples of Indian silk, both yarn and cloth would be displayed to the European market. By the time of the Colonial and Indian exhibition the improved products were available.

During and after the exhibition, the attention of Europe's manufacturers was sought as India's improved output was promoted. Within a year Bengal silk was fetching much higher prices, and the reinvigoration of *tasar* production was also successful. Fifteen years later it was pronounced to be a settled and vigorous industry, supplying markets in Europe and America, thereby providing employment for many thousands of workers.

Displaying India

It was the Colonial and Indian Exhibition of 1886 that gave an impetus to the compilation of the previously disparate records of India's goods. It was the first exhibition when anything like a complete economic survey of the British Empire was attempted and the first occasion when a complete art survey of India had been put in place. The system of assessment had begun in Paris in 1878 and carried on ever since, but for the first time a comprehensive series of samples lined the walls of the Exhibition Courts in 1886. One aim in doing this was to collate in one volume or economic ledger, information that was hitherto scattered through the multiple reports and records which crowded the walls of every official library, as well as the separate series of other publications compiled at various times by private individuals.

The Colonial and Indian Exhibition occupied a prime site of 22 acres in South Kensington; the buildings occupied 10 acres. The India section was the leading area and the Silk Court was the dominant court in the India section. Its displays celebrated India's goods, technical skills and designs. As the displays were fundamental to future commercial success they were planned to be spectacular. At the Exhibition's opening ceremony, held in the Albert Hall, the Queen's throne was covered in Indian embroideries and the canopy was of Indian cloth of gold. The India section, which was divided into five parts, attempted to cover a complete survey of art manufactures in the displays. As the Preface to the Exhibition catalogue stated, it was seldom the practice for any Indian artisan to keep any stock of his wares in hand. This was particularly the practice for complex silks, as the raw materials were costly. Almost every single exhibit had to be specially ordered by a government official.

Objects were exhibited in the lavish settings of a recreated Indian palace and Durbar Hall (or Hall of Audience) designed by Caspar

Purdon Clarke, with the objective of showing a typical royal Indian residence. The palace courtyard was approached through a massive stone archway, designed by Major J. Keith and presented by the late Maharaja Sindhia to the South Kensington Museum, who lent it for the purposes of the exhibition. Around three side of the courtyard were arranged shops, in which native artisans plied their trades. Figure 9 illustrates the stone archway and a corner of the courtyard. Opposite the gateway was a spacious hall of columns through which the palace was approached. The hall was entirely panelled with carved pine, which demonstrated how decoration in India was applied to architectural details on walls and ceilings (see Figure 10). The hall was hung entirely with *phulkaris* (a distinctive form of silk embroidery) and printed cottons. The decor was widely admired and it was assumed that this magnificent display alone would give an impetus to the demand for India's goods.

Throughout the India section intricately carved wooden screens and reconstructed great stone gateways, characteristic of the architecture of the various provinces, provided elaborate backdrops for the textiles. The screens were either contributed by the native Princes or made at the order of the government of India, local Indian committees and the Royal Commission. The buildings were hung with fabrics to show how they would be used in an Indian setting.

Undoubtedly one of the most interesting and popular features of the Exhibition was the forecourt of the palace, where the public flocked to watch Indian craft workers demonstrate their skills. The important and recent improvements in silk production were practically demonstrated in this central court. Silk reeling, dyeing, printing, spinning and weaving were all to be seen on a daily basis. During certain times during the exhibition silkworms were to be seen spinning their cocoons, while a silk reeler from Lyons, and, therefore, an artisan with high expectations, who was engaged by the Royal Commission, demonstrated that superior silk was being exported from India now that a better system of yarn production had been adopted.

The magnificent range of 200 silk fabrics and other related items was arranged mainly in cases and displayed in the garden vestibule. The collection consisted of the widely used cultivated silks and the lesser-known wild silks such as the *atlas, eria* and *muga* types. The display was arranged according to the region of origin rather than by class or type, which had been the case at earlier exhibitions. The Silk Court, therefore, was organised to reflect the unique characteristics of centres of excellence. This new system had been tried in a huge Calcutta exhibition the previous year and proved to be successful. This method of display worked particularly well for silk, as India had

9 The Colonial and Indian Exhibition, London 1886, stone archway and corner of courtyard with Indian shops.

10 The Colonial and Indian Exhibition, London 1886, Durbar Hall.

increasingly developed specialisations of products and labour skills. Each region typically produced a distinctive silk cloth or yarn that was specific to that part of India and the classification system was designed to reflect that. It allowed the relationship of silk types or technologies to one another to be clearly observed. The result was a range of displays which represented a region's distinctive output, and celebrated differences as much as similarities.

Exhibitors were offered a commemorative medal and diploma in an attempt to institute this non-competitive classification system. This avoided the more competitive, wide-ranging survey based on cloth types, with awards for the best of type. For as the catalogue stated: in some cases only one or two families in a single locality managed the production of an exclusive cloth. Such displays could, however, only be attempted if all the goods exhibited were of a high standard. Maps were conspicuously displayed showing the position, area and population of that region of India to which each section related. An indexed collection of many specimens of the principle raw materials such as fibres and dyes produced throughout India was also displayed to familiarize the public with its vast natural wealth. This system of classification had an inherent logic, which meant that it was simple to compile and study. The new system mixed aesthetic and economic concerns, giving a more complete sense of India's rich and diverse silk tradition. Most of the items were typical of the designs of their district. This had the added advantage of indicating with considerable clearness the changing composition and character of manufactures, which differ from one part of India to another. The vast Indian subcontinent, with its different languages, beliefs and traditions, would have been virtually unknown to many of its own citizens. Even between one village and another there were different nomenclatures for silk products or techniques. All the exhibits were catalogued in detail with a view to providing important product information to Indian and European manufacturers and consumers, not just a classification for its own sake.

The Silk Court exhibited huge lengths of complex and costly silks in the form of saris, shawls, turbans and other items of traditional Indian dress. There was clear evidence that very high technical standards were maintained as particularly fine specimens were on display. They were the products of centres of excellence across India, each with highly skilled communities, many of which continued to trade long after the official end of the empire. The collection was displayed so that the rich, glowing colours, complex techniques and lavish use of gold and silver made a dramatic impact. It proved to be a great attraction, not only to the ordinary visitors, but also more particularly to those with an interest in the silk industry. We know from an examination of the silks that survived from these displays, that deep, glowing colours would have provided a rich, sensual environment; red was the predominant colour. Most of the items were large lengths of silk; saris of 7–9 metres in length, turbans of up to 4 metres in length and shawls up to 5 metres square. There were satins, brocades, gold and silver *kincobs*, silk *bandhani*, fine plain weaves of undyed golden tasar and densely stitched embroideries. The majority of the exhibits were unsewn items of clothing; there were a few tailored pieces, however, including a long black satin coat, richly embroidered in gold; an emerald green satin *kurta* (tunic), also embroidered in gold; and a number of gold embroidered caps. There were two costly *patola* in the collection; bridal saris of great complexity.

The decision to display the silks in an opulent setting was a calculated one. The management of the silk displays aimed to reflect India's richly diverse and complex culture. The silks were magnificent in their own right; rich colour combinations and liberal use of gold and silver thread signified wealth and intricate skills. The setting needed to be equally splendid for them to be seen in the right context. Figure 11 shows a lavish interior setting at the exhibition. The textile maker's expertise was matched by the wood carver's and stonemason's ability. The combination added up to an image of a prosperous India, which was capable of producing the best goods then available – an important message to give out. British consumers needed to be torn away from their preference for French luxury goods; India had luxury aplenty and its history of silk production was a longer one.

Exhibitions and artisans

India's skilled artisans were to be observed weaving and reeling silks and interacting with visitors in lavish surroundings. The spectacle of highly skilled makers performing throughout the duration of the 1886 Exhibition caused great interest. Demonstrations of fine skills offered insight into a little known culture and created opportunities for communication between citizens from far-flung corners of the empire. Normally invisible, these workers who were masters of their craft, enjoyed the positive reactions of visitors who openly admired their publicly performed skills. The producers of complex silk cloths were chosen not to represent their country as a whole but to promote the Indian silk trade, aspects of which needed urgent marketing. These were not passive, subordinate people, but dynamic – actively involved in demonstrations for the benefit of their own industries. They represented ambition, planning for the future and willingness to accept

11 The Colonial and Indian Exhibition, London 1886, interior.

change within reason. There was a lot at stake and they took the opportunity to help shape their silk industry.

It was also a celebration – a public observance of time-honoured techniques that were meant to continue. At the same time they could reveal how recent advances had improved silk yarns, thereby reconciling tensions over quality between Indian producers and European manufacturers. India's silk yarns were demonstrably improved to the higher standards demanded by European manufacturers. Most importantly, English manufacturers had the potential to use them to produce silk fabrics that would match the French silks and overturn their competitive advantage. The fact that a French silk reeler could be observed demonstrating India's improved yarns was a masterstroke of marketing. It clearly signified that if the French, with their own means of silk production and demanding standards were using Indian yarns, then they satisfied the highest criteria; here also was a ready market outside the empire as well as within it.

The demonstrations by Indian craftsmen were not the first ever seen in London. Only the previous year A.L. Liberty had organised displays of Indian textiles in Battersea, along with demonstrations of weaving and printing by Indian artisans brought over for that purpose. Organising the labour and transportation for the demonstrators had been a highly complex task in itself, as makers from different castes did not usually mix when in India.

The Austrian artist Rudolf Swoboda painted the portraits of five of the Indian artisans who attended the 1886 Exhibition. Queen Victoria commissioned the paintings and thought them 'Beautiful things'.[13] The images eloquently capture a great sense of the individuality and diversity of the makers. The artist focused on their faces and distinctive headwear, made from a wide variety of closely observed textiles, rather than the surroundings of the exhibition. The work is of a high quality and the results are sensitive and powerful. Since then they have hung in a long hall of what was the private residence of Queen Victoria: Osborne House on the Isle of Wight.[14] The Queen invited all the craftsmen from the Exhibition to lunch at Windsor Castle; thirty-four of whom were from India.

Visitors

After the Great Exhibition of 1851 there was a rise in visitor numbers for international exhibitions. Visitors had a vital part to play at these events and were the focus of the displays and demonstrations. (Figure 12 shows the Hyderabad screen area with visitors.) They had the opportunity to see at first-hand a version of a flourishing Empire with authentic goods and genuine artisans in impressive settings. Displays and demonstrations were not static historical pageants for the entertainment of passive observers; they were making visible, and therefore comprehensible, commercial and social links that were usually hidden from view. Different visitor groups filled different niches in society and in turn benefited in various ways. Those visitors who were manufacturers, artisans and/or consumers were meant to experience the displays in ways that would strengthen trade benefits for all the nations taking part. In the case of those visitors who were training for work in the English textile industry it was hoped to stimulate a sense of 'good' design through the observation of the universal principles evident in India's textiles. The displays and demonstrations were also structured to some degree to guide the opinion

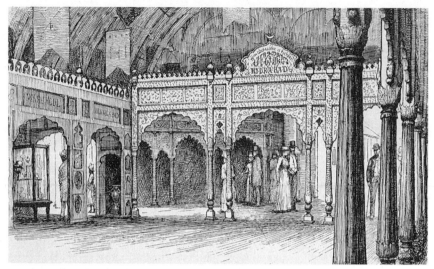

12 The Colonial and Indian Exhibition, London 1886, Hyderabad screen.

of the consuming public by providing them with material evidence of luxury goods. They were not intended to be mystified where silk was concerned, but educated and turned into consumers of English cloth made from Indian silk yarns. In the process it was hoped that they would then actively reject French silks, which had for so long dominated English consumption.

By making traditional complex weaving and dyeing skills an accessible public display, exhibition organisers were making the otherwise hidden causal chain more intelligible to the consumer. Thus the economically important aspects of trade between India and England were clearly revealed as connecting processes. As the makers were visibly linked to the finished silks, the potential consumers could observe that this was an ongoing, everyday activity which conflated real individuals' lives within and between England and India. Where displays of Indian silks were concerned there was evidently a shared viewpoint, which both India and England wished to endorse: that the silks could simultaneously serve both English and Indian objectives. National as well as colonial visions were not mutually exclusive and commonly agreed solutions to problems made sense where the silk trade was concerned.

Exhibition publications

Throughout the *Descriptive Catalogue to the Indian Silk Court*, written by Thomas Wardle, the context and heritage of Indian silk production was given, including detailed references to the ancient history of textiles and the demands for them by other cultures. Where possible indigenous Indian names were used. Taxonomies that arose from botanical and etymological classifications were universal by then and were used throughout. The catalogue gave Wardle an ideal opportunity to express his thoughts about India and its people. The *Journal of Indian Art* published the following extract from the catalogue, which summed up the warmth and depth of feeling:

> No one can pass through the length and breadth of India without being greatly impressed by two things: first, its enormous population; second, the excellence of its handicraft work with a love of ornamentation, so wonderfully and patiently wrought out, whether it be in metals, stone, wood, ivory, or textile fabrics. The importance of preserving to these clever and patient people their trades and industries cannot, in my opinion, be over-estimated; beside this I have endeavoured to show in this paper how much England can do for India by stimulating the people in Bengal, and other parts where silk can be produced, to the production of a much greater supply of the raw material. Her dyes are also beautiful, and ought to find a ready application in Europe both for silk and cotton. I have no doubt that the Colonial and India Exhibition will be of great service in showing the West what an enormous variety of raw material India is capable of producing. A practical and unselfish regard for her welfare will constitute the strongest bonds of Empire Federation and enable us to look upon our Indian fellow subjects in the spirit happily embodied and expressed by Mr Edwin Arnold in his sonnet preface to his 'India Revisited'.

There followed an extract from Arnold's sonnet.[15]

The *Journal of Indian Art*, whose purpose was mainly educational, ran a series of special monthly numbers for the duration of the 1886 exhibition. They included numerous articles on historical methods of manufacture, many of which were devoted to Indian textiles with detailed illustrations, and many in full colour. The *Journal* had been launched under the patronage of the government of India in 1884, and received liberal contributions from Residents and those officials who were able to supply illustrations. Its aims were to call attention to Indian manufacture with illustrations of the best available type: 'To call attention of the public and ultimately artisans and dealers to the artistic qualities in older work, the absence of which in some recent efforts is a common cause of complaints.' It also aimed to serve the commercial purposes of popularising arts 'too frequently regarded as merely curiosities of craftsmanship'.[16] The *Journal of the Royal Society of Arts* also covered the Exhibition in some detail. The following is typical:

It was evident that a vast amount of trouble was taken to make displays worthy of our great Asiatic Empire by officers whose names the public have never heard. The liberal manner in which the native princes and gentlemen of India responded to the invitation to the executive president of the royal commission was remarkable and it was this which mainly made the India Court the most attractive in the Exhibition.

India occupied about one quarter of the whole exhibition space. Figure 13 illustrates the impressive Jeypore gateway. The Silk Court under Thomas Wardle's management received particular mention, with the comment that, 'Very modest claims were made by Mr Wardle for the silk court.'[17] Special conferences on India's natural resources were organised and were also very successful. The Royal Commissioners produced a series of over 20 reports, which resulted from the series of committees of learned people, which were held throughout the three-month duration of the exhibition.

Manchester's Royal Jubilee Exhibition, 1887

Manchester's Royal Jubilee Exhibition was a massive undertaking, which took place on the Old Trafford site of the celebrated Manchester Art Exhibition of 1858. The Jubilee exhibition covered 45 acres. (Figure 14 shows a bird's-eye view of the exterior of the elaborate buildings.) Although it was held only a year after the Colonial and India Exhibition in London, Manchester's event did not set out to cultivate a colonial atmosphere. It was less about the empire, as it was about trade in general, which needed more than the empire as its marketplace in order to survive. The prime purpose of the silk sections was to promote the ailing silk industries in both England and India – a rescue operation for both, underpinned by a humanitarian motivation. Figure 15 is an illustration of the opening ceremony, which clearly shows it was a grand occasion. The exhibition committee allocated the same amount of space to the silk section as it did to the giant cotton industry and it was judged to be excellent. A complete overview of the industry was presented from silkworm eggs, through all the preparatory processes, to the manufactured cloth and yarn in all its diverse forms. The displays featured silk fabrics from many countries, including ancient and contemporary English cloth. Figure 16 shows general interior scene, which indicates the splendour of the event.

The collection of Indian silks that had been displayed in London the previous year was displayed at the Manchester event, with the addition of further silk items sent over from India. The detailed descriptive catalogue, written by Thomas Wardle, Chairman of the silk section, described the Indian silk thus:

13 The Colonial and Indian Exhibition, London 1886, Jeypore gateway.

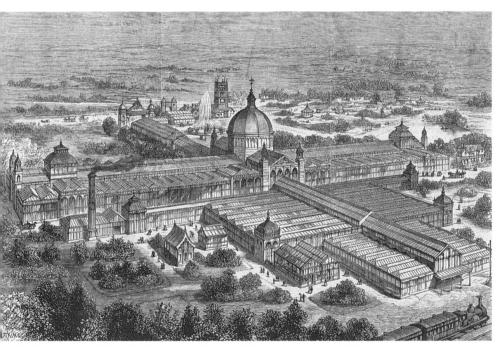

4 Bird's-eye view of Royal Jubilee Exhibition buildings, Manchester, 1887.

[133]

This collection possesses a high value in an aesthetic and pecuniary sense. One notable feature of this series of silk 'attire' is the variety and beauty of the borders which surround almost every piece of stuff. For richness and harmony of colouring, for originality and positive wealth of design power, these borders stand out as triumphs of the designer's art.[18]

We know from the exhibition catalogue the order in which the Indian silks were exhibited in Manchester. Unlike the displays at the Colonial and Indian Exhibition, they were displayed according to type, not according to region. The first textile to be seen was a costly *patolu* wedding sari (see colour plate 6) – the impact of this long length of richly patterned silk alone must have been huge. The *patolu* was followed by a group of more than fifty elaborate brocades, many of which were sumptuous *kinkhabs*, with their lavish use of gold and silver thread. Next was the section devoted to the *bandhani* – a demanding tie-dye process. Mixed silk and cotton fabrics followed, with their vibrant multicoloured patterns. They were succeeded by a richly coloured group of saris, scarves and shawls; all of which demonstrated different dyeing techniques using a variety of silk cloths, many with gold woven into their borders.

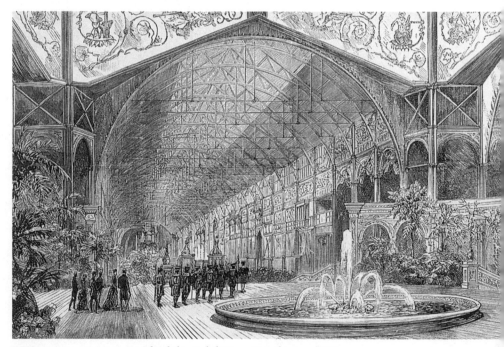

15 Opening ceremony, Royal Jubilee Exhibition, Manchester, 1887.

This diverse range included an orange shot silk formed from a mix of yellow and crimson threads, plaids of yellow and black, an indigo sari thickly brocaded with a red, white and yellow *buti* designs and a refined border pattern, and one particularly interesting sari that was differently coloured (red and yellow) on each side of the heavy satin double cloth. There were also a number of finely woven *tasar* silk *chadars* (shawls) with their understated aesthetic derived from the undyed, natural golden colour of the wild silk, enhanced with simple, narrow woven borders. The woven textiles were followed by a group of embroideries: large shawls of different weaves densely covered with fine stitching, many with mirror work. Colour plate 8 shows an indigo silk satin *odhani* (shawl) from Kutch, densely embroidered with multi-coloured silk threads and mirror glass. Colour plate 9 is a detail of the shawl showing one of four central motifs. There were also embroidered scarves, turbans, a long satin coat, a satin *kurta*, hats, bodice pieces and sari borders. There were a very few examples of block-printed silk. This display must have looked spectacular and was recorded as impressive. The textile trade press was enthusiastic, with the *Textile Recorder* reporting the display as 'a source of pleasure and delight'.[19]

6 Interior, Royal Jubilee Exhibition, Manchester, 1887.

The collection, assembled by Thomas Wardle in India, represented the costliest fabrics produced for India's internal market. On the whole they were professionally made pieces, which would have been commissioned for specific occasions. The collection demonstrated examples of the fine artisan skills then in use for textile production in India. They confirmed an understanding of universal principles of design and practised control over demanding techniques. A notable and distinguishing feature, which can be clearly observed in the surviving pieces, is the use of rich colour combinations. The complete mastery of dyeing, in terms of evenness, depth of colour and striking colour contrasts is immediately evident. The display would have provided saturation of intense colour along with the luxurious use of precious metal threads.

Most of the handmade Indian silks were not obviously related to the mass-produced, printed cotton goods for which Manchester was noted. It would have been impossible, moreover, to profitably reproduce these types of silk textiles in England. What was their purpose, therefore in Manchester? Undoubtedly this stunning collection was intended to make political points, as well as aesthetic and economic ones. One significant intention was to direct the public's attention, especially that of English consumers, to the distinct possibility that England could make high quality silks, using India's yarns and design principles. As at the Colonial and India Exhibition, India's raw materials were highlighted as eminently suitable for the production of luxury silk goods. By choosing to display the most dramatic and costly examples, rather than the more obvious printed pattern sources for Manchester's printed cotton industry, the silks were intended for those luxury markets then dominated by imported French goods. At that time British consumers were exercising their preference for French silks to the tune of £12 million per annum. Such a loss to English manufacturers could be reversed, preventing an annual loss of revenue and preserving threatened jobs, if England could only claim a greater share of the international silk market. Discerning consumers evidently preferred the French approach to textile design, an approach that acknowledged that textiles needed well-drawn patterns and good colour combinations. An evident understanding of complex patterns and control over rich colouring was clearly evident in these displays of Indian silks.

The displays of Indian silks in London and Manchester were also exposing possibilities for English textile design education. Throughout the period under discussion, there was a great deal of debate about design education and the appropriateness of design-related courses. To demonstrate the most magnificent and technically difficult of India's silk textile production, despite its reliance on very basic technology, was to demonstrate excellence through contrast. Thomas Wardle and many other textile manufacturers knew what design education lacked in England. In an endeavour to counteract poor textile design, he was reinforcing the arts and crafts ideals, which were already influencing design education. He was not advocating a return to hand-making per se, but was indicating principles that were little understood in England. Costly Indian silks demonstrated techniques that could not be profitably transferred to factory production; nor were they ever intended to be used for that purpose. Rather they were the antithesis to the structural and aesthetic incoherence of many mass-produced objects, a result that was thought to stem from the separation of design from the processes of production. In addition, of course, there was a strong element of Arts and Crafts philosophy, which was sympathetic to India's traditions. A number of pivotal spokespersons from the movement promoted India's designs and Manchester had fostered an Arts and Crafts approach to teaching in its art school. One of the incentives to be gained from studying India's textiles at first hand was the inspiration to make beautiful work. Through his activities Thomas Wardle aimed to make the English consumer hunger for designs that drew on the lessons illustrated by India's best examples. They offered different ways out of the decline evident in both the English and Indian silk trades.

Thomas Wardle thoroughly understood the relationship that existed between exhibitions, museums, industry, consumerism and design education. Trade, not taste, was his driving force, but in the end it amounted to much the same thing if the consumer's taste was for those objects that displayed characteristics of universal design principles; as the preference for the more expensive French silks would seem to suggest. Manufacturers, at home and abroad, advocated the study of textiles from other cultures and eras in order to understand their underlying principles. Wardle publicly argued a case for keeping the Indian silk collection in Manchester as a teaching collection and recommended that a permanent home should be found for it in the textile-producing region. At that time there was no trade museum in Manchester. In the event, a large portion of the Indian silk display was donated to the Whitworth Institute, now the Whitworth Art Gallery, Manchester.

This group of silk textiles was a remarkable teaching collection for a number of reasons. First, the size and quality of the range of silks provided a unique opportunity to study a complete range of India's silk production for its internal market, and an unbroken tradition of considerable skills. Second, many of the items were complete garments. Third, many large lengths were available for study – some sari lengths were up to 9 metres long. This meant that a clear examination of horizontal, vertical, diagonal pattern repeats, central panel designs, corner treatments, joins, borders, etc., could be observed. The textiles also provided the opportunity to view edgings and fringing, some of which were woven in; others were attached and, therefore, separate textiles in their own right. One large piece, could, therefore, offer combinations of techniques and possibly demonstrate how different patterns were combined in one garment. There was, moreover, a remarkable opportunity to assess the weight and drape of the cloth and to consider how it might be worn.

The opportunity to study techniques over a large expanse of fabric provided an occasion to marvel at the basic technology, which had produced such large and challenging silks. To achieve such fine weaves of different types, with an evenness of dye on such a large scale was clearly admirable. The high standard of the silks meant that they displayed exemplary qualities in all areas of silk textile production. In one *patolu* alone the finest dyeing and weaving skills were to be observed (see colour plate 6). Wardle's description of this demanding technique was the first ever known in English. His observations highlight the complexity of the process thus:

> It is woven with warp and weft which have been separately tied and dyed in the *bandhana* process. The dyer takes a small bundle of warp which has been dyed in the lightest colour found on the warp in the finished process, and draws a pencil line across it at measured distances according to the design to be produced. His wife then ties the silk, along the spaces marked, tightly round with cotton thread, through which the dye will not penetrate. It is then dyed in the next darker colour found upon the warp, and the process is repeated until the darkest colour is reached. The weft is then treated in the same way, being so tied and dyed that in the loom, when it crosses the warp, each of its colours may exactly come in contact with the same colour in the warp. The little bundles of warp have next to be arranged in the loom by the weaver, who then takes the little bundles of weft one at a time, using each in its own place throughout the design.[20]

Wardle and many others firmly believed that Indian dyers were the best in the world and their colour technology was masterly, thereby providing excellent models for textile design education. A sound knowledge of colour theory was considered to be the overwhelmingly important element of a good design; something for which the French were particularly noted. Apart from the natural golden tones of the undyed wild silks, most of the items in the collection displayed a rich and diverse treatment of colour. On the whole, the colour combinations were rich and striking. Red, in its many hues, was dominant. A number of pieces were unpatterned and relied on an unbroken expanse of rich colour for their impact. The liberal use of gold and silver threads was mostly combined with crimson silk to form costly *kinkobs*. The embroideries were mainly large items from noted centres of excellence and included a number of exceptionally fine examples of stitching and design. The use of pattern was also a most interesting aspect of this collection. Pattern derived from construction techniques such as weaving, and from surface embellishment such as printing and embroidery. Historic, symbolic and traditional motifs were utilised in many intricate ways.

What these textiles clearly demonstrated was appropriate design principles. Although they were not meant to be copied they were certainly intended to be understood. The lessons to be learnt from them were to be absorbed then applied in a way that would express an English approach to design. In this respect they worked in parallel to the collections in South Kensington Museum and complimented the Forbes Watson collection of small pieces of Indian textiles in Manchester, the Manchester School of Art collection and the small Horsfall collection of silk brocades, also in Manchester. The driving force behind each different collection was trade in its widest sense. The documentary evidence that survives indicates that in their collections and displays of Indian silks the intentions of each separate institution were broadly the same. Collectively they indicate a remarkable continuity in their aims and solutions.

This remarkable collection of Indian silks remains in Manchester at the Whitworth Art Gallery and still functions as a source of inspiration to those training for Britain's textile industries. It is an outstanding legacy from two major international exhibitions and clearly demonstrates the timelessness of India's design heritage.

Manchester's success stimulated Glasgow to hold a similar event, and the impressive 'Indian' pavilion, produced in ceramic by Royal Doulton (see figure 17) was used again on the Glasgow site. Both cities have continued to benefit from these events. Their museums still hold treasures directly sourced from the exhibitions. The long-term benefits at numerous levels fulfilled the aims of experts and officials who were determined to use exhibitions to promote lasting change. This was also the case in India, notably in Calcutta, where the International Exhibition provided the core collection for a revived public museum.[21] Lord Curzon of Keddleston, Viceroy and Governor General of India continued the tradition and included a large display of Indian textiles at the Delhi Imperial Durbar in 1903. Superintendents and curators of various museums in India sent loan collections. George Watt compiled a catalogue of Indian art for this event as a systematic guide and to facilitate future research in India.

17 Royal Doulton's Indian Pavilion, Royal Jubilee Exhibition, Manchester, 1887.

Conclusion

Exhibitions created the ideal marketplace, a non-competitive arena with ideal conditions of luxurious displays, demonstrations of impressive artisanal skills and the finest raw materials. The effect of displaying India, with its participating artisans from a vast and varied sub-continent, implied a nation with a coherent culture, heightened creative awareness and ancient trading history. Displays and demonstrations made public that which was often hidden from sight; the processes shown in demonstrations and the goods made comprehensible the various mercantile and shared aspects of the complex trade throughout the empire. In both England and India, furthermore, producers were also consumers, they had mutually dependent roles to play in the imperial marketplace. For those participating Indians, exhibitions provided a very good opportunity to travel as 'citizens' of the empire in a way that would not otherwise have been possible, and in the process to expand their design repertoire.

On a personal level, Thomas Wardle gained publicity and admiration for his company, a knighthood for his work with India's silk industry, the *Chevalier de la Legion d'Honneur de France, Officier d'Academie de France*, Indian accolades, medals from the Manchester Royal Jubilee Exhibition, and up to a dozen more for other silk-related activities. The official role of Honourable Superintendent of the Indian

Silk Court of the Indian and Colonial Exhibition added to Wardle's standing. It allowed new opportunities for his expertise to be utilised, presenting a wider cultural context in which to operate; sanctioning him as an expert beyond the industrial sector. As Chairman of the Manchester Exhibition's Silk Section he gained further authority, which reinforced his recommendation that the Indian silk collection be kept for teaching purposes. On the back of the overwhelmingly successful and profitable Manchester Jubilee Exhibition, he helped form the Silk Association of Britain and Ireland and became its first President.

International exhibition displays unquestionably influenced the formation, development and use of public collections of textiles in England and India. Wardle's vision included the provision of open access to the best textiles for those training for the English textile industries, in the region where they lived and worked. In the case of Manchester, Wardle recommended that a permanent teaching collection should be established at the Whitworth Institute and it still serves as such today. Local access meant that more people training for the textile industries could see and examine the Indian silks at first hand. Close inspection of the pieces was an important consideration for those in textile production. Even though Manchester was the heart of the cotton industry, silk manufacturing still continued in the region and the universal design principles and inspirational use of colour were also appropriate to cotton. Although for the most part the collection housed in Manchester remained there, a number of key pieces were loaned for major temporary exhibitions at prestigious addresses in London, which Wardle organised in order to boost the silk industry at the end of the nineteenth and the beginning of the twentieth century.

The South Kensington Museum, now the Victoria and Albert Museum, gained many of its core collections as a result of international exhibitions held in London. Accession registers reveal whether they were purchased or donated after the events closed. Although the bulk of the collections remained in London, a series of travelling collections went out to the provinces. Macclesfield School of Art and Manchester Municipal School of Art both had large displays of Indian silks loaned from South Kensington. It is possible to identify from the records which items were circulated. In the case of Indian silks they are known to have been costly and complex examples, chosen to travel around the country, demonstrating good design principles as well as the finest dye technology, weaving and embroidery techniques.

Art and technology colleges in English regions where silks were produced housed these travelling displays regularly. They gave students and tutors, as well as local manufacturers and public, the opportunity to see at first hand, pieces from major exhibitions. Although it was intended that they should influence design and technological education in those regions where English silk was produced, it was not intended that the designs should merely be reproduced. There is evidence in surviving examples of students' work from Bradford and Macclesfield, which clearly show an affinity with samples of Indian silks: the designs and techniques have, however, been interpreted with an English sensibility. It is quite apparent that many of the students' designs have a colour palette that owes a great deal to the influence of Arts and Crafts Movement. Many colleges formed their own study collections and some had already received the Forbes Watson volumes of Indian textiles, which were also the result of Great Exhibition displays and purchases. (See colour plate 10, which illustrates a Macclesfield student's design, which is a clever dovetailing of both Arts and Crafts and Indian influences.)

Where silk was concerned, a codependent imperial marketplace could not be enough. Thomas Wardle thought globally, realising that consumers demanded goods from beyond the confines of the empire; and the only way that that trend could be reversed was to offer comparable or superior goods. He was also aware that increasing competition from the Far East meant that India's raw materials needed a wider market. France, a major silk-producing nation and England's major rival, was targeted by Wardle as a potential market for India's wild silks in the 1870s as he had ambitions for Indian silks that were more international than they were imperial.

The splendour of the past was, therefore, used to safeguard the future. The lavish exhibition sites for Indian silks were more than attractive stage settings. They were pointed reminders of India's noble past as well as its present. Sophisticated and lavish settings grounded Indian silks in an opulent and ancient heritage, a legacy that equalled the grandeur of the French, yet the Indian silk tradition was longer and more comprehensive. While India's historical designs and skills were admired as a sign of continuing high standards, maintained over centuries, it was also necessary to demonstrate that India's artisans had progressed where the latest reeling technology was concerned. Overall, the past and the present were successfully combined and signalled a challenge to French silk supremacy. The displays as object lessons were a complete success. There were lessons here too for British manufacturers, of course.

Thomas Wardle knew that design and technical skills could be taught; they were not specific to the French, but were down to a good design education system and understanding of universal design principles. Demystifying the aesthetic and commercial processes through direct observation demonstrated to exhibition visitors that this was the case. Educators were clearly expected to consider these lessons.

Manufacturers and consumers could examine raw silk materials of many types and obtain technical information about them, observe artisans in action and see cloth being woven, printed and embroidered, with both the latest technology and ancient tools in operation. Britain and India, nevertheless, needed to devote more effort to the scientific study of sericulture. Wardle wanted it elevated as a serious study, linked to higher standards of technical education in order to overcome production difficulties. He was convinced that, in order to regain and then retain a leading trade position, original research was needed. Collective action was essential as the problems were now too vital to be left to individuals. The combination of the superior objects on display and the learned publications produced by exhibition committees tangibly reinforced what was possible for both England and India. The combined efforts of manufacturers, educators and museum officials bore fruit, English silk goods did benefit from improved designs and in their turn they even influenced the French consumer, who recognised the improved designs and began selecting English silk.

Notes

1   The dye is applied directly to the cloth by a brush or 'pencil' before it oxidises; only small amounts could be applied at any one time.
2   Desmond, 1982, p. 165.
3   Ibid.
4   Birdwood, 1878.
5   *The Lady's World*, 1887, pp. 349–52.
6   *Journal of Indian Art*, Vol. 1, No. 1, 1886, p. 48.
7   In 1884–85 the value of exports of Indian silk was Rupees 46,35,613 while that for imported silk was Rupees 74,75,633, *Proceedings of a Conference on Silk*, Calcutta, 1886, p. 6.
8   Buck, 1886, p. 7.
9   Wardle, 1887, p. 8.
10   Ibid.
11   Ibid.
12   Wardle, Manchester, 1887.
13   Mathur, London, 2002.
14   They were exhibited in December 2002 at the National Portrait Gallery, London, for the first time since the Exhibition.
15   Wardle, *The Journal of Indian Art*, Vol. 1, Nos 1–16, 1886, pp. 115–23.
16   Ibid.
17   The *Journal of the Royal Society of Arts*, 23 September 1886.
18   Wardle, 1887.
19   *Textile Recorder*, 14 May 1887, p. 2.
20   Wardle, Manchester, 1887, p. 43.
21   'Museums and Exhibitions', resolution from the proceedings of the government of India, Department of Revenue and Agriculture, *Journal of Indian Art & Industry*, 1884–86, p. 6.

CHAPTER SEVEN

The Arts and Crafts Movement and Indian silk

The Arts and Crafts Movement was originally a British response to the generally poor state of the decorative arts and the exploitative conditions that produced them. In the latter half of the nineteenth century a disparate group of artists and designers found a common aim in their belief in the equality of the fine and applied arts. The 'Movement' as it was later called, had its origins in the writings of Pugin and Ruskin and centred on the practical application of their ideas. The designs and theories of William Morris were also profoundly influential. A central tenet was the notion that personal fulfilment could be achieved through honest workmanship and decent citizenship.

The creation of a number of craft guilds and societies, along with the Arts and Crafts Exhibition Society (1887), helped to consolidate and promote shared values that were based on socialist and utopian ideals. The ideals were rooted in the belief that 'society produces the art and architecture it deserves'.[1] English vernacular buildings and interiors were considered the ideal and successful design was that which considered the properties of the material to be used and the object's ultimate purpose. The result was a great interest in design and a revival of craft skills, which had a considerable effect. Ideals were made visible in artist's and architect's designs for buildings, interiors and textiles for both furnishings and dress. The battle for aesthetic reform was one part of a wider moral campaign concerned with social reform, which found expression in diverse, often national interpretations in industrialised Europe and America in the late nineteenth century.

The Arts and Crafts Movement had a lasting effect on British, European and American design, contributing to the great revival of the decorative arts that was evident across Europe from about 1890. Although the Movement was anti-industrial to a large extent, prominent designers of the Arts and Crafts Movement and like-minded English textile manufacturers collaborated in mutually beneficial ways, which helped the Movement to progress. Technical and design developments by industrialists were often due to symbiotic, creative relationships with designers. Leading creative members of the Movement gained employment through the support of manufacturers who commissioned and produced their designs in a sympathetic manner. Besides which, a number of artists and designers became interested in the moral issues relating to industry. Aware of the poor conditions of many factory operatives, they criticised exploitative factory conditions and sought out those manufacturers who were in accord with their social, as well as aesthetic aims.

Members of the Arts and Crafts Movement also had a profound effect on design education (see Chapter Two). Designers and manufacturers encouraged the educators, many of whom were in agreement with the aims of the Movement. Some designers, who were also educators, brought practical experience to their teaching and publications. Influences were spread through publications and by other means; the designer and theorist Owen Jones instituted a medal for student textile designers; some supportive manufacturers were examiners of students' work. Charles Holme, a Bradford businessman financed *The Studio* (in 1893), a sympathetic and influential journal which supported Arts and Crafts values. The *Studio* illustrated a number of Thomas Wardle's products and carried articles on British silks by A.L. Liberty. The journal also ran prize competitions in order to encourage good design practice. Holme, who lived in Morris's Red House for a time, travelled to Japan with A.L. Liberty, and to India in the 1890s.

A growing interest in the designs of the near and far east, along with changes in some consumers' taste, 'those who were wealthy and design conscious',[2] were related factors which contributed to the climate of change. This consumer group showed an increasing interest in natural colours and softer fabrics, which led to a resurgence of interest in Indian silks. New and rapidly changing approaches to fashionable dress, with its simplified silhouette, focused interest on the designs of textiles, helping silk maintain its popularity for certain items of clothing in the face of robust competition from cotton. The increased demand for fluid, plainly woven silks, with hand-dyed and printed rather than woven designs, accessories and lace, ribbons, braid and embroidery thread in soft tones, contributed to the demand for 'art manufactures'. New variations in interior design also had a significant impact on designs for furnishing textiles. Moreover, during this period a number of like-minded retailers were providing vital outlets for the goods that these consumers were demanding. The increased numbers of department stores dedicated whole sections to selling silks; huge quantities of Indian silk piece goods were imported for direct sale to customers. Oriental designs generally became extremely familiar and were demanded in their indigenous forms, and in European versions.

A pivotal figure in this milieu was Arthur Lazenby Liberty, a huge promoter of the Arts and Crafts Movement and advocate of English silks; he was also interested in design education. When the Paris branch of Liberty opened in 1890, at 38, avenue de l'Opera, it nurtured a growing respect for English textiles on the continent. From that time the distinctive designs were increasingly in demand throughout Europe.[3] Samuel Bing, who retailed Liberty fabrics through *Maison de L'Art Nouveau* in Paris declared 'When English creations began to appear a cry of delight sounded throughout Europe. Its echo can still be heard in every country'.[4] Other retailers in England such as F.B. Goodyer, who established the Aesthetic Gallery for Art Fabrics, in Bond Street, London, held exhibitions of English silks, while retailers in Europe and agents in America, Canada and Australia carried the textiles over a wider area. Recognising their importance a number of European museums formed collections of Liberty fabrics at this time.[5]

Liberty's shop, founded in Regent Street, London, in 1875, was an influential and necessary outlet for English made goods as well as imported Asian commodities. It was one of the first retailers to actively promote English silks, stocks of which were always available. Moreover, Liberty & Co. held many educative exhibitions, with accompanying catalogues, of historic and contemporary textiles, many of which highlighted English and Indian silks. Exhibitions of English silks were held in 1881, 1891, 1896, 1902, and in 1888 a room was set up for a Spitalfields weaver to hold weaving demonstrations. In 1885, the year before the Colonial and Indian Exhibition, the retailer brought over 45 Indian artisans, including 7 skilled in textile crafts, to demonstrate their skills at the Indian Village Exhibition in the Albert Palace, Battersea. Demonstrations took place in a recreated Indian village, which was constructed to show different types of Indian architecture and visitors were encouraged to meet the textile makers; three embroiderers, a silk spinner, silk weaver, silk twister and a cotton and silk printer.[6] A.L. Liberty also instituted an improved school of colouring and design.[7]

Liberty had become increasingly dissatisfied with the fugitive dyes on the silks he imported from India. Like William Morris he turned to English companies to obtain traditional dyeing techniques. His partnership with Thomas Wardle was one of his greatest achievements; between them they developed a highly successful range of art colours using silks, natural dyes and ancient methods from India. Liberty, who was thought to have developed his appreciation of colour through handling Eastern productions such as Chinese embroideries, Persian carpets and Indian textiles also helped to established a preference for the softer shades in the 'art colours' range. This aspect of the company was vitally important to its success and was mentioned extensively in promotional material. Wardle & Co. became a major supplier to Liberty, also providing vast quantities of printed and dyed Indian silk cloth from the store's beginning. The beautiful, delicate shades became world famous as 'Liberty's art fabrics'. Surviving Liberty catalogues clearly show the importance of Indian silks to the company. Extant pattern books from the Wardle company contain samples of 'tussors', 'corahs', 'mysore' silks, cottons and velveteens, which were either dyed or printed for Liberty.[8] Most of Wardle's 'Mysore silk' designs for Liberty are thought to be 'exact reproductions of old Indian textiles'. Research for 'authentic' designs was undertaken for Liberty at the Indian Museum in London.[9] The designs were generally small floral repeat patterns, printed in various colours or gold on a cream ground. They were given names which were evocative of the East, such as 'Allahabad Marigold', 'Poonah Thistle', 'Chamba Chrysanthemum' and 'Rangoon Poppy'.

The silk was hand-woven in India then dyed and hand-block printed to commission in Leek. Liberty, in addition, sold 'Tussur' silk in its natural golden colour from the beginning; it was used for clothing and light furnishings. When it became available in the new art colours demand grew. Liberty and Wardle joined forces to promote the new colours by using dramatic window displays in the Regent Street shop, where they became a well-known sight. 'Tanjore Lotus', an Indian *tasar* silk woven with a lotus pattern, imported and dyed by Wardle & Co., became the Liberty trademark until it was replaced by the now familiar peacock feather motif; this was first shown at the Royal Manchester Jubilee Exhibition in 1887.

Within a very short period, this creative collaboration received high acclaim. A display of Indian silks, dyed and printed by Thomas Wardle for Liberty, was shown at The Paris Universal Exposition of 1878. Indian textiles mainly inspired the designs; they were dyed and hand-block printed with fast colours, using Indian wood blocks from the India Museum, or they were adapted from Indian and Persian patterns, printed onto *tasar* and Mysore silk hand-woven in India. The response was overwhelmingly enthusiastic – even a French fashion journal was moved to describe them as 'the best finished silks we have seen'.[10] When the exhibition closed the silks were purchased for South Kensington Museum.

As Wardle had his own retail outlet in New Bond Street, London, and as both men were importing and retailing Indian silks in its various forms, he needed to maintain a carefully balanced relationship with Liberty. Liberty commissioned a great deal of printing and dyeing from Wardle; therefore, they needed not to appear as rivals in the retail sector. They continued to collaborate and benefit the English and Indian silk industries in different ways. Liberty loaned Wardle some of his exceptional examples of old Indian silks for the 1887 Royal Jubilee Exhibition, in Manchester. When Thomas Wardle was appointed as the first President of the newly formed British Silk Association in 1887, A.L. Liberty was appointed as the Vice-President.

Designs

In the last quarter of the nineteenth century there was a marked change in English textile design, although this affected a relatively small sector of the market: that which followed the growing fashionable trend for 'artistic' interiors and fashionable dress. English manufacturers were encouraged enough by the positive climate to purchase designs from the increasing numbers of freelance, avant-garde designers and architects who were following a particular aesthetic goal. As individuality was cultivated there was no overall style that dominated the Arts and Crafts designs, but there were shared values and influences which manufacturers, designers and educators alike acknowledged. This led to British textiles being acclaimed in Europe for their excellence and originality of design.

The theories developed by William Morris and other leading designers made a major contribution to the changes taking place. Naturalistic, three-dimensional designs, which had dominated textiles for so long, were rejected in favour of two-dimensional patterns, which were considered to be more appropriate to the flat planes of a cloth's surface. A major characteristic was the use of eastern patterns as a source for inventive new designs. This development can be perceived, both in the techniques and aesthetics, in the many surviving silk cloths and designs of the period. Stylised plant forms were endlessly popular, sinuous floral stems provided a structural framework that linked pattern elements together. They followed what Morris described as the 'universal acceptance of continuous growth'.[11] Repeating patterns were based on stems or branches following a diagonal axis or were placed within a network of diamond-shaped structures. Along with turnover (mirror-image) designs, these were ancient schemes, which were given a new sensibility, providing approved formats that survived well into the Art Nouveau period. William Morris argued that structure was a crucial element in successful pattern design, giving 'a wall against vagueness' by using 'definite form bounded by firm outline'.[12] His influence can be observed in finely detailed, two-dimensional compositions, typical of designs demanded by wealthy middle-class consumers.

William Morris, who had learnt of Wardle's dyeing expertise, approached him in 1875; Wardle had by then gained a good reputation as a leading dyer. He and Morris had many interests in common and their collaborations made a major contribution to the history of dyed and printed textiles. Both men were keen to perfect natural dyeing, particularly indigo dyeing, the most demanding of all processes, which was in danger of disappearing, as it was such an unpredictable method. Morris travelled to Leek a number of times between 1875 and 1878, staying at the Wardle family home, socialising, walking and fishing with Wardle and working at his Hencroft site in the town. Together with Wardle's workmen he experimented with vegetable dyeing in one of the dye houses, where three experienced workers were allocated to his use. Morris learnt a great deal about printing and dyeing there and Wardle printed all of his early textile designs at Leek: Acanthus, African Marigold, Bluebell, Carnation, Honeysuckle, Indian Diaper, Iris, Little Chintz, Marigold, Peony, Pomegranate, Snakeshead and Tulip. Wardle & Co. also dyed the embroidery silks, wool cloth, velvets and wool yarn for Morris's weaving and carpets. Colour plate 11 shows some colour trials of early William Morris designs hand-block printed by Wardle & Co. onto *tasar* silks during this experimental period.

Morris provided a useful model for Wardle, and both ran successful businesses upholding many of Ruskin's theories as guidelines. As Ruskin argued in *The Two Paths*, 'It should be one of the first objects of all manufacturers to produce stuffs not only beautiful and quaint in design, but also adapted for everyday service, and decorous in humble and secluded life.'[13] Wardle upheld Ruskin's views and produced well-designed, beautiful and practical goods, not meretricious designs simply because they were more profitable. Ruskin also suggested that 'you must remember always that your business, as manufacturers, is to form the market, as much as to supply it'.[14] Taking on some of Ruskin's other theories he also set forth 'to publish what will educate as it adorns'.[15]

He was certainly not the type of manufacturer described as morally degenerate by Ruskin, bent on driving the labouring classes into cultural and material poverty. Nor did he fit the picture of a complacent employer, indifferent to the needs of his workforce. We know that when Morris was acquiring his dyeing skills and experimenting at Wardle's dye works in Leek, he complained that Wardle's dyers would not bend to his will. Of one worker Kay, who had thirty years of dyeing experience, Morris complained: 'I believe he thinks we can't do without him and that he can do anything he pleases', clearly indicating that the dyers were used to a degree of autonomy and had established their own tradition of working.[16] This suggests that Wardle valued his worker's tacit knowledge and although Morris was greatly admired, he did not worship him as others did; the designer was only one expert among others in a team dedicated to the day-by-day reality of developing new products.

Wardle was always driven by the notion that he could produce a superior product and his production processes were constantly being improved in order that this could be realised. The challenge of working with such a man as Morris called into play a lifetime of knowledge for Wardle. It would seem that both men were using the experience for slightly different ends but doubtless both enjoyed the intellectual and entrepreneurial challenges involved and ultimately there were mutual benefits.

A great deal of technical and design development was taking place at Leek and this continued throughout Wardle's long working life. Companies of international repute gave Wardle significant commissions and a number of foremost designers had their designs put into production there. Designers needed good printers and dyers to be part of the creative process in order that their design concepts could be successfully translated throughout the different production procedures and then into finished goods. The limitations of the manufacturing processes could otherwise adversely influence the outcomes. Wardle quite evidently put his theories into practice; he was a creative thinker and played an innovative role in developing designs for his company as well as experimenting with dyes and colour combinations for others. His was a constant search for high quality that he knew the market demanded, and which produced textiles that were internationally acknowledged to be of excellent quality and considered to be beautiful things. They were demanded by a certain type of consumer, and received accolades at prestigious international exhibitions. He encouraged those designers who were sympathetic to the aims of the Arts and Crafts Movement and continued with methods of production that utilised the individual's craft skills and allowed for the practice of judgement in his workforce. He would never have been allowed to exhibit in Arts and Crafts exhibitions had he not upheld the same principles as the other members.

In between his visits to Leek, Morris instructed Wardle by letter and their correspondence documented their hopes and failures in detail.[17] The following extract from Morris demonstrates their expectations: 'We want to get something quite different from the ordinary goods in the market. This is the very heart of our undertaking since we felt quite certain that the ordinary manufacturer throws away precious opportunities that the national [Natural?] fibres and dyeing drugs give him.'

Morris who was notoriously critical evidently admired Wardle's outlook as follows:

> I fully understand the value of working in open day with an honourable and sympathetic person like yourself and am quite prepared to support you by any means in my power. I am also as you must know most deeply impressed with the importance of our having all our dyes the soundest and best that can be, and am prepared to give up all this part of my business which depends on textiles if I fail in getting them so. However, I don't in the least see why I should talk about failure, which is after all impossible, as I have no doubt you feel yourself.

Although Morris clearly admired Wardle, their correspondence reveals that there were many anxieties over dyeing. That Wardle persevered with Morris's requests over many years is clear evidence of his commitment to ideals over profit. He eventually took on much of Morris and Co.'s dyeing and printing including the dyeing of yarn for woven textiles. The collaboration was successful and Morris was sufficiently encouraged to request a more extensive range of products from Wardle's firm.

The series of over 60 letters between Morris and Wardle is enlightening as it reveals many common passions – notably a shared admiration for Eastern and Indian textiles. Without doubt, each reinforced the other's interest and Indian textiles provided them with models of excellence in printing, dyeing, weaving, embroidery and carpet making. They were valued for their superiority of colour palette, arrangement of design elements, craftsmanship and continuity of tradition. Although Indian textiles were readily available, Parry argues that Morris was more directly influenced by the Indian textiles that Wardle imported, and also probably indirectly affected by the Indian influences on Wardle's own products.[18] Wardle & Co. block-printed a number of designs by William Morris, many of which display a marked Indian character, both in their design motifs and colouring; they were 'Indian Diaper', 'Snakeshead', 'Little Chintz' and 'Pomegranate'. More subtle references to Indian patterns can be seen in other designs by Morris. These are characterised either by the use of particular motifs or by a recognisably Indian colour scheme: 'Marigold', 'Larkspur', 'African Marigold' and 'Honeysuckle', were designed by Morris and hand-block printed by Wardle onto different types of silk which was hand-woven in Indian. They were exhibited in the British India section of the Paris Exhibition in 1878.

With such a wide range of experimental dyeing undertaken it was perhaps inevitable that problems did arise. Blue, the least successful and technically the most difficult colour, continually evaded Wardle who would only settle for the highest quality. Indigo gave the most satisfactory shades but required a laborious preparation process. Wardle experimented with indigo using all his knowledge as a chemist but never completely overcame its inherent difficulties. Throughout his trials he was inspired by the results which Indian dyers achieved. Although interested in all aspects of textile design it was colour that was his overriding passion; both Morris and Wardle felt it lay at the heart of successful textile design. Had colour in textile design not been a subject that deeply concerned him it is unlikely that he would have persevered with Morris's demands. Morris wrote to him outlining the qualities of a first-rate textile designer. The qualities were listed as:

1 He must have a general feeling for art, especially for its decorative side;
2 He must be a good colourist;
3 He must be able to draw well: i.e. he must be able to draw the human figure, especially the hands and feet;
4 He must know how to use the stitch of the work. Unless a man has these qualities, the first two of which are rare to meet with and cannot be taught, he will turn out nothing but bungles disgraceful to everyone concerned in the matter.[19]

The Wardle and Morris correspondence is scattered with references to ancient textiles and the value of museums and textile collections. Like Wardle, Morris admired ancient textiles and had studied them in the South Kensington Museum. Wardle later confirmed that Morris's power as a designer had partly been acquired 'through the study of olden artistic work'.[20]

As Wardle became increasingly involved with matters beyond the immediate running of his dye works, Morris wrote despairingly that Wardle was letting the quality of his work slip. This seems unlikely as he did not separate out his business practice from his ideals but continually strove for perfection in dyeing and printing. He was ethically consistent and was not searching for anything that was not also a concern of Morris. He was a member of the Art Workers' Guild, an early committee member of the Arts and Crafts Society, a frequent exhibitor and he printed designs by many of the prominent Arts and Crafts designers.[21] Surviving evidence in the form of textiles and paper designs demonstrates the versatility of his company.[22] He printed an elaborate design by L.F. Day onto velveteen in 1888 and one of

Wardle's finest fabrics, the complex 'The Four Seasons' by Walter Crane, was printed onto silk in 1893. It was considered a tour de force, and shown at the Arts and Crafts exhibition that year. Wardle summarised his work with Morris and the difficult conditions imposed on him, as something he never wished to experience again.

Despite the various problems the Wardle-Morris collaboration was clearly instructive for both men. Long after their business association had ended Wardle referred to Morris in intimate terms and freely acknowledged that his advances in printing were due to Morris's influence.[23] Despite the high calibre of the silk and the designs from avant-garde designers, Wardle's Hencroft Works faced financial difficulties during the 1890s. During the same period the Churnet Works, which employed 74 men, was not making a profit and was kept running out of regard for the workers and their families.[24]

Was Wardle so very different from other manufacturers in the silk trade? He paid tribute to Ruskin and Morris often, discussed their theories at length and upheld them as models for the *entire* textile industry when he lectured, for instance to other manufacturers, educators or students. Furthermore, Wardle's thoughts were widely known and acted upon. This would not have been the case if his ideas had been completely at odds with those of his fellow manufacturers and those who were training the workforce. Wardle was neither idiosyncratic nor operating in a vacuum. In working with prominent designers he was following a practice similar to that of other prominent textile manufacturers such as Alexander Morton,[25] G.P. Baker,[26] Benjamin Warner[27] and Turnbull and Stockdale.[28] All of these leading industrialists were committed to a business practice that embraced Arts and Crafts values. All were noted for their sound knowledge of design, interest in traditional hand techniques and an understanding of how colour worked in a textile. The same manufacturers owned collections of Indian textiles, which were a strong force in the development of their companies' designs. Moreover, like Morris and Wardle, they all placed great emphasis on educating the workforce. Benjamin Warner purchased a number of designs from art school students, deliberately fostering links between education and manufacturing.

Wardle's work with William Morris has been broadly documented but Morris always overshadowed him; to reverse the trend is interesting. This study of his contemporary reveals Morris as less of an isolated figure and even as less radical than some have suggested. Morris has been credited with 'having almost single-handedly reformed public taste and revolutionized the domestic interior'.[29] As a man driven by the need to put wrongs right, Wardle made every effort to write and speak to the widest audience, all the time demonstrating his independence of thought. Moreover, he was often called to speak publicly on what were evidently shared concerns with other manufacturers. As a retailer, with a shop at 71 New Bond Street, London (from 1882 to 1888), he was aware of consumers' demands, and as a chemist he communicated knowledgeably with other scientists. Many of his lectures were delivered to leading art and design schools throughout the country, others were published and were available to an international audience. Overall he was a practical man who could see the advantages of traditional methods and dovetailed these with the benefits of modern developments. He was not sentimental but spoke from first-hand knowledge. Idealism was tempered by the realities of making a living. In this combination lay the strength and the value of his opinion.

The Leek Embroidery Society

As part of his promotion of Indian *tasar* silk, Thomas Wardle called on the skills of his wife Elizabeth, who founded the Leek Embroidery Society in 1879. She devised a form of embroidery that employed the qualities of *tasar* floss (untwisted) silk, having found that its long lustrous fibres made it particularly suitable for needlework. Elizabeth Wardle had regular contact with William Morris when he visited her home and was clearly aware of the influence that Morris had on needlework design. Morris developed close links with the Leek Embroidery Society, designing a number of pieces for it, including a carpet.

The Leek Embroidery Society became a notable one and Thomas Wardle was spurred on by the growing interest in Arts and Crafts embroideries to develop his dyeing of *tasar* yarn using natural dyes. This new use of the silk was to have a major impact on its demand and was acknowledged to have significantly increased Indian exports.[30] Leek embroidery had its own department in Thomas Wardle's shop in New Bond Street, in William Morris's shop in Oxford Street, London and Liberty & Co. Regent Street, London. Leek embroidery was developed in a kit form, the base cloth was block-printed with an embroidery design and sold complete with the appropriate silk threads – the design was then stitched by the customer at home. Partly due to the growing success of the Arts and Crafts Movement, there was already an increasing demand from embroiderers for a soft, lustrous thread in a subtle range of colours. Moreover, embroidery was a major feature of fashionable dress for women and children, and remained so until the First World War.

Surviving pieces of Leek embroidery show clearly how Elizabeth Wardle experimented with the lustrous *tasar* thread and used the deep vegetable dyes to great effect. A distinctive Leek style evolved based on simple stitch techniques that created rich textures. The base cloth chosen as a backdrop for the ecclesiastical pieces was often a brocaded silk with a woven self-coloured pattern. Many of the embroidered motifs were appliquéd onto the silk and did not necessary relate directly to the brocaded design underneath; the effect created was luxurious. The embroiderers both developed their own designs and received commissions from noted designers and Arts and Crafts architects who were seeking textiles and vestments to compliment their church designs. Walter Crane, William Morris, Norman Shaw, John Sedding, Gerald Hawsley and John Rigby, among others, provided designs for the Leek Embroidery Society. Colour plate 12 shows a detail from a Leek embroidery with Indian *tasar* silk thread worked onto woven silk brocade, which is typical of the ecclesiastical designs. Secular designs were usually repeat patterns hand block-printed onto *tasar* silk, hand-woven in India. The stitching generally followed the printed pattern. Leek embroidery was also applied to plain *tasar* silk, woollen cloth, velvet and velveteen.

The main appeal of the Leek embroidery lay in its beautiful colouring. Thomas Wardle dyed the Indian *tasar* silk yarns to the exact subtle shade required using vegetable dyes. The rich appearance of Leek embroidery was obtained by the use of densely packed stitches that maximised the lustre of floss silk with its long filaments. The thread could be stitched in such a way that it reflected light in different directions. Simple knots were occasionally used, as were spangles; the practice of outlining some of the motifs with couched gold thread emphasised the sumptuous treatment. The placing of motifs close together added to the opulent effect. Designs often contained scrolling elements and diaper patterns that were influenced by Indian designs, which were very suitable for enrichment with floss silk embroidery. Colour plate 13 shows a panel of Leek embroidery entitled 'Indian Poppy'. It demonstrates the use of the lustrous Indian *tasar* thread and the range of delicate shades that could be produced. The design was hand-block printed in a brick red by Thomas Wardle, onto an undyed *tasar* silk cloth woven in India. The rich lustre of the stitching forms a contrast against the natural deep gold of the matt *tasar* silk cloth.

As well as utilising designs from some leading Arts and Crafts designers, many of the Leek embroideries owed their inspiration to Indian textiles. Some were direct copies of Indian patterns or were inspired by their colour schemes or motifs. Colour plate 14 is an example of such a design, which was used as a border. Through her embroidery designs and their colouring Elizabeth Wardle was acknowledged as having contributed to the growing interest in the adaptability of India's designs.[31] In 1881 Sir Philip Cunliffe Owen, a friend of the Wardles and director of South Kensington Museum, opened an exhibition of Leek embroidery. He also designed an embroidery for the Society. It was a prestigious event. Alongside the Leek exhibits were 7 pieces by William Morris; and the Royal School of Needlework sent 43 pieces for display. The exhibition catalogue described numerous pieces of Leek embroidery with an evident influence from Indian designs. The scrolling lines of many Indian patterns translated well to this form of needlework and Indian fabrics were fashionable at that time. Moreover, Thomas Wardle had returned from India in 1886 with sketches he had made of the ancient Ajanta cave paintings, and was inspired to produce designs from them. 'Ajanta' was produced as both an embroidery on a cream tasar silk ground stitched in terracotta, moss green and lapis lazuli blue, generously highlighted with gold thread, and also as a block-printed velvet.

Conclusion

The surviving textiles, designs and documentation clearly demonstrate that there was a great deal of necessary collaboration between the aesthetic avant-garde and a number of leading textile manufacturers in the last third of the nineteenth century. Although William Morris was outstanding as a designer, he was not alone in his stance against shoddily produced goods, or the struggle to find appropriate designs, and he had much in common with a number of leading designers and manufacturers. His role as a designer, who became personally involved with the demands of production, was matched in its intensity by producers such as Thomas Wardle, who became involved with the theory behind design as well as the techniques.

The material outcome of the Arts and Crafts Movement, in design terms, was, moreover, less radical than some of its ideals. In fact the success of the textiles was predicated on their fulfilling particular design conventions that had been employed in some cultures for centuries. It is reasonable to presume that this was a factor that helped to raise the status of English textiles abroad. Furthermore, the particular aesthetic that developed as a result of the movement, along with many of its associated ideals, was promoted in art and technical colleges. Colour plates 1, 2 and 10 show woven silks designed by students at Macclesfield College of Art, c.1910; they are a blend of Indian design and Arts and Crafts influence, which has produced an English sensibility. At this point, the Art Nouveau style was in vogue and it was also characterised by naturalistic plant and flower motifs and designs with sinuous curving lines.

Throughout the period of the Arts and Crafts Movement, the consumer was at the centre of the picture. Commercial success rested on satisfying a section of the English middle classes, who needed to be dissuaded from buying foreign goods. It was often textile manufacturers who provided the all-important bridge between the designer and the consumer. Furthermore, this was not short-lived: a number of Arts and Crafts designers and silk manufacturers maintained successful working relationships well into the 1930s. However, in the case of silk, it was possibly consequential that some manufacturers were sympathetic to the Arts and Crafts cause. Silk manufacture retained more hand processes due to its nature, and as a consequence silk remained as a luxury commodity affordable only by the wealthy.

Wardle was able to uphold many Arts and Crafts principles, as shoddy goods and exploitation were subjects about which he felt deeply. His intention was always to produce goods of the highest standard and this included good design. He was a manufacturer whom Morris knew could operate within the commercial world, yet who was principled and held socially responsible opinions rather than being governed solely by the profit motive. Commitment to these principles had important implications for his business; and he recognised that he had a duty to supply the public with well-made and appropriately designed goods at fair prices. Furthermore, his proposals for design improvement were rooted in his concerns with an unstable global industry and the elimination of poverty, which was often a related feature. In their combined efforts, European commercial and entrepreneurial advances accommodated both English and Indian interests. Indian silk producers and officials collaborated with English enterprise, as it was beneficial to do so. Otherwise events such as the Indian and Colonial Exhibition of 1886 and Manchester's Royal Jubilee Exhibition would not have had the extensive displays of Indian silks that they did.

Like other upholders of Arts and Crafts principles, Wardle believed in the power of beauty to enrich everyday life for all and not just for the privileged few, and he remained convinced that beauty could be found in all manner of everyday things if they were well made. Good textile design, therefore, offered more than utilitarian possibilities. Beautiful designs were provided for those consumers who wanted an alternative to mainstream textile production. In particular, he had formed very strong opinions on colour, to the extent that he felt a professorship in colour theory should be created. He justified his comments by explaining the therapeutic value of good colour and colour combinations, which could give harmony to all aspects of life. As he stated: 'All decorative work has for its object the increasing of the

happiness of life, the output of coloured and patterned work must
be artistic if to be lasting and pleasant in the living with it.'

Notes

1   Naylor, 1990 (first published 1971), p. 7.
2   Banham, Macdonald and Porter, p. 107.
3   Parry, London, 1988, p. 133.
4   Naylor, 1990 (first edition 1971), p. 113.
5   Morris, p. 33.
6   *The Illustrated London News*, 12 Nov. 1885.
7   Liberty archives, Westminster City archives, London.
8   Wardle's pattern books, with details and samples of dye trials, are housed at the
    Whitworth Art Gallery, Manchester, and the Victoria and Albert Museum.
9   Adburgham, 1992, p. 42.
10 *La Mode Illustree.*
11 Quoted in Gillow, 1988, p. 4.
12 Ibid.
13 Ruskin, Lecture Three: 96, 'Modern Manufacture and Design', *The Two Paths*,
    1887, p. 129.
14 Ibid.
15 Ibid., p. 132.
16 November 1875, Sir Thomas Wardle Papers, Duke University, Durham, NC, USA.
17 Ninety letters from Morris to Wardle date from 3 August 1875 to 20 October 1881
    (one from 1896). Two letters are from Jane (Burden) Morris to Wardle. The corre-
    spondence documents their business relationship in great detail. It is now in the
    Special Collections Library, Duke University, Durham, NC, USA.
18 Parry, London, 1996, p. 260.
19 Sir Thomas Wardle Papers, Duke University, Durham, NC, USA.
20 Stated in a lecture by Wardle: *Tissue or Textile Printing as an Art*, at Manchester
    Municipal School of Art Museum.
21 Designs by Butterfield, Crane, Day, Doran, Mawson, Miller, Reuter, Solon and
    Voysey were printed by Wardle.
22 Examples of the companies products are in the Whitworth Art Gallery, Manches-
    ter and the Victoria and Albert Museum, London.
23 On Morris's advice Wardle had sent his youngest son to the Manchester School of
    Art. Under Mr Willis, he then attended South Kensington before becoming a part-
    ner in the Leek firm, continuing the family printing business with his brother. His
    designs show the utility of a thorough training in the leading art schools.
24 Jacques, Staffs, 1996, p. 106. During this period this site was managed by Arthur
    Wardle, son of Thomas.
25 A collection of Indian textiles donated by the Morton family to the Whitworth Art
    Gallery, Manchester.
26 Baker, Tucker and Co. were importers of Indian silk goods, and silk printers at one
    point. Baker was knowledgeable on Indian textile production and published an
    extensive work on printed cotton textiles: *Calico Painting and Printing in the East
    Indies in the XVII–XVIII Centuries*, 1921. Part of the Baker archive of Indian
    textiles is now housed in the Indian and South-East Asian Department of the
    Victoria and Albert Museum.
27 Owen Jones produced at least sixteen designs for woven silks for Warner. They
    clearly show his theories of textile design.
28 L.F. Day was the chief designer for this firm for many years.
29 Banham, Macdonald and Porter, London, 1991, p. 81.
30 Yusuf Ali, Allahabad, India, p. 7.
31 The Silk Industries of India and the Life and Work of Sir Thomas Wardle, JP, FCS
    FGS. *Journal of Indian Art & Industry*, 1909.

CHAPTER EIGHT

Legacies

Textiles have been the most prominent of the many goods that have passed between East and West. The wealth of several nations has depended on their designs, which often reflected both national and international values. For centuries the West assimilated Asia's materials, techniques and designs, and the ancient textile traditions, particularly those of India, are now confirmed as major influences on English textile development. We cannot conceive of European textiles today without taking into account the enduring influence of India's textile traditions on Western manufactures. This Indian legacy was acknowledged by a wide range of provincial and metropolitan institutions as well as by influential individuals. The range of material and documentary evidence surviving in many English archives testifies to the commitment to designs based on universally accepted principles over many centuries. The long history of India's textile influence stretches back to classical times and this makes the study of silk history a rich field with considerable scope.

Western manufacturers frequently and publicly considered Indian textiles as superior to their European counterparts. During the latter half of the nineteenth century this admiration grew, and Indian textiles had a major influence on the English silk industry. They were upheld as exemplars, which demonstrated to designers, industrialists, artisans, theorists, educators and consumers alike, good design principles, inspirational use of colour and the highest standards of technical excellence. Theoretical interest in Indian design continued throughout the nineteenth century as noted English figures published works that reinforced existing trends. A number of authors assumed a wider viewpoint, which also considered the society that produced the cloth. Theories arising out of India's textile tradition were rigorously promoted by a number of influential members of the Arts and Crafts Movement, including William Morris, Walter Crane and L.F. Day. Even

John Ruskin, with his rigid views on British imperialism, declared his admiration for Indian textile designs. The great champion of Turner's work paid Indian artisans his highest compliment, when he compared the painter's masterpieces with 'colours in an Indian design'.[1] In one lecture, in which he discussed examples of Indian decorative art held in many English institutions he stated:

> [F]or the teaching of design, there are, I suppose, none in their kind more admirable than the decorated works of India. They are, indeed, in all materials capable of colour – wool, marble, or metal – almost inimitable in their delicate application of divided hue, and the fine arrangement of fantastic line . . . the love of subtle design seems universal in that race, and is developed in every important implement that they shape, and every building that they raise.[2]

Although members of the Arts and Crafts Movement aimed to raise the level of the applied arts to that of the fine arts, it proved difficult to do this where Indian art and design was concerned, where the situation was reversed. Although Indian design was greatly admired, Indian painting and sculpture was generally related to that nation's belief system; as such Ruskin did not accept them. This aspect alone highlights the complex and paradoxical nature of the subject. And, as Mitter argues, the Western world has still to find a way to appreciate the values of Indian art in its own context and in its own right.[3]

Many of William Morris's quintessentially English designs were inspired by and included recognisably Indian features. They were ideological models for him in many respects and he saw in them an important educative force. He supported George Birdwood who alerted him to the fact that Indian craft skills, along with the communities that produced them, were in danger of disappearing. Idealised versions of Indian village communities were then contrasted with a critical judgement of Western industrialisation. When Birdwood was working in the Indian medical service, he had documented the complex dress codes he encountered there, detailing the reasons for them, and actively campaigned for the preservation of native dress, arguing that it was threatened by the impact of European fashion.

Birdwood was particularly knowledgeable of Indian silks and documented them in great detail, along with the complexity of the historical and contemporary textile trade; from village level to the global export market. He admired Indian textiles for their coherent colour schemes, the scale of the motifs and prodigious technical expertise. He was totally convinced that the Indian approach to design was superior to English and French models. A publication such as Birdwood's provided a framework of scholarship and established Indian textiles in international mainstream history at that time. His publication indicates that traditional methods of production were still widely practised to a high standard.

Traditional Indian culture was considered to be superior by more than one authority. India's customs were acknowledged as advantageous, even enviable; and their textiles became ideological models signifying a traditional way of life. Tradition was commonly accepted to have protected an unbroken design practice, which could be traced back to antiquity. India's textiles assumed a distinctively pedagogical role, which positively influenced the European textile industry and commerce. Thomas Wardle's humility in acknowledging the superiority of Indian textiles in many respects, while bringing his own expertise to aid their continuation, is a case in point. His actions exemplify the healthy relationship between two cultures: East and West, and aesthetics and science. The relationship was one between equals addressing aesthetic and technical problems against a background of shared values and mutual respect.

The emphasis in this book is on collections of Indian silk textiles surviving in England and it demonstrates that the silks were clearly more than a design repertoire for the export trade. They were far from being merely exotic objects of curiosity, or aspects of a fashionable 'Oriental' phase. They were the subject of intelligent appreciation and scholarly enquiry in many cultures outside India, including Britain. The very visible evidence of costly and technically complex Indian silk textiles in English collections is a powerful indicator of continuing traditional textile skills that were still practised. Silk production was still much in evidence, and traditional symbolic designs continued to be produced to a very high standard throughout the nineteenth century and the beginning of the twentieth century. The same collections demonstrate the widespread interest with which these textiles were regarded in a number of spheres.

The numerous textile collections that were established in England were one aspect of the rich cultural exchange that was England's strong historical connection with India. The collections were one means by which India's designs were disseminated during the period researched for this publication, although this had not previously been clearly established. They were frequently the legacy of major international exhibitions, which were time and again the stimulus, as well as the source, of core collections in public museums in England and India. Exhibits and their associated knowledge were disseminated to various institutions in order that they might leave a long-term inheritance beyond the short life of the exhibition: many can still be seen today particularly in the provinces, where they provided much needed

longer lasting access. Indian textiles were seen as sufficiently import-
ant to be among the first items to form the core collections of South
Kensington Institute (now the Victoria and Albert) Museum and the
Whitworth Institute (now the Whitworth Art Gallery).

Until the 1860s, the South Kensington Museum had relatively few
textiles, other than the fine contemporary Indian silks, that were an
important indicator of their status. Very few other textiles were displayed other than those exhibiting 'false principles of design'; in contrast, the Indian fabrics displayed 'true principles'.[4] The Museum
acquired those objects that were already a source of public interest; at
the time of the museum's founding there was a great fascination with
India for a number of reasons. Generally there was increasing interest
in archaeology, anthropology, ancient languages and the origin of the
human species; they combined to highlight India as a place of extreme
antiquity, possibly the 'cradle of the universe'. Since the eighteenth
century, numerous volumes had been written on Indian culture and
English artists had travelled and recorded life there in picturesque
paintings and drawings. Moreover, the East India Company had been
trading in textiles since the early seventeenth century and many Indian
designs and techniques had become very familiar and covetable. As
a great deal of interest in India existed before the Great Exhibition
of 1851, there was an expectant audience for Indian manufactures.
The Great Exhibition, however, served interests that went beyond the
gratification of curiosity; and Indian exhibits became the focus of
debates on appropriate design. An examination of the literature produced by prestigious theorists involved with both the Exhibition and
the founding of the Museum of Ornamental Art, reveals a prodigious
knowledge of Indian manufactures, especially textiles.

A mass of evidence indicates the importance that museum textile
collections had for the English textile industries. It was some time
after the founding of the South Kensington Museum, however, before
textile collections in provincial centres of manufacturing became established. They were then closer to manufacturing bases and consequently
of more direct use to those connected with industry. The Forbes
Watson volumes, *The Textile Fabrics of India*, were in essence a series
of mobile museums, which furnished many provincial towns with a
wide range of India's indigenous textile products, albeit in small pieces.
This collection now provides us with valuable dating criteria, which
demonstrates that high standards of a very wide range of craft skills
relating to most branches of textile production were still practised in
the mid-nineteenth century.

Among other things, the curators, theorists, educators and industrialists were using collections to demonstrate that there was no

mystery to understanding good design. There in museums and in exhibitions were superb examples of design practice, exemplified in India's textiles. It was only necessary for the modern English designer and artisan to examine them and comprehend their underlying principles. By working with the same spirit of awareness, using the best of materials, it was thought that they too could produce well-designed fabrics for the international market. Through the same displays the public was also being offered demonstrations of design coherency that was purposely instructive. Indian designers did not produce meaningless, eclectic patterns or apply motifs in a haphazard, meretricious manner. What was evident in the Indian tradition was a complete understanding of the nature of raw materials, the ability to work with them in a way that utilised and expressed their qualities along with an evident consideration of the function of the cloth. All factors that were all too evidently absent from many mass-produced English textiles.

One purpose of this book has been to provide an account of those exemplary silk textile collections, particularly the significance of the provincial archives, which for the first time have been identified as manifestly important. It has aimed to clarify the means by which India's silk textiles were made available to English silk manufacturers through collections that were formed to stimulate the English and Indian silk trades – a subject relatively unexplored. The range of interconnected issues and policies surrounding such collections embrace aspects of English design education, collecting and exhibiting, design theory and manufacturing. By drawing heavily on contemporary qualitative and quantitative evidence in the form of data, objects, texts and other visual material, important aspects of a major international industry and its trading activities have been identified and pieced together. The point of departure for this research has been the object, at every point the research into English and Indian silk history has been anchored in the tangible reality of the silk textiles surviving in these collections. A central aspect of the task has, however, been the formation of an historical context for understanding these objects.

It is significant that more woven and embroidered Indian silks were initially collected for major collections than any other Indian fabric type, for example printed cotton fabric, possibly because printed cottons were widely known. Many English cotton manufactures had utilised Indian motifs for a considerable length of time, even exporting their version of them to India. Since one of the primary purposes of the museums was didactic why did they acquire so many elaborate and costly silk textiles, created with a wide range of demanding artisanal skills? It was unlikely that these cloths were intended to be adapted to machine production – the very area of English manufacturing that was rapidly increasing and causing so much design-related concern. Because of the complexity of many of the designs, many of the silk brocades would have taken a master weaver in India between six and twelve months to produce a sari length. Why therefore, include such elaborate pieces in museum collections? The evidence suggests that they were intended to work as exemplars. The major collections were formed when debates over appropriate design were raging. Manufacturers were calling for the provision of regional textile museums to assist their understanding of successful design. A better understanding of design principles was considered to be necessary for competitive advantage in an industry that faced fierce competition from foreign imports. Countries that were well provided with regional textile collections produced many of the textiles imported into Britain and English manufacturers openly acknowledged the particular advantage of these resources as global commercial trading was a fact of daily life.

It was widely acknowledged that they demonstrated sound principles from which artisans, manufacturers and consumers could learn. The exquisite colour combinations evident in these examples were their primary advantage, as good colouring was vital for successful textile production. These examples, furthermore, were produced using natural dyes. Important lessons were to be learnt from this aspect alone – lessons that many considered as imperative in order to counteract the harsh tones of chemical dyes which were proliferating in the English textile industry and infiltrating India. The superior examples of hand technology also functioned as counterpoints to shoddy, machine-made goods, reinforcing the notion that mass production had almost ruined English craft skills, which many considered were in danger of disappearing.

Moreover, given the evidence of the surviving objects and the concerns expressed in the latter half of the nineteenth century, it is reasonable to assume that such a concentration of Indian silks in important textile collections may have been a deliberate strategy to shake the supremacy of the French. France was England's main competitor in silk production and French silks made for the luxury markets were openly acknowledged to be supreme. The fact that many of the Indian silks in collections were the costliest and technically the most complex available may have been a political gesture – a calculated offensive against the French. The expanse of gold brocades and other elaborate silks, furthermore, indicated a luxury market in India to which the French manufactures had no access. Such long-standing technical mastery would have been provocative for French manufacturers, particularly as these silks were made within the British

Empire, signifying imperial status and conspicuous consumption in no uncertain terms. Such examples were calculated to shake the English consumer's loyalty to French products, widening their experience of the silk products of the British Empire. Therefore, there was a lot at stake when these textiles were collected. Moreover, their role was symbiotic as they were expected to demonstrate new possibilities for the Indian and English silk industries alike.

Showing the best examples that India could produce using its indigenous silks, in exhibitions and thereafter in major museums, was another calculated effort on the part of Indian and English governments designed to draw attention to the great possibilities of India's raw materials. To a large extent these efforts paid off. English and French manufacturers increasingly imported their raw materials from India, once production problems had been overcome.

Although stimulated by collections of India's silk textiles and their role in English silk manufacturing, this publication does not pretend to be an exhaustive record of either country's silk industry. It restricts itself to an analysis of those events which moulded the main lines of development during a period of empire when both the English and Indian silk industries were experiencing severe difficulties. The intention is to sketch in the major features and trends, in order to locate the pivotal collections historically. Detailed trade figures, particularly those from India, were difficult to obtain and more research here would obviously be useful. Archive material has, nevertheless, permitted a partial reconstruction of the international silk industry in the nineteenth century, an area that up to now has not been fully explored. This evidence shows that numerous economic factors such as severe trade depression in both India and England influenced the acquisition of Indian silks for collections in England. Anxiety over competition with France was coupled with debates on design principles and design education.

Archival study has revealed that both complex and simple silk cloths from India were collected. Whether this was due entirely to economic imperatives is not possible to say. It can confidently be stated, however, that an interest in India's designs increased in England during the period between 1830 and 1930. This interest took different forms. At times it focused on different aesthetic and technical aspects, particularly the understanding of dyes and the skilful use of colour – a vital aspect for the English silk textile trades and their competition with France. At others times the symbolic nature of the designs, or the nature of the society that produced them provided models for an idealised, traditional way of life. Indian design at one point was a focal point in theoretical discussions on design, and its perceived underlying principles were held to be superior to those of the 'advanced' industrial countries of Europe.

Although the book is primarily concerned with objects, the task of establishing the criteria against which the qualities of textiles were assessed required analysis of a large selection of contemporary texts. They emanated from different sectors such as education, industry and aesthetic theory, and from different nations, and yet they occupied common ground in their interpretation of events relating to silk textile design. For, although the object alone can be a seemingly irrefutable item of evidence in some aspects, it was also necessary to consider theories and concepts relevant at the time the textiles were produced, in order to fully understand their cultural context and aid interpretation. Of course, even an engagement with the past via both objects and documents cannot guarantee that objective knowledge will emerge. Nevertheless, writers from a variety of backgrounds upheld Indian silks as exemplars. Furthermore, there was much cross-referencing; educators referred to museums, theorists referred to educators, and manufacturers to consumers and so on; a clear indication that there were shared values.

In the light of the findings of this research, the relative absence of the important role of Indian design in cultural and design history texts demands some explanation. In the course of an evaluation of the relevant literature, it became increasingly apparent that late-twentieth century histories of nineteenth-century design have given little attention to the role that Indian design played. There are several dimensions to this. It could be argued that this has been due to a lack of awareness of primary evidence in the form of the objects themselves, along with the secondary evidence that supports them. It might be the case that design historians have been ignorant of the nineteenth-century literature on design, in which Indian textiles were represented in a positive manner in discussions relating to the 'good' design debates and design education.

Certain commentators have tended to emphasise the passivity of Indian manufacturers during the period of empire. This view runs the risk not only of being deeply patronising, but continues to promote the universality of notions of Eurocentric superiority and Indian inferiority in the period. This view cannot embrace the evidence in the form of objects and texts discussed in this book, or accommodate the complex relationships that made up the Anglo-Indian textile trades. Moreover, it has served to discourage more positive accounts of Anglo-Indian collaboration. This has done a great disservice to the history of Indian design, helping to marginalise it and leaving a skewed Eurocentric history as dominant. As Das Gupta argued, what happened in India was subject to internal forces as well as to external ones.[5] The history of both the English and the Indian silk industries was one of cyclical changes, booms and slumps, before and throughout the era of empire. Colonialism did not always involve systematic control and exploitation. In the case of silks there were serious imperatives for both nations to collaborate and encourage silk production in England and India alike. Trade had its own agenda and regional factors often overrode national concerns. The point here is not to judge the impact of the British Empire on India, or on international commerce, since this embodies vast and valid concerns, which go beyond the scope of this publication. Rather the aim is to highlight evidence that acknowledges the mutually beneficial nature of the West's debt to India and India's debt to the West, as is evident in silk textile history during the period of Empire.

The relationship between West and East is a theme that has been much discussed in post-colonial studies and this has fuelled an interest in reassessing Britain's colonial past. This interest has not extended to issues surrounding textile design, however, even though it is a particularly germane area of investigation. Indian textile designs need to be part of this activity, not only because they were a major component of early trade and imperialism, but also because they had a major and positive impact on European design development that is still current. Although there was a variety of opinion stemming from many participants in nineteenth-century industry, education and museums, the superiority of Indian design and technical skills, particularly in the understanding of dyes and the use of colour, was constantly emphasised. Such admiration was hardly typical of the assumptions about the Orient, which Said argued were prevalent, and which he sums up thus: 'everything in it was, if not patently inferior to, then in need of corrective study by the West'.[6] Edward Said's *Orientalism* was a landmark publication that stimulated debate on aspects of the West's relationship with the Islamic East. Said argued that the essence of Orientalism is the ineradicable distinction between Western superiority and Oriental inferiority. With a few important exceptions,[7] post-*Orientalism* publications do not include design and design historians have, for the most part, failed to challenge Said's arguments, although the material evidence and a scholarly corpus provides us with the tools with which to do so.

The positive dimensions of English views of India may have been overlooked due to an uncritical dependence on texts that stress the total disruption of the Indian textile trades as a result of the hegemonic British. One outcome of this is that the positive role of Indian and other influences on Western design is downplayed if not ignored by theoreticians. Greater critical attention needs to be paid to the ways in which theory is uncritically accepted. For as Good cautions, hegemony can lie in theory itself, which is now 'in the process of dissolving the discipline it was originally supposed to theorize'.[8] The value placed on Indian design has, therefore, yet to be fully explored in this context. MacKenzie, who disagrees with Said's theory, clearly points out that there is a far greater variety of opinion than Said allows for and argues that at its height 'imperialism, far from coinciding with a down-grading of the arts of the subordinate peoples of the East ... actually coincided with a new appreciation.[9] As Vanke so cogently explains,[10] and as the evidence used for this book demonstrates, nineteenth-century English decorative design stands out as an area which contradicts the original Saidian thesis particularly strongly and forms part of a serious objection to Said's approach in general. Stewart confirms this and categorically affirms that until these post-colonial discourses are 'undermined, no true picture of empire can emerge'.[11] There needs to be room made to accommodate the variety of cultural exchanges that happened, 'and which formed and re-formed both coloniser and colonised'.[12] The evidence presented here indicates that post-colonial theories have not been examined with sufficient care. India's historic past was acknowledged by many as a noble one and its continuation of a traditional way of life was seen as a positive, even enviable, force. Although the presence of the English in India gave them varying degrees of direct or indirect control, the involvement of men like Thomas Wardle, with his ideological position and technical expertise used for the benefit of India's silk trade, was collaborative. Wardle's respect for the Indian craft worker was unstinting in its praise. Not to recognise this as such would indeed be patronising to the Indian producers, who knew well the value that was placed on their goods in the West, and the importance of the Western market to their economy.

It is hoped that the evidence presented here will allow future researchers to better understand the specifics of India's strengths during the period of British rule; strengths that were acknowledged, admired and fostered in Europe. We know that English silk manufacturers and artisans could experience the highest quality Indian silks in all the major centres of production. The presence of extraordinary collections of Indian textiles in the provinces and in London presented opportunities to examine closely not only technically complex silk goods, but also alternatives to the standard European design repertoire. The presence of collections of similar textiles in different types of English institutions indicates the application of a set of widely-acknowledged principles to the process of selection and recording, adding another layer of meaning to the individual items. Furthermore, although most of the collections remained separate, yet each is also now changed through the revelation of their shared history. The cumulative nature of the evidence can now be recognised as their conjoint history is revealed, confirming the key importance accounted to Indian design across many fields.

Some recent texts dealing with the development of museums and their culture since the eighteenth century have tended to focus on the theatrical, triumphalist, aspects of display, emphasising the appropriation of goods from unwilling or unknowing parties. This has tended to remove collections of objects of commerce, such as textiles, from their mundane but most important context: the marketplace and industry. Accounts, which have concentrated on more emotive issues such as appropriation or domination at work in the formation of European museum collections, fail to acknowledge the practicalities of international trade. This suggests an obsession with one-way global relationships of inequality, which distorts interpretations. Whilst appropriation and domination may be important issues, they are not automatically pertinent to discussions of Indian goods. India has, since records began, been continuously referred to as a trading nation. Its textiles were, for millennia, produced for foreign markets as well as domestic ones, and exported accordingly. There was a sophisticated awareness of international trade well before the existence of the European East India companies. Interpretations that do not acknowledge this fact obscure the vital connections between commerce and culture, trade and scholarship and the role of design within these. The evidence used to write this book demonstrates the economic importance accorded to Indian textiles in the nineteenth century, through the firm interconnections between museum collections, manufacturing, education and consumption. In fact, Indian textiles were more the subject of admiration than appropriation.

It is hoped that this book has demonstrated that Indian silks were admired by English textile manufacturers both for their technical and aesthetic attributes, and for their ability to help undermine French supremacy in European silk production. Archival evidence also indicates that at key times English textile designers took inspiration from both India and the Arts and Crafts Movement. The result was a melding of attributes from both, producing an English sensibility in silk designs, which considerably affected European designs. This was what Wardle, and others such as Morris, Jones, Crane and Day hoped for.

The book does not merely question the conventional view of how Indian design was regarded in nineteenth-century England. It also questions the blanket acceptance that English textile design was uniformly degenerate in the period, and the common assumption that the Arts and Crafts Movement was totally at odds with all English textile manufacturing. Both of these widely-held views have contributed to some narrowly focused analyses of nineteenth-century English textile design. Such interpretations have served to reinforce the notion that matters of 'good' design were of little importance to the generality of nineteenth-century textile manufacturers. The evidence assessed here contests this view and suggests that recent histories fail to reflect just how much attention the campaigns to improve design received from nineteenth-century textile manufacturers.

An important area for further consideration, which this study suggests, is the issue of the ruination of India's handicrafts. That British rule ruined Indian handicrafts is an established view.[13] This research suggests at the very least that this position needs qualification. Two points in particular need reiterating. Firstly, the complex craft skills needed to produce silk goods of the highest order were still in evidence during the period under review. Secondly, 14 million people earn their living today by handloom weaving fine cloth in India and contribute to the economy.[14] Recent exhibitions have demonstrated that highly sophisticated artisanal skills are still producing the finest textiles based on traditional designs.[15] The enduring nature of India's traditional designs and skills are, furthermore, still a touchstone for today's designers, makers and consumers in the West and the East.

Lastly, and perhaps most importantly, research into India's archives would aid our understanding of the Indian perspective on a process that has been approached in this publication predominantly from the English end of what was a two-way relationship.

Notes

1 Mitter, 1977, p. 242.
2 Ruskin, 1859: a lecture given at the Museum of Ornamental Art.
3 Mitter, 1977, p. viii.
4 Persian textiles also acted as exemplars, along with Chinese, although they were fewer in number.
5 Das Gupta, 1979. Das Gupta was director of the National Library of India and historian of Asia's sea-borne trade of the seventeenth and eighteenth centuries.
6 Said, 1985 (reprinted 1991), pp. 40–1.
7 MacKenzie, 1995; Sweetman, 1987.
8 Good, 1996, p. 535.
9 MacKenzie, 1995, p. 107.
10 Vanke, 1998.
11 Stewart, *Jute and Empire*, p. 193.
12 Ibid., p. 194.
13 *Inter alia*, Head, 1988, pp. 118, 121; Chhachhi, 1983, p. 39.
14 *Hand Made in India*, The Crafts Council, London, 1998, p. 11.

15 The Crafts Council's touring exhibition *Hand Made in India*, presented contemporary Indian crafts to a British audience, demonstrating how they have responded to new markets and changing ways of life. The textile exhibits demonstrated how fresh influences and techniques have been absorbed; yet the outcome was unmistakably Indian. The Crafts Council, London 1998, *Minakar*, was an exhibition that showed contemporary Indian silk and precious metal textiles. They demonstrated a level of technical and artistic excellence which recalled the highest skills practised in the past. Martand Singh, ed., *Minakar: Spun Gold and Woven Enamel*, The National Museum, New Delhi, India, 1997; the British Museum, London, 1999.

BIBLIOGRAPHY

MANUSCRIPTS

Bradford and Ilkley Community College, Textile Archive

Volumes of students' work books, c.1900–10: lecture notes, course details relating to drawing, design, colour and technical exercises, samples of woven cloth. Examples of students' work sent for examination.
Textile Manufacturer, *Textile Recorder* and *Textile Society Journal*.
John Forbes Watson, *Textile Fabrics of India*, first and second series.

Leek, Staffordshire, The Nicholson Institute

Transcripts of Thomas Wardle's papers, including:
  Address: *English Art and Industries*, to students, School of Art, Burslem, Staffs, 1887.
  Address: *The Relationship Which Should Exist Between Art Schools and Technical Instruction*, Fenton, North Staffs, 1891.
  Address: *Tissue or Textile Printing as an Art*, Manchester Municipal School of Art, 1899.
  Address: *Education and Causes of Unemployment*, Technical School, Halifax, 1905.
  Address: Bath Technical School, 1907.
  Address: *Art and the Revival of the Silk Trade*, Macclesfield, 1908.
  Address: *The Relation of Design to Such Craft Teaching as May be Undertaken by Technical Schools*, The Art Workers Guild, n.d.
  Address: *Education and Art*, School of Art, Stoke-on-Trent, n.d.
  Address: *Arts and Crafts and Industries*, at Newcastle-under-Lyne, n.d.
  Address: Tunstall Technical School, Staffs, n.d.
  Address: Royal Female School of Art, n.d.
  Address to Hanley Arts and Sketching Club, n.d.
  Address to students at Bradford Technical College, n.d.
  Address to students of the Technical Institute, Halifax, n.d.
  A lecture: *The Wild Silks of India*. Given before the Society of Arts, 1880.
  A paper: *On Several Species of Silk Fibre, and on the Silk Industry*, read before the Society of Colourists, the Technical College, Bradford, 8 May 1885.
  A paper: *The Depression in the English Silk Trade and its Cause*, n.d.
  A paper: *Art as Applied to Weaving and Printing of Textile Fabrics*, read before the Royal Society of British Architects, London, n.d.
  A paper: *The History and Development of Pattern-Designing in Textiles*, read before the Society of Arts, London.

A paper: *On Silks Eastern and Western*, The School of Archaeology, Cambridge, n.d.

A paper: *On the Present Development of Power-loom Weaving of Silk Fabrics at Lyons*, read before the Weaving and Power-loom Committee, 1891.

A paper: *Secondary Education and Technical Instruction*, Municipal Technical College, Bradford, 1903.

Report on the English Silk Industry, 1886. For the Royal Commission on Technical Instruction.

Report on the Silks Exhibited in the Colonial Sections of the Colonial and Indian Exhibition 1886. Issued under the supervision of Council of the Society of Arts 1887.

Correspondence: Leek Embroidery Society.

London

Victoria and Albert Museum, Indian and South East Asia Department Archive

Circulation Catalogues of the Collections of Works Circulated. Press mark: V & A 1855:0001.

Inventory of Art Objects (slip books) 1852/53/54/55/56/57/58–63/64–75.

Inventory, 1889.

The India Museum Inventory of Examples of Indian Art and Manufactures transferred to the South Kensington Museum, 1880.

Inventory of the Indian Section, South Kensington Museum. Objects acquired in the year 1880, Nos 1–35, 1880.

Indian and South East Asia Department: textiles survey, 1988.

Transcript: *Proceedings of a Conference of Silk held in the Office of Revenue and Agricultural Department of the Government of India*, at Calcutta, 8 January, 1886.

The British Library, Oriental and India Office Collections

L/E 1–10 Economic Dept. Records, 1786–1950.

L/E/5/67 Reports on Indian industries, 1884–98.

L/E/5/68 Petitions against Indian import duties on cotton goods, 1875–76.

L/E/7/138 Report of a Conference held in the Commercial Room of the Imperial Indian Court of the Colonial and Indian Exhibition. Sections include:

16 June 1886 'Indian Fibres suitable for Textile Purposes', pp. 1–6.

18 June 1886 'Indian Silk and Silk Substitutes', pp. 1–3.

7 July 1886 'Indian Dyes and Mordants', pp. 1–4.

L/E/7/138, Files 1784–1855. Correspondence: Subject – Colonial and Indian Exhibition.

L/E/7/213/–39. 1890 Application from T. Wardle for a silkworm collection for the Grosvenor Museum, Chester.

(217) 1890, Proposed Silk Exhibition, application from T. Wardle.

L/E/7/247/(950) Transcript: Wardle, T., Lecture to the Royal Society of Arts, 1891.
(950/91) R.S.7C. Minute Paper: Thomas Wardle's lecture on Tussur Silks, 1891.
ZLE7/2/ 165, 480, 1480, 1929, 1940, 2023, 2839. Revenue statistics and Commerce Department Register, 1883 (No. 165, 18/19 January, Correspondence Thomas Wardle, subject dyestuffs.
Letter to Wardle, 16 Feb.
480. 6 Feb., Wardle's report on dyestuffs of India.
1480. 9 July Talk, subject: Indian fibres, silk reeling machine for India.
(1929) 21 August Letter from T. Wardle. Subject: tussur silk reeling machine.
(2839) 10 Dec., Letter from T. Wardle. Subject Industrial development of silk.
Collection of silks presented to Lyons Chamber of Commerce.
ZLE 7/3 1310, 1916, 2229.
ZLE /7/6/775.
L/E/7/478 Revenue and Statistical Papers 1903. References to the Kashmir silk industry, Sir T. Wardle.
Z/E/4/68 (1247–48; 881–2) Proposed Exhibition of Products, International Exhibition, Dublin, 1853.
Z/L/E/3/1–40 Correspondence with India, 1820–1924.
Z/L/E/75 Catalogue.
Z/L/E/7/1–64 Departmental papers, 1882–1929.
V/17/1, I.S. a 80/3 Annual Statement of the Sea-borne trade of British India with the British Empire.

Macclesfield, Cheshire, Macclesfield Silk Museum's archive

Report on the English silk industry, 1885.
Transcript: Royal Commission on Depression in Trade. *Report of Evidence of a Deputation from Macclesfield on the Decline of the English Silk Trade,* 1886.
Reports of the Silk Association of Britain and Ireland.
Reports of the Macclesfield Silk Manufacturers' Association.
Minutes of the Macclesfield Higher Education Committee.
Reports of the Macclesfield District Free Trade Union.
Notes: Macclesfield Silk Trade Protection Association.
Reports; Silk Trade Members of the Macclesfield Chamber of Commerce.
Papers: Society of Arts, Examinations in Silk Manufacture.
Papers: Silk Supply Association.

Manchester

John Rylands University Library of Manchester

Serial Holdings
Abstract relating to British India, London HMSO – 963509, 208480/3, 1865–6/1874–5/1869–9/1877–8; 1904.

BIBLIOGRAPHY

Manchester Central Reference Library

LC. Ref. 659. 152094272085 Roy. Official Catalogue of the Royal Jubilee Exhibition, *Manchester City Art Gallery Archive*.

The T. Horsfall Collection:

The Study of Beauty, paper read to Manchester Field Naturalist's Society, 1883.

List: of art objects purchased in India for the Art Museum (Ancoats) by permission of the Lords of the Committee of Privy Council on Education, by Mr Casper Purdon Clarke, 11 June 1883.

Horsfall Acquisition Book: textiles 1882–87.

T. Horsfall's printed papers:

Committee notes: 'An Art Museum for Manchester' 1877.

'Ancoats Art Museum', 3/9/1888.

John Ruskin (a letter from) LXXIX, in *Fors Clavigera* IV.15.

Newspaper articles relating to the 'Horsfall' museum.

Manchester Regional College of Art Archive
(Manchester Metropolitan University Library)

707.1142.733 MAN

British Parliamentary Papers: Report and papers relating to the state of Head and Branch Schools of Design, together with the first Report on the Department of Practical Arts 1850–3. Irish University Press. Design IV.

Report of the Proceedings at the Annual General Meeting, held in the Lecture Room of the Royal Manchester Institution, Bond Street, 15 January 1844 (With a list of donors and annual subscriptions).

Notes on the History of the School by Benjamin Love, 1839.

Minutes of Annual General Meetings 1844–55.

Annual Reports 1883–91.

Committee Records.

Report by the Director of Design – Walter Crane, 28 July 1895.

A draft of *'Suggestions'*, March 1893.

Reports of the Education Committee of the Manchester Corporation 1892–1912.

The Whitworth Institute

Transcripts of over 60 letters from William Morris to Thomas Wardle, 1875–96.

Minutes of the Inaugural Meeting of the Manchester Whitworth Institute, 17 July 1890.

Minutes of the Council 1895–1900, Vols A, B.

Minutes of the Council 1904, Vol. C.

Minutes of the Council 1915 (including Minutes of the Art Sub-committee).

Manchester Whitworth Institute Catalogue 1894.

Stafford, Staffordshire Record Office

D538/C/1/40 [4/A/26] W.S. Brough: *A History of the Leek Silk Industry*, 1907.

D538/C/1/76 [4/A/65] Correspondence with Sir Thomas Wardle on the affairs of Wardle and Company, Silk Manufacturers in Leek, 1883–84.

Oldham Library, local history archive

PR.1 Oldham School of Art: curriculum details.
PX.QYK Fine Art and Industrial Exhibition Handbook, 1 August 1883.
PXYK. 9, Minutes of Manufacturers Committee for the above.
PX:QYK. 9, Minutes for the 1883 Exhibition, 5 vols (handwritten).
PX542, Bound volume of 1883 Exhibition lists. Indian fabrics, p. 65.

USA

Duke University, Durham, North Carolina: Rare Book, Manuscript and Special Collections Library.
296-01-1, Microfilm: *Sir Thomas Wardle, Papers.* Including photographed copies of the original letters from William Morris to Thomas Wardle.

Unpublished theses

Longdon, George, *Further Education in Macclesfield, 1835–1945* (MEd, Manchester University) 1980.
Vanke, Francesca, *British Cultural and Aesthetic Relationships with the Decorative Arts of the Islamic Orient, with special reference to Ceramics, 1851–1914.* The London Institute, Camberwell College of Arts, 1998. Unpublished PhD thesis.

CORRESPONDENCE

Dr Tirthankar Roy, Indira Gandhi Institute of Development Research, Bombay, India, 24 February, 2000.

SECONDARY SOURCES

Albanr, Keith, *The Language of Pattern*, London, Thames & Hudson, 1974.
Ali, Abdullah ibn Yusuf, *A Monograph on Silk Fabrics*, The Calico Museum of Textiles, India, 1900.
Appadurai, Arjun (ed.), *The Social Life of Things: Commodities in Cultural Perspective*, Cambridge, Cambridge University Press, 1986.
Arasaratnam, S., 'Weavers, Merchants and Company: The Handloom Industry in South-eastern India, 1750–1790', pp. 175–200, in M.F. Mazzaoui (ed.),

Textiles: Production, Trade and Demand, Ashgate, Variorum, Aldershot, 1998.

Arizoli-Clementel, Pierre, Catalogue. *The Textile Museum, Lyons*, Lyons, Musée et Monuments de France, 1990.

Art Treasures Examiner, Exhibition Catalogue, Manchester, 1857.

Ashbee, C.R., *Should We Stop Teaching Art?*, New York, Garland Publishing Co., Reprinted 1978 (1st edition 1911).

Ashenhurst, Thomas R., *Weaving and Designing Textile Fabrics*, London, Cassell & Co., 1883.

——, *Design in Textile Fabrics*, London, Cassell & Co., 1881.

——, *Design and Colouring in Fancy Vestings: Textile Recorder* 1889, p. 212.

——, Ibid. Oct. 1889, p. 158.

——, Ibid. Nov. 1889, p. 135.

Askari, Nasreen and Crill, Rosemary, *Colours of the Indus: Costumes and Textiles of Pakistan*, London, Merrell Hilberton, 1997.

Auerbach, Jeffrey A., *The Great Exhibition of 1851: A Nation on Display*, New Haven, Yale University Press, 1999.

Bag, Sailendra Kumar, *The Changing Fortunes of the Bengal Silk Industry 1757–1833*, Calcutta, S.K. Bag, 1989.

Baker, George P., *Calico Painting and Printing in the East Indies in the XVII– XVIII Centuries*, London, 1921.

Bal, Mieke, 'Telling Objects: A Narrative Perspective on Collections', pp. 97– 115, in J. Elsner and R. Cardinal (eds), *The Cultures of Collecting*, London, Reaktion Books, 1994.

Baldry, A. Lys, 'Manchester School of Art', *The Studio*, Vol. 15, pp. 105–8.

Balfour-Paul, Jenny, *Indigo*, London, British Museum Press, 1998.

Banham, Joanna, Macdonald, S. and Porter, J., *Victorian Interior Design*, London, Cassell, 1991.

Barnard, Nicholas and Gillow, John, *Traditional Indian Textiles*, London, Thames & Hudson, 1991.

Barnes, Ruth, *Indian Block-Printed Textiles in Egypt*, Oxford, Clarendon Press, 1997.

Barnes, Ruth and Eicher, Joanne (eds), *Dress and Gender: Making and Meaning*, Oxford, Berg, 1992.

Barringer, Tim and Flynn, Tom (eds), *Colonialism and the Object: Empire, Material Culture and the Museum*, London, Routledge, 1998.

Bayley, Stephen, *Commerce and Culture*, London, Penshurst Press Ltd, 1989.

Bean, Susan S., 'The American Market for Indian Textiles, 1785–1820: In the Twilight of Traditional Cloth Manufacture'. Conference Paper, *Textiles in Trade*, Proceedings of the Textile Society of America, Biennial Symposium, 14–16 September 1990, Washington DC.

Beer, Alice Baldwin, *Trade Goods: A Study of Indian Chintz*, Washington DC. Smithsonian Institution Press, 1970.

Bell, Quentin, *The Schools of Design*, London, Routledge & Kegan Paul, 1963.

Bennet, C.A., *History of Manual and Industrial Education 1870–1917*, Illinois, Manual Arts Press, 1937.

Bennett, Tony, *The Birth of the Museum: History, Theory and Politics*, London, Routledge, 1995.

Berg, Maxine, *The Age of Manufactures, 1700–1820: Industry, Innovation and Work in Britain* (2nd edition), London, Routledge, 1994.

——, 'New Commodities, Luxuries and their Consumers in Eighteenth Century England', pp. 63–85, in Maxine, Berg and Helen, Clifford (eds), *Consumers and Luxury: Consumer Culture in Europe 1650–1850*, Manchester, Manchester University Press, 1999.

Bhavnani, Enakshi, *Decorative Designs and Craftsmanship of India*, Bombay, India, D.B. Taraporevala Sons & Co. PVT. Ltd, 1974.

Birdwood, Sir. C.M. George, *The Handbook to the British Indian Section of the Paris International Exhibition*, London, Offices of the Royal Commission, 1878.

——, *The Industrial Arts of India*, In association with the Indian Section of South Kensington Museum, London, 1880.

Blair, Sheila and Bloom, Jonathan, *The Art and Architecture of Islam 1250–1800*, Yale University Press, 1994.

Bosence, Susan, *Hand Block Printing and Resist Dyeing*, London, David & Charles, 1991.

Brett, David, 'The Management of Colour: The Kashmir Shawl in a Nineteenth Century Debate', *Textile History*, Vol. 29, M0 2, 1988, pp. 123–33.

——, 'The Interpretation of Ornament', *The Journal of Design History*, Vol. 1, No. 2, p. 103.

Briggs, Asa, *William Morris: Selected Writings and Designs*, London, Penguin, 1962.

Brown, Clare, *Silk Designs of the Eighteenth Century*, London, Victoria and Albert Museum, 1996.

Brown, Percy and Watts, George, *Arts and Crafts of India*, New Dehli, Cosmo Publications, 1904. Reprinted 1979.

Brunner, J.T. and Ellis, T.E., *Public Education in Cheshire*, Manchester, 1891.

Buck, Ann, *Victorian Costume*, London, Herbert Jenkins, 1961.

Bühler, Alfred, Fischer, Eberhard and Nabholtz, Marie-Louise, *Indian Tie Dyed Fabrics*, Ahmedabad, Calico Museum of Textiles, 1980.

Bury, Hester, Catalogue: *A Choice of Design: 1850–1980. Fabrics by Warner and Sons Limited*, Purley Press, 1981.

Buss, Chiara (ed.), *Silk and Colour: Colezione Antonio Ratti*, Grafiche Mazzucchelli, Spa, Milano, 1997.

Butler, Anne, *The Batsford Encyclopaedia of Embroidery Stitches*, London, Batsford, 1979.

Calderi and Montecchi, Catalogue: *Photographs of Gems of the Art Treasures Exhibition*, London, 1858.

Calico Museum of Textiles, *Textile Trade of India with the Outside World* Gallery Notes, Ahmedabad, India, 1998.

Calloway, Stephen, *The House of Liberty: Masters of Style and Decoration*, London, Thames & Hudson, 1992.

Cannadine, David, *Ornamentalism: How the British saw their Empire*, London, Allen Lane, The Penguin Press, 2001.

Catalogue of the Art Treasures of the United Kingdom, London, 1857.

Cawthorne, Nigel, *The Art of India*, London, Hamlyn, 1997.

Chandra, Bipin, *Towards a Reinterpretation of Nineteenth Century Indian Economic History, Indian Economy in the Nineteenth Century*: A Symposium, Delhi, The Indian Economic and Social History Association, Delhi School of Economics, 1969.

Chapman, Stanley, 'David Evans & Co., The Last of the Old London Textile Printers', *Textile History*, Vol. 14, No. 1, 1983, pp. 29–56.

——, 'Vanners in the English Silk Industry', *Textile History*, Vol. 23, No. 1, 1992, pp. 71–86.

Charlesworth, Neil, *British Rule and the Indian Economy: 1800–1914*, London, Macmillan, 1982.

Charpigny, Florence, 'The French Silk Industry', conference paper, *Ars Textrina*, Leeds University, 1995.

Chaudhuri, K.N., *The Trading World of Asia and the English East Indian Company, 1660–1760*, Cambridge, Cambridge University Press, 1978.

——, 'The Structure of the Indian Textile Industry in the Seventeenth and Eighteenth Centuries', pp. 33–84, in T. Roy, *Cloth and Commerce: Textiles in Colonial India*, N. Delhi, Sage, 1996.

——, *Trade and Civilisation in the Indian Ocean: An Economic History from the Rise of Islam to 1750*, Cambridge, Cambridge University Press, 1997.

Clifford, Timothy, Catalogue: *A Century of Collecting: Manchester City Art Galleries*, Manchester, 1983.

Cohen, Steven, 'A Group of Early Silks', *Marg*, Vol. 46, No. 3, Bombay.

Cole, A., *Ornament in European Silks*, London, B.B.T. Batsford, 1899.

Cole, H.H., *Catalogue of the Objects of Indian Art Exhibited in the South Kensington Museum* (2 vols), London, 1880.

Coleman, Donald C., *Courtaulds: An Economic and Social History* (Vol. 1), Oxford, Clarendon Press, 1969.

Colley, Linda, *Britons: Forging the Nation, 1707–1837*, London, Vintage, 1992.

Collins, Louanne, *Silk Museums in Macclesfield*, Macclesfield Museums Trust, 1989.

Collins, Louanne and Stevenson, Moira, *Silk: Sarsanets, Satins, Steels & Stripes*, Macclesfield Museums' Trust, 1996.

Cookson, H.C., *Monograph on the Silk Industry of the Punjab, 1886–87*, Punjab, 1887.

Coote, Jeremy and Shelton, Anthony, *Anthropology, Art and Aesthetics*, Oxford, Clarendon Press, 1992.

Cottereau, Alain, 'The Fate of Collective Manufacture in the Industrial World: The Silk Industries of Lyons and London, 1800–1850', pp. 37–73, in C. Sabel and C. and Z. Jonathen (eds), *The World of Possibilities: Flexibility and Mass Production in Western Industrialisation*, Cambridge, Cambridge University Press, 1997.

Crane, Walter, *The Claims of Decorative Art*, London, Lawrence & Bullen, 1892.

——, *The Bases of Design*, London, G. Bell, 1898.

——, *Line and Form*, London, G. Bell, 1900.

Crill, Rosemary, *Indian Ikat Textiles*, London, Victoria and Albert Publications, 1998.

——, *Oxford Asian Textiles Group Newsletter*, No. 6, Feb. 1997.

——, 'Vaishnavite Silks: The Figured Textile of Assam', *Marg*, Vol. 46, No. 3, Bombay, 1995.

Cundall F. (ed.), *Reminiscences of the Colonial and Indian Exhibition 1886*, London, 1887.

Das Gupta, A. *Indian Merchants and the Decline of Surat*, Weisbaden, Germany, 1979.

Davis, C.S. (ed.), *History of Macclesfield*, Manchester, Manchester University Press, 1961.

Davis, John, ' "A Most Important and Necessary Thing": An Arts and Crafts Collection in Manchester', *The Journal of the Decorative Arts Society: 1850 to the Present*, No. 18, Autumn, 1994, pp. 15–22.

Day, Lewis Foreman, *The Anatomy of Pattern*, London, 1887.

——, *The Application of Ornament*, London, 1888.

——, *Nature in Ornament*, London, 1892.

——, *Pattern Design*, London, 1903.

——, *Nature and Ornament*, London, 1908–9.

Denvir, Bernard, *The Late Victorians: Art, Design and Society 1852–1910*, London, Longman Group Ltd, 1986.

Desai, Chelna, *Ikat Textiles of India*, Tokyo, 1988.

A Descriptive Catalogue of the Arts and Crafts Museum, Municipal School of Art, Manchester, MCMIII.

Desmond, Ray, *The Indian Museum, 1801–1879*, London, HMSO, 1982.

Dhamija, Jasleen and Jain, Jyotindra (eds), *Handwoven Fabrics of India*, Ahmedabad, 1989.

——, 'Woven Silks of India', *Marg*, Vol. 46, No. 3, Bombay, 1995.

Dhamija, Jasleen, 'Paithani Weaves', *Marg*, Vol. 46, No. 3, Bombay, 1995.

Dhamija Jasleen, Eicher, Joanne B. (ed.), *Dress and Ethnicity*, Oxford, Berg, 1995.

Elsner, John and Cardinal, Roger, *The Cultures of Collecting*, London, Reaktion Books Ltd, 1994.

Emery, I. and Farington, Anthony, *Primary Structure of Fabrics*, London, Thames & Hudson, 1994.

——, *Trading Places: The East India Company and Asia, 1600–1834*, London, The British Library, 2002.

Faulkner, Peter (ed.), *Arts and Crafts Essays*, Bristol, Thoemmes Press, 1996.

Federico, Giovanni, *An Economic History of the Silk Industry, 1830–1930*, Cambridge Studies in Modern Economic History 5, Cambridge University Press, 1997.

Feltwell, John, *The Story of Silk*, Stroud, Alan Sutton, 1990.

Ferro, Marc, *Colonization: A Global History*, London, Routledge, 1997.

Fine, Ben and Leopold, Ellen, *The World of Consumption*, London, Routledge, 1997.

Forbes Watson, John, *Textile Manufactures and the Costumes of the People of India*, London, Eyre and Spottiwoode, 1866.

Forty, Adrian, *Objects of Desire: Design and Society 1750–1980*, London, Thames & Hudson, 1989.

Gaddum, H.T., *Silk: How and Where it is Produced*, Manchester, 1949.

Gay, Peter, *Pleasure Wars: The Bourgeois Experience*, London, Harper Collins, 1998.

Geoghegan, J., *Silk in India, Some Account of Silk in India, Especially of the Various Attempts to Encourage and Extend Sericulture in that Country*, Calcutta, Office of the Superintendent of Government Printing, 1872.

Gibbs-Smith, C.H., *The Great Exhibition of 1851: A Commemorative Album*, London, HMSO, 1950.

Gillow, Norah, *William Morris: Designs and Patterns*, London, Bracken Books, 1988.

Gittinger, Mattiebelle, *Master Dyers to the World*, Washington DC, The Textile Museum, 1982.

Glazier, Richard, *Historic Textile Fabrics: A Short History of the Tradition and Development of Pattern in Woven and Printed Stuffs*, London, Batsford, 1899. Reprinted 1922.

Gombrich, Ernest H., *The Sense of Order*, London, Phaidon Press, 1992.

Good, Graham, 'The Hegemony of Theory', *University of Toronto Quarterly*, Minos, 41Q65, pp. 534–55, 1996.

Goody, Jack, *The East in the West*, Cambridge, Cambridge University Press, 1996.

Gosh, G.K. and Gosh, S., *Indian Textiles Past and Present*, New Delhi, APH Publishing, 1995.

Goswamy, B.N., *Indian Costumes in the Collection of the Calico Museum of Textiles*, Ahmedabad, 1993.

Greenhalgh, Paul, *Ephemeral Vistas: The Expositions Universelles, Great Exhibitions and World Fairs*, Manchester, Manchester University Press, 1989.

Gregory, Richard L., *Eye and Brain*, London, Weidenfeld & Nicolson, 1990.

Guy, John and Swallow, Deborah (eds), *Arts of India 1550–1900*, London, Victoria and Albert Museum, 1990.

Guy, John, *Woven Cargoes: Indian Textiles in the East*, London, Thames & Hudson, 1998.

Hall, Margaret, *Indian Painted and Painted Fabrics*, Ahmedabad, S.R. Bastikar, 1971.

——, *Indian Textiles from the Embroiderers Guild Collection*, Catalogue: London, 1986.

Hampson, Mary, *Macclesfield's Heritage is Silk*, Macclesfield, Silk Heritage, 1980.

Hann, Michael and Lin, X., Catalogue: *Symmetry in Regular Repeating Pattern*, Leeds, The University Gallery, 10–12 July 1995.

Harris, Jennifer (ed.), *5000 Years of Textiles*, London, British Museum Press, 1993.

Harrison, M., *Art and Philanthropy*, Manchester, Manchester University Press, 1986.

Harte, Negley (ed.), *Fabrics and Fashions: Studies in the Economic and Social History of Dress*, Leeds, Pasold Research Fund, 1991.

Harvey, Charles and Press, Jon, *William Morris: Design and Enterprise in Victorian Britain*, Manchester, Manchester University Press, 1991.

Harvie, Christopher, Martin, Graham and Scharf, Aaron (eds), *Industrialisation and Culture*, 1830–1914, London, Macmillan, Open University Press, 1970.

Haynes, Douglas, 'The Dynamics of Continuity in Indian Domestic Industry: *Jari* manufacture in Surat, 1900–1947', pp. 299–320, in T. Roy (ed.), *Cloth and Commerce: Textiles in Colonial India*, Sage Publications, New Delhi, 1996.

Head, Raymond, 'Indian Crafts and Western Design from the Seventeenth Century to the Present', *The Royal Society of Arts Journal*, January 1988, pp. 116–31.

Hemneter, Ernst, 'The Castes of the Indian Dyers', pp. 51–4, *CIBA Review* 2, October 1937.

Herzig, Edmund, 'The Iranian Raw Silk Trade and European Manufacture in the Seventeenth and Eighteenth Centuries', pp. 27–44, in M.F. Mazzaoui (ed.), *Textiles: Production, Trade and Demand*. Aldershot, Ashgate Publishing Ltd, 1998.

Hill, C.P., *British Economic and Social History: 1700–1975*, London, Edward Arnold, 1977.

Hinsley, Curtis M., 'The World as Marketplace', pp. 344–65, in I. Karp and S. Lavine (eds), *Exhibiting Cultures*, Washington DC, Smithsonian Institution Press, 1991.

Hooper, Luthe, *Silk: Its Production and Manufacture*, London, Pitman & Sons Ltd, 1927.

Hooper-Greenhill, Eilean, *Museums and the Shaping of Knowledge*, London, Routledge, 1992.

Horsfall, Thomas C., *An Art Gallery for Manchester*, 1877.

——, *Art in Towns and Villages*, 1878.

——, *The Study of Beauty and Art in Large Towns*, 1883.

——, *The Manchester Art Museum*, 1891.

——, *The Need for Art In Manchester*, 1910.

——, *The Place of Adoration, Hope and Love in Town Life*, 1910.

Hoffenberg, Peter, *An Empire on Display*, California, University of California Press, 2001.

Howard, Constance, *Twentieth Century Embroidery in Great Britain*, Batsford, 1981.

Hurst, George H., *Colour: A Handbook of the Theory of Colour*, London, Scott, Greenwood & Co., 1900.

Irwin, John, *The Kashmir Shawl*, London, Her Majesty's Stationery Office, 1973.

——, Catalogue: *Art and the East India Trade*, The Victoria and Albert Museum, London Autumn, 1970.

Irwin, John and Brett, Katherine, *Origins of Chintz*, London, HMSO, 1970.

Irwin, John and Jayakar, Pupul, *Textiles and Ornaments of India*, New York, Museum of Modern Art, 1956.

Jacques, Anne, *The Wardle Story*, Leek, Staffordshire, Churnet Valley Books, 1996.

——, 'Leek Embroidery', *Embroidery*, Vol. 39, No. 1, Spring, 1988.

——, 'Thomas Wardle and the Kashmir Silk Industry', *Staffordshire History*, pp. 105–17, The Local History Unit, Keele University.

Jain, Rahul, *Minakar: Spun Gold and Woven Enamel*, Textile Art, New Delhi, 1997.

Jeremiah, David, *A Hundred Years or More*, Manchester, Manchester Polytechnic, 1980.

——, Catalogue: *Object Lessons: A College Collection of Art, Craft and Design, 1840–1980*, Manchester, Manchester Polytechnic, March 1982.

Jervis, Simon, *Dictionary of Design and Designers*, London, Penguin Books, 1984.

Jones, Owen, *The Grammar of Ornament*, London, Bernard Quaritch, 1856 (reprinted 1997).

Journal of Decorative Art, 'A Visit to the Manchester School of Art', pp. 181–4, Dec. 1888.

Journal of Design and Manufactures, 'Mousselines de Laine', No. 1, March 1849.

——, 'Counsel to Practical Designers for Woven Fabrics', p. 146, No. 1, March 1849.

——, 'Selected Patterns for Dress', No. 1, March 1849, pp. 22–3.

——, 'Printed Garment Fabrics', No. 7, Sept. 1849, pp. 104–5.

——, 'Selected Patterns for Dress', Vol. II, No. 8, Oct. 1849, p. 771.

——, 'Reports on the Schools of Design', March–August 1850.

Journal of Indian Art, 'Preface', Vol. 1, Nos 1–16, 1885–86.

——, Wardle, T. 'The Indian Silk Culture Court at the Colonial and Indian Exhibition', Vol. 1, No. 1, p. 48.

——, Gupta, B.A., 'Thana Silks', Vol. 1, No. 5, pp. 33–6.

——, Baden-Powell, B.H., 'Difficulties of Art Manufacture', Vol. 1, No. 5.

——, No. 8, 'Colonial and Indian Exhibition Notes', pp. 63–4.

——, No. 11, 'Colonial and Indian Exhibition', p. 77.

——, No. 12, 'The Embroidered Camel Saddle', p. 91.

——, No. 12, 'Notes on the Colonial and Indian Exhibition', p. 40.

——, No. 16, 'The Baroda Court: Fabrics', p. 130.

——, Nos 2, 4, Cookson, H.C. 'Monograph on the Silk Industries of the Punjab 1886–87'.

Journal of Indian Art & Industry, Mookerji, Baboo and Nitya, Gopal, 'The Silk Industries of Moorshedabad', No. 38, April 1892.

——, 1907, 'Textiles', p. 13.

——, 1909, 'Memoir of Sir Thomas Wardle', pp. 5–8.

——, 1909, 'The Silk Industries of India' (obituary for T. Wardle), pp. 8–13.

Kaplan, Flora, *Museums and the Making of Ourselves: The Role of Objects in National Identity*, London, Leicester University Press, 1994.

Karp, Ivan and Lavine, Steven D., *Exhibiting Cultures: The Poetics and Politics of Museum Display*, Washington DC, Smithsonian Institution Press, 1991.

Kasamitsu, Toshio, 'British Industrialization and Design Before the Great Exhibition', pp. 77–95, *Textile History*, Vol. 12, Leeds, The Pasold Research Fund, 1981.

Keighley, Mark, *Woven With Wisdom and Skill: The History of the Bradford Textile Society, 1893–1993*, Bradford, 1993.

Kendrick, A.F., 'Woven Fabrics at the Whitworth Art Gallery, Manchester', *The Connoisseur*, pp. 20–8.

Kidd, Alan G., *City, Class and Culture: Studies of Cultural Production and Social Policy in Victorian Manchester*, 1985.

King, Brenda, 'Cresta Silks: The Textiles of the 1930s', *The Textile Society Magazine*, Vol. 15, 1991, pp. 24–6.

King, Donald, *British Textile Design in the V & A*, London, Tokyo, 1980.

King, Donald and Rothstein, Nathalie, *Textile Design in the Victoria and Albert Museum*, Tokyo, 1980.

King, Donald and Levey, Santina, *Embroidery in Britain from 1200–1750*, Victoria and Albert Museum, 1993.

Klingender, Francis D., *Art and the Industrial Revolution*, St Albans, Herts, Paladin, 1975.

Krishna, Rai and Krishna, Ujay, *Benaras Brocades*, Ahmedabad, 1966.

Krishna, Ujay, 'Flowers in Indian Textile Design', *Journal of Indian Textile History*, No. 7, Ahmedabad, 1967, pp. 1–20.

Lardner, D., *A Treatise on the Origin, Progressive Improvements and Present State of Silk Manufacture*, London, 1851.

Laughton, Jane, *Origins of the Silk Industry*, Macclesfield, CMA, Educational Project.

The Leek Times, 'Warden of the Silk Industry', 14 March 1903.

Lemire, Beverly, *Fashions Favourite: The Cotton Trade and the Consumer in Britain, 1660–1800*, Oxford, Pasold Studies in Textile History, Open University Press, 1991.

Levey, Santina M., *An Elizabethan Inheritance: The Hardwick Hall Textiles*, The National Trust, 1998.

Lewis, Reina, *Gendering Orientalism*, London, Routledge, 1996.

Leyten, Harrie (ed.), *Illicit Traffic in Cultural Property*, The Netherlands, Royal Tropical Institute, Museums Against Pillage, 1993.

Little, Linda and Spink, Molly, *The Handloom Weavers*, Macclesfield, CMA, Educational Project.

Lowengard, Sarah, 'Colours and Colour Making in the Eighteenth Century', pp. 103–17, in M. Berg and H. Clifford (eds), *Consumers and Luxury: Consumer Culture in Europe 1650–1850*, Manchester, Manchester University Press, 1999.

Lynton, Linda, *The Sari: Styles, Patterns, History and Techniques*, Thames & Hudson Ltd, 1995.

——, 'Victorian and Edwardian Designs in East Indian Hand-woven Saris', *Surface Design Journal*, Vol. 18, No. 1, Fall, 1993, California.

MacCarthy, Fiona, *William Morris: A Life for our Time*, London, Faber and Faber, 1994.

Macclesfield Courier and Herald, 18 July 1851, p. 55.

——, 18 October 1851, p. 4.

——, 15 September 1866, Collections of Specimens of the Textile Manufactures of India, p. 1.

MacDonald, Stuart, *The History and Philosophy of Art Education*, University of London Press, 1970.

——, 'Articidal Tendencies', pp. 14–22, in D. Thistlewood (ed.), *Histories of Art and Design Education: Cole to Coldstream*, London, 1992.

Macfie, A.L., *Orientalism*, Longman, London, 2002.

MacKenzie, John M., *Orientalism: History, Theory and the Arts*, Manchester, Manchester University Press, 1995.

Malmgreen, Gail, *Silk Town: Industry and Culture in Macclesfield: 1750–1835*, Hull, Hull University Press, 1985.

Manchester Whitworth Institute, Catalogue, Manchester, 1894.

Mathias, Peter, *The First Industrial Nation: An Economic History of Britain 1700–1914*, London, Methuen, 1969.

——, *The Transformation of England*, London, Methuen, 1979.

Mathur, Saloni, *An Indian Encounter: Portraits for Queen Victoria*, Catalogue, The National Gallery, London, 2002.

Mehta, G., *Indian Textiles*, New York, Metropolitan Museum of Fine Art, 1986.

Mehta, Rustum J., *Masterpieces of Indian Textiles*, Bombay, D.B. Taraporevala Sons & Co., Private Ltd, 1970.

Mendez, Valerie and Parry, Linda, *The Victoria & Albert Museum's Textile Collection: British Textiles from 1900 to 1937*, London, V & A Museum, 1992.

Miller, Lesley Ellis, 'Education and the Silk Designer: A Model for Success', conference paper, *Ars Textrina*, Leeds University, July 1995.

——, 'Manufacturers and the Man: A Reassessment of the Place of Jacques-Charles Dutillieu in the Silk Industry of Eighteenth Century Lyons', *Textile History*, Vol. 29, No. 1, Spring, 1998, pp. 19–40.

Mitter, Partha, *Much Maligned Monsters: History of European Reactions to Indian Art*, Oxford, Clarendon Press, 1977.

Morrell, Anne, *The Techniques of Indian Embroidery*, London, B.T. Batsford, 1994.

Morris, Barbara, *Inspiration for Design: The Influence of the Victoria and Albert Museum*, London, Victoria and Albert Museum, 1986.

——, *Liberty Design: 1874–1914*, Chartwell Books Inc., 1989.

Morris, William, *News From Nowhere and Other Writings*, London, Penguin, 1993.

——, *The Collected Works of William Morris*, Longman Green & Co. 24 vols, 1910–15.

Mukharji, T.N., *Art Manufacturers of India*, Glasgow, 1888.

Murphy, Veronica and Crill, Rosemary, *Tie-dyed Textiles of India*, London, Victoria and Albert Museum, 1991.

Nabholz-Kartaschoff, Marie-Louise, *Golden Sprays and Scarlet Flowers*, Kyoto, Shikosha Publishing, 1986.

Naish, John P., 'The Connection of Oriental Studies With Commerce, Art and Literature during the 18th and 19th Centuries', *Manchester University Egyptian and Oriental Society Journal*, Vol. 15, 1930, pp. 33–9.

Naylor, Gillian, *The Arts and Crafts Movement*, London, Trefoil, 1990 (first published 1971).

Norris, Jill, *The Last Handloom Weavers*, Macclesfield, Macclesfield Museums' Trust, 1996.

Osborne, Harold (ed.), *The Oxford Companion to the Decorative Arts*, Oxford, Clarendon Press, 1975.

Page, Bunny and Taylor, Louise, Catalogue: *Handmade in India*, London, The Crafts Council, 1998.

Paine, Sheila, *Embroidered Textiles*, London, Thames & Hudson, 1990.

Parry, Linda, *William Morris*, London, Victoria and Albert Museum, 1996.

——, *Textiles of the Arts and Crafts Movement*, London, Thames & Hudson, 1988.

——, *William Morris Textiles*, London, Weidenfeld and Nicolson, 1983.

——, *British Textiles 1850–1900*, London, Victoria and Albert Museum, 1992.

Patni-Bhawmick, Madhurima, *Brocades of Ahmedabad*, Ahmedabad National Institute of Design, 1992.

Pearce, Susan M., *Museums Objects and Collections: A Cultural Study*, Leicester, Leicester University Press, 1992.

Phillips, Peter and Bunce, Gillian, *Repeat Patterns*, London, Thames and Hudson, 1993.

Poni, Carlo, 'Fashion as Flexible Production: Lyons Silk Merchants in the Eighteenth Century', pp. 37–73, in C. Sabel and J. Zeithin (eds), *The World of Possibilities: Flexibility and the Mass Production in Western Industrialisation*, Cambridge, Cambridge University Press, 1997.

Poovaya-Smith, Nina, 'Keys to the Magic Kingdom', pp. 111–28, in T. Barringer and T. Flynn (eds), *Colonialism and the Object*, London, Routledge, 1998.

Poynter, E.J., Decorative Art: Lectures in Art, 1873.

Priestley, J.B., *English Journey*, London, Mandarin, 1994.

Prown, Jules, ' "Mind in Matter": An Introduction to Material Culture Theory and Method', pp. 133–8, in S. Pearce (ed.), *Interpreting Objects and Collections*, Routledge, 1994.

Reach, Angus B., *Manchester and the Textile Districts*, Helmshore Local History Society, 1972.

Redgrave, Gilbert R., 'Textile Fabrics at the South Kensington Museum', *The Art Journal* 1889, pp. 329–221.

Redgrave, Richard, *Supplementary Report on Design at the Great Exhibition*, London, W. Clowes, 1852.

——, 'Report on Design', *The Illustrated Magazine of Art*, Vol. 1, 1853.

Reilly Valerie, *Paisley Patterns: A Design Source Book*, London, Studio Editions, 1989.

Rifkin, Adrienne, 'Success Disavowed: The Schools of Design in Mid nineteenth-century Britain: (An Allegory)', *Journal of Design History*, Vol. 1, No. 2, 1988, pp. 89–102.

Roberts, Beamont, 'Design and Colour in Fancy Vestings', *The Textile Recorder*, 15 Oct. 1888, pp. 134–5.

——, 'Design and Colour in Fancy Vestings', *The Textile Recorder*, 15 Nov. 1888, pp. 158–9.

——, 'Design and Colour in Fancy Vestings', *The Textile Recorder*, 15 Dec. 1888, pp. 183–4.

——, 'Designing and Manufacturing', *The Textile Recorder*, 15 April 1889, pp. 268–9.

Robinson, Sir John C., *Treasury of Ornamental Art*, London, Day & Son, 1857.

Rothstein, Natalie (ed.), Catalogue: *From East to West: Textiles from G.P. & J. Baker*, London, Victoria and Albert Museum, 1984.

Roy, Tirthankar, 'Introduction', pp. 11–32, in *Cloth and Commerce: Textiles in Colonial India*, New Delhi, Sage Publications, 1996.

Rudzki, Dorothy, 'Paisley Designs in Fabric and Fashion', Part III, in *Ratti and Paisley*, New York, Fashion Institute of Technology, 1986.

Ruskin, John, *Modern Painters* (Vol. 1), 1856.

——, *The Two Paths*, London, George Allen, 1887.

——, 'Fors Clavigera', in *Selections From the Writings of John Ruskin*, Second Series, 1860–88, London, George Allen, 1893.

Said, Edward W., *Orientalism: Western Conceptions of the Orient*, London, Penguin Books, Ltd, 1978. Reprinted 1991.

Schoeser, Mary and Dejardine, Kathleen, *French Textiles*, London, Laurence King, 1991.

Schoeser, Mary and Rufey, Celia, *English and American Textiles*, London, Thames & Hudson, 1989.

Schoff, W.H. (ed.), *The Periplus of the Erythraean Sea: Travel and Trade in the Indian Ocean, By a Merchant of the First Century*, New York, Longmans, 1912. Reprinted New Delhi, Oriental Books, 1974.

Scott, Phillipa, *The Book of Silk*, London, Thames & Hudson, 1993.

Shrigley, Ruth (ed.), Catalogue: *Inspired by Design: The Arts and Crafts Collection of the Manchester Metropolitan University*, Manchester, 1994.

Siegelaub, Seth, *Bibliographica Textilia Historia*, Amsterdam, International General, 1997.

Skelton, Robert, 'The Indian Collection 1798–1978', *Burlington Magazine*, CXX (902), pp. 297–304, May 1978.

Silk Journal and Rayon World, 'An Exhibition of Textile Designs', pp. 24–5, Nov. 1930.

——, 'Assam Silk Industry', p. 28, Feb. 1931.

——, 50 Years of Silk Dyeing', Gilbert C. Wardle, pp. 67–9, March 1937.

Silk and Rayon Users Association, *The Silk Book*, London, 1951.

Somers-Cocker, Anna, *The Victoria and Albert Museum: The Making of the Collection*, Leicester, Winward, 1980.

Spurr, David, *The Rhetoric of Empire*, Durham, NC, Duke University Press, 1994.

Stephenson, C. and Suddards, F., *Ornamental Design for Woven Fabrics*, London, Methuen Ltd, 1897.

Stobart, Jon, 'Textile Industries in North West England in the Early Eighteenth Century', *Textile History*, Vol. 29, No. 1, Spring, 1998, pp. 3–18.

Swallow, Deborah, 'The India Museum and the British-India Textile Trade in the Late nineteenth Century', *Textile History*, Vol. 30, No. 1, Spring, 1999, pp. 29–45.

Swallow, Deborah and Guy, John, *The Arts of India*, London, Victoria and Albert Museum, 1990.

Sweetman, John, *The Oriental Obsession: Islamic Inspiration in British and American Art and Architecture 1500–1920*, Cambridge, Cambridge University Press, 1988.

Swift, John, 'The Arts and Crafts Movement and Birmingham Art School, 1880–1900', pp. 23–37, in D. Thistlewood (ed.), *Histories of Art and Design Education: Cole to Coldstream*, London, 1992.

Szygenda, Lynn, 'Eastern Influences on European Textiles', *Embroidery*, Vol. 39. No. 3. Autumn, 1988, pp. 128–9.

Tarlo, Emma, *Clothing Matters: Dress and Identity in India*, London, Hurst, 1996.

The Metropolitan Museum of New York, Catalogue: *Orientalism: Visions of the East in Western Dress*, 1994.

The Textile Manufacturer, 15 Sept. 1877, 'Museums of Trade Patterns', pp. 277–8.

The Textile Recorder, 15 May 1883, 'The Yorkshire College', pp. 12–13.

——, 15 June 1883, 'Huddersfield Technical School and Mechanics' Institute', p. 36.

——, 14 July 1883, 'Manchester Technical School and Mechanics' Institution', pp. 60–1.

——, 15 October 1883, 'Textile Institutes', pp. 130–1.

——, 15 October 1883, 'Bradford Technical College', pp. 128–9.

——, 15 March 1884, 'The North-West Oriental Art Weaving Factory, Agra, p. 249.

——, 15 March 1884, 'Suggestive Designs', p. 249.

——, 14 June 1884, 'The Royal Commissioners' Report on Technical Instruction', p. 26.

——, 15 September 1884, 'Education in Industrial Art', p. 104.

——, 15 October 1884, 'Industrial Education in England, a Myth', p. 122.

——, 15 December 1884, 'Textile Schools', p. 180.

——, 15 January 1885, 'Instruction in Designing in Schools of Art', pp. 202–3.

——, 15 July 1885, 'Haste to the Wedding', p. 50.

——, 14 December 1885, 'The Design Sells the Cloth', p. 161.

——, 15 June 1886, 'Indian and Colonial Exhibition', p. 33.

——, 15 June 1886, 'Indian and Colonial Exhibition', pp. 62–3.

——, 15 July 1886, 'Indian Silk Cultivation', pp. 38–9.

——, 14 August 1886, 'Conferences at the Indian and Colonial Exhibition', p. 60.

——, 15 October 1886, 'The Indian Textile Industries', p. 91.

——, 15 December 1886, Preface; notes on the superiority of English design over French', p. 1.

——, 15 December 1886, 'English Trade in India', p. 170.

——, 1887, 'Our Industrial Race with Foreign Countries', pp. 182–3.

——, 15 May 1888, 'On the Syllabus and Examinations in Cloth Manufacture: Macclesfield', p. 138.

——, 15 June 1888, 'Textile Colouring', pp. 6–7.

——, 15 July 1888, 'Treatment of finished goods in India', pp. 40–1.

——, 15 July 1888, Preface: 'Notes on Increasing Textile Industries in India', p. 1.

——, 15 August 1888, 'Failure of the Present Elementary Education System', p. 51.

——, 15 September 1888, 'Sunday work in Indian Mills', p. 87.

——, 15 November 1888, 'Factory workers in India', pp. 98–9.

——, 15 November 1888, 'Factory Hours in India', p. 146.

——, 15 November 1888, 'Mill Extension in India', p. 146.

——, 15 January 1889, 'The Bombay Millowners' Association', p. 195.

——, 15 January 1889, 'The Manchester Technical School', pp. 206–7.

Tomlinson, B.R., *The Economy of Modern India, 1860–1970*, The New Cambridge Modern History of India, Vol. III, Cambridge University Press, 1993.

Twomey, Michael, 'Employment in Nineteenth-century Indian Textiles', *Explorations in Economic History*, p. 37, 1983.

Tylecote, Mabel, *The Mechanics' Institutes in Yorkshire and Lancashire to 1851*, Manchester, Manchester University Press, 1951.

Varron, A., 'Fashion and the Silk of Lyons', *CIBA Review*, No. 6, Basle, pp. 181–6.

——, 'The Development of Lyons as the Centre of the French Silk Industry', *CIBA Review*, No. 6, Basle, pp. 174–80.

——, 'The Organisation and Importance of the Silk Industry of Lyons', *CIBA Review*, No. 6 Basle, pp. 187–93.

Vergo, Peter, *The New Museology*, London, Reaktion Books Ltd, 1989.

Victoria and Museum, *Demand for the Exotic: English Wood-block Printed Furnishing Fabrics 1790–1810*, Exhibition Information, 31 January to 9 October 1994.

Victoria and Albert Museum, *A Brief Guide to Oriental painted and Printed Textiles*, Catalogue, London, HMSO, 1950.

Victoria and Albert Museum, *Fashionable Cultures: Ethnic Influences on Western Fashion*, Education Department Study day, 13 February 1999.

Wainwright, Clive, 'Morris in Context', pp. 352–61, in L. Parry, *William Morris*, London, Victoria and Albert Museum, 1996.

Wardle, Thomas, *Handbook of the Collection Illustrative of the Wild Silks of India, in the Indian Section of the South Kensington Museum, with a Catalogue of the Collection and Numerous Illustrations*, London, Eyre and Spottiswood, for HMSO, 1881.

——, *Kashmir: Its New Silk industry with some Account of its Natural History, Geology and Sport, with Notes of a Visit to the Silk producing District of Bengal in 1885–6*, London, Simkin, Marshall, Hamilton, Kent & Co., 1904.

——, *On the Entomology and Uses of Silk: With a List of the Families, Genera, and Species of Silk Producers, Known up to the Present Date,*

North Staffordshire Naturalist's Field Club and Archaeological Society, post 1889.

——, *On the Present Development of the Power Loom Weaving of Silk Fabrics at Lyons*, Manchester, W. Harris, 1893.

——, 'A Paper on the Relationship Which Should Exist Between Art Schools and Technical Instruction', delivered to Fenton Art School, North Staffordshire, *The Staffordshire Advertiser*, January 1891.

——, Catalogue: *The Silk Court: Exhibits of the Government of India and the Royal Commission*, Colonial and Indian Exhibition, 1886.

——, Catalogue: *The Silk Section*, The Royal Jubilee Exhibition, Manchester, 1887.

——, *Specimens of Fabrics Dyed with Indian Dyes. Also known as An Examination of the Dyes and Tans of India for the Government of India*, also *The Blue Book*, 1882.

Warner, Frank, *The Silk Industry: Its Origin and Development*, Manchester, Dranes, 1921.

Washburne, Dorothy and Crowe, Donald W., *Symmetries of Culture: Theory and Practice of Plane Pattern Analysis*, Seattle, University of Washington Press, 1988.

Watson, John Forbes, *The Textile Manufacturers and the Costume of the People of India*, London, W.H. Allen & Co., 1867.

Watt, George, *The Commercial Products of India*, London, His Majesty's Secretary of State for India in Council, John Murray, 1908.

Weiner, Annette and Schneider, Jane (eds), *Cloth and Human Experience*, Washington, Smithsonian Institution Press, 1989.

Werner, Alex, 'Artists as Educators', Journal of the Decorative Arts Society', No. 13, pp. 14–18.

White, Dorothy, *Bradford College*, Bradford, 1978.

The Whitworth Art Gallery, The First Hundred Years, *Catalogue*, Manchester, September 1988.

Wiener, Martin J., *English Culture and the Decline of the Industrial Spirit 1850–1980*, New York, Penguin Group, 1981.

Wilde, John Peter, *Berenike, 1998*, The Textiles, First Interim Report.

Wills, John E. Jr., 'European Consumption and Asian Production in the Seventeenth and Eighteenth Centuries, in J. Brewer and R. Porter (eds), *Consumption and the World of Goods*, London, Routledge, 1993/4.

Woods, Christine, 'In Search of the Silkmen', *The Textile Society Magazine*, Vol. 15, 1991.

Woods, H.J., 'The Geometrical Basis of Pattern Design', Parts 1–4, *Journal of the Textile Institute, Transactions*, 1935, Nos 26–7.

Wyatt, M.D., *Industrial Arts of the Nineteenth Century at the Great Exhibition* (2 vols), 1851–3.

Yelland, Zoe, *Traders and Nabobs: The British in Cawnpore 1765–1857*, Salisbury, Michael Russell (Publishing) Ltd, 1987.

Zannier, Claudio, 'Current Historical Research into the Silk Industry in Italy', *Textile History*, Vol. 25, No. 1, 1994, pp. 61–78.

INDEX

Note: 'n' after a page reference indicates the number of a note on that page.